Praise for *Opting Back In*

"Pamela Stone and Meg Lovejoy show clearly how women's cheerful language of reinvention following 'opting out' veils status anxiety about their children's future in an age of increasing income inequality and disillusion with the family-hostile and often sexist atmosphere in high-stakes, high-status jobs."
— Joan Williams, Professor of Law and Director of the Center for WorkLife Law, University of California Hastings College of Law

"Vividly captures the dilemma facing professional women wrestling with family obligations. Sympathetic and incisive, this book is a must-read for anyone who wants to understand the personal and public toll America's lack of family policy enacts even on the advantaged."
—Sharon Sassler, Professor of Policy Analysis and Management at Cornell University and coauthor of *Cohabitation Nation*

"Demonstrates how the personal decisions of a group of elite women reverberate throughout our social world and become consequential both for those equally privileged and those with far fewer advantages. Beautifully written and impeccably organized."
—Margaret K. Nelson, Hepburn Professor Emerita of Sociology at Middlebury College and coauthor of *Random Families*

"This book provides keen insights on challenges professional women face as they exit careers and later attempt to reestablish them. Founded on rich data and crisply written, it is a must-read for anyone interested in work-family concerns."
— Stephen Sweet, Executive Officer, Work and Family Researchers Network

"*Opting Back In* is a book that we badly need. Stone and Lovejoy probe the lives of the very women who could and should be earning the same high salaries and leading the same companies and law firms as their male counterparts but are not. They demonstrate where and how the pipeline of female talent leaks, while also identifying paradoxes of privilege that reinforce existing power structures. It should be required reading at professional schools across the country."
—Anne-Marie Slaughter, CEO, New America

A **NAOMI SCHNEIDER** BOOK

Highlighting the lives and experiences of marginalized communities, the select titles of this imprint draw from sociology, anthropology, law, and history, as well as from the traditions of journalism and advocacy, to reassess mainstream history and promote unconventional thinking about contemporary social and political issues. Their authors share the passion, commitment, and creativity of Executive Editor Naomi Schneider.

The publisher and the University of California Press Foundation gratefully acknowledge the generous support of the Barbara S. Isgur Endowment Fund in Public Affairs.

May 30, 2021

Opting Back In

To Jayne—
whose friendship
and support sustained
me through the ministry
of this book and beyond.

xoxo

Pam

Opting Back In

*What Really Happens When Mothers
Go Back to Work*

Pamela Stone and Meg Lovejoy

UNIVERSITY OF CALIFORNIA PRESS

University of California Press
Oakland, California

© 2019 by The Regents of the University of California

Library of Congress Cataloging-in-Publication Data

Names: Stone, Pamela, author. | Lovejoy, Meg, author.
Title: Opting back in : what really happens when mothers
  go back to work / Pamela Stone and Meg Lovejoy.
Description: Oakland, California : University of
  California Press, [2019] | Includes bibliographical
  references and index. |
Identifiers: LCCN 2019006654 (print) | LCCN 2019009633
  (ebook) | ISBN 9780520964792 () | ISBN 9780520290808
  (cloth : alk. paper)
Subjects: LCSH: Women—Employment re-entry—United
  States. | Work and family—United States. | Choice
  (Psychology) | Life change events.
Classification: LCC HD6054.2.U6 (ebook) |
  LCC HD6054.2.U6 S76 2019 (print) |
  DDC 331.4/40973—dc23
LC record available at https://lccn.loc.gov/2019006654

Manufactured in the United States of America

26   25   24   23   22   21   20   19
10   9   8   7   6   5   4   3   2   1

In memory of Ruth Sidel
For her heart, smarts, wit, and integrity, and for the
gentle mentorship that advanced so many women's
careers, including my own
Pamela Stone

For my mother
Determined, impassioned—a forerunner and role model
Meg Lovejoy

Don't think about making women fit the world—think about making the world fit women.

Gloria Steinem

CONTENTS

ILLUSTRATIONS

FIGURES

TABLES

ACKNOWLEDGMENTS

Our greatest thanks, first, to the forty-three women who made this book possible for their extraordinary generosity in sharing their stories not once, but twice. Their reflectiveness and surprising candor about how their lives had unfolded since the first time we came knocking, a decade earlier, form the bedrock of this study.

We might never have reached out to these women, however, had it not been for the remarkable group of Stone's undergraduate and graduate students who formed our research team: Katherine Cross and Lira Skenderi, then at Hunter College, and Lisa Ackerly Hernandez, Erin Maurer, and Robin Templeton of the sociology doctoral program at the Graduate Center of the City University of New York (where Cross is now a student). We owe them a huge debt of gratitude for their outstanding research assistance, which ranged from interviewing and initial coding to transcription and recordkeeping. Their interest in the topic, coupled with their incredible energy, intellect, competence, and creative sociological imaginations, was inspiring, and their collective insights and commentary on our emerging findings inform and enrich this book.

We also want to thank our editor, Naomi Schneider, for her unflagging support—and patience—in seeing this book through to publication.

Indeed, it is because of Naomi's advice and advocacy that this research resulted in a book rather than an epilogue. We cannot thank her enough for her many contributions to making this book immeasurably better and for being such fun to work with.

Funding provided to Stone by Hunter College's Presidential Research Grants, Roosevelt House Fellow Research Grants, and PSC-CUNY Research Awards was also critical to making the research a reality. In addition to the aforementioned research assistants, we want to thank others who provided important backstage support. For their literature review, preliminary qualitative data analysis, and transcription prowess, thanks go to Meghan Amato, Nicole Rios, and Nichole Whitney. For carrying out quantitative data analyses with accuracy, speed, and endless patience for "one more run," our thanks to James Guerra.

We would also like to thank those whose careful review and editorial advice on our initial manuscript improved and clarified our prose. Special thanks go to Dawn Raffel, editor extraordinaire, for helping us smooth over the rough patches, and to our reviewers, for their careful reading and instructive comments.

Stone would like to acknowledge the many people who supported and encouraged her along the way, sometimes simply by listening enthusiastically. Particular appreciation goes to Judith Warner of the Center for American Progress for taking an early interest in this research. Her *New York Times Magazine* cover story building on what were then preliminary findings helped convince Stone of the research's broader appeal and book potential. She thanks Jennifer Raab, president of Hunter College, for her ongoing interest in the issues this book addresses and for providing opportunities to bring her work to a larger audience. Thanks also goes to Stone's department colleagues at Hunter and the Graduate Center, especially Janet Gornick and Karen Lyness, and her colleagues on the Life and Leadership research project she's been fortunate to be part of at Harvard Business School: Robin Ely, Colleen Ammerman, Laurie Shannon, and Elizabeth Johnson. Stone spent a semester as a visiting scholar at Stanford University's Clayman

Institute for Gender Research, which came at a pivotal moment and facilitated completion of some of the research fieldwork as well as informing some of her early thinking about the project. A particular debt of gratitude goes to Director Shelley Correll and Executive Director Lori Mackenzie for their support in making this wonderful opportunity available and for innumerable small kindnesses throughout her stay there. Stone benefited greatly from feedback she received on presentations of preliminary findings at conferences and seminars at Harvard Business School, Stanford, and University of Southern California.

For their friendship and support of many kinds, Stone would like to thank Lisa Cornish, Cynthia Rhys, Tonia Johnson, Jackie Carroll, Katie Shah, Peggy Northrop, Lesley Seymour, Kris Klein, the Crystal Lake gang (Jayne Booker, Catherine Bosher, Wendy Jay Hilburn, Linda Jenkins, Celeste Gentry Sharp, and Laura Meyer Wellman), Sara Cousins, Jeff Stone, Janet Giele, and Jean O'Barr. Her family has always been her biggest booster. For putting her priorities in front for the last couple of years, Stone will always be grateful to her husband, Bruce Schearer. Not just moral support, Bruce took on so much more to enable her to write. Her sons, Alex and Nick Schearer, also pitched in, with both creative and technical support. Stone feels fortunate to have such loving, talented, generous, and caring men in her life, and her sons give her hope for the future about the very issues this book addresses.

Lovejoy would like to thank her mother, her earliest role model of what can be accomplished when women challenge the status quo. Both parents, one an artist and the other a scientist, helped grow her sociological imagination with their love of learning and their desire for a better world. Lovejoy is grateful to her sociological colleagues and graduate school mentors Karen Hansen and Gail Dines for helping to deepen her understanding of and commitment to feminism and the intersectional politics of class and gender. Thanks also to her (now former) colleagues at the Institute on Assets and Social Policy, especially Jessica Santos, who often inspired her with their commitment to systemic, root cause inquiry and to moving beyond analysis to solutions.

She also benefited from helpful feedback from colleagues on preliminary findings presented at various sociological conferences and seminars over the years.

Lovejoy thanks her friends, especially Maria Carrig, for their endless patience and support during the long journey that was this book. But the biggest debt of gratitude goes to Jonathan Martin, Lovejoy's longtime partner (and sociologist in his own right), for his unerring encouragement, deep political acuity, and helpful feedback over the years, and for helping her believe that men too can be feminists.

Finally, we would both like to acknowledge past and present feminist scholars and activists (too numerous to be named), who have inspired our critique of the way things are and our vision of the way things could be.

Introduction

MINDING THE GAP

It was another day in paradise in Silicon Valley—the perfect cloudless blue-sky weather matching the perfectly manicured Mediterranean landscaping of the upscale office park. But inside, there was no mistaking the sense of unease in the air, equal parts anticipation and anxiety. Dozens of women, most forty-somethings, some a bit younger, a few older, filled the large windowless meeting hall. They were here to attend a panel about resources for "career returners," the organizers' label for women like them who had stepped away or pulled back from careers and now wanted to return to the workforce. The event was exclusive: many women in attendance were graduates of top-tier graduate and professional schools such as Harvard, Stanford, the University of Chicago, or Cornell. This wasn't their only similarity. Residents of the affluent communities nearby, most were white, with a sprinkling of Asian American women and Latinas, all dressed in a style that combined business casual with soccer mom.

An impressive and confident-looking bunch, they nonetheless had about them a kind of "first day of school" demeanor—eager, but with a trace of tentativeness and tempered expectations. They chatted as they waited for the program to begin, exchanging alma maters, and sharing why they were here and where they were in their thinking about returning to work. They were open about their insecurities and about the challenges facing them ("I have to figure out what I want to do"), and welcomed the chance to compare notes with other women similarly situated.

Once the program began, women listened attentively and actively with many knowing nods of recognition as panelists offered advice and shared their own personal stories about returning to work or helping other women to do so. While speakers set an upbeat tone of support and encouragement, they were also cautionary. They warned, for example, of the very real specter of ageism, especially in the Bay Area, where, as one expert noted, only half-jokingly, "it starts not at forty or fifty, but over twenty-five." The program was well received, but worries surfaced in the Q&A. One of the first questions from the floor, the one that had women sitting up straighter and leaning forward to hear the answer, was also the one that gave panelists their only pause: "What do I do about the gap in my résumé?"

RÉSUMÉ GAPS AND RESEARCH GAPS

This is a question to which there are no easy or ready answers. Historically, women have long taken time out from work, particularly during the childbearing years, but they didn't have MBAs from the best schools or sterling prequit résumés chronicling their employment at the best firms. The problem these women are grappling with is of relatively recent vintage, born of the so-called opt-out revolution, identified and provocatively named by journalist Lisa Belkin in the early 2000s.[1] Belkin depicted this phenomenon as reflecting the emergence of a new traditionalism by which women chose domesticity out of preference, not constraint. This interpretation was challenged, by our own and others' research.[2] However, there is no question that in identifying a group of highly qualified and credentialed women who had walked away from successful professional careers, she was on to something new and different and resonant. Like the women at the seminar, some seek to find their way back—not just back to work or a job, as was the case for earlier generations of women, but to *professions,* occupations defined by continuity and commitment, against which résumé gaps are a glaring red flag.

Organizations like the one that sponsored this program are springing up to assist career returners, who've also caught the attention of the popular press,[3] but most are in start-up mode themselves and, however well-meaning, have a shallow reservoir of experience on which to base their advice. Nor is there much research on the subject, either to provide how-to guidance to women as they navigate reentry or to address larger questions: What proportion of women who've "opted out" seek to return to work?[4] What motivates them to do so? What are they looking for? What's the process of returning to work like? What kind of a reception will they receive from prospective employers? Will they be able to reenter and relaunch their career? Which strategies work, and which ones don't work?

In opting out (typically defined as a career break of at least six months, during which women are out of the paid labor force and primarily engaged in taking care of home and family), women knowingly risk their prospects for returning to the workforce, let alone their former jobs. Recent trends show that in any given year only about 20 percent of college-educated married moms with children younger than eighteen have opted out and are at home full-time. While a recent fine-grained analysis found that women graduates of elite schools were slightly more likely than those from less elite schools to opt out, both groups showed high rates of labor force participation—68 and 76 percent, respectively. However, mothers cycle in and out of work over the course of their childbearing years. Taking this into account, the fraction *ever taking a sustained break* is much larger than the cross-sectional statistics imply. Studies of women graduates of highly selective schools, comparable to the women we study, who are especially well positioned for successful careers, show that on the order of 30 to 40 percent report ever having taken time out from them. A recent study of Harvard Business School alumnae, who one can safely assume are as ambitious and career focused as they come, revealed similarly that while 10 percent of those with kids were currently at home, 30 percent of mothers had at some time been home full-time.[5]

Taking a break or work hiatus is risky enough, and one of the reasons, no doubt, that the opting-out phenomenon has garnered so much attention, but for professionals the potential downsides of doing so are especially high given the lucrative and prestigious nature of their work. We can only gauge and fully appreciate the extent of that risk and the associated costs—whether they can find work at all and how far they might fall from the high-flying jobs they left—when we know what happens when they seek to opt in by returning to work. Their efforts, and the success or failure of these efforts, lay bare the potential riskiness of the opt-out strategy, as well as highlight the brave new world in which these women are pioneers or perhaps guinea pigs.

Has their gamble paid off? Can professional women return to work after time out for motherhood? Under what terms and with what consequences? Do they even want to return to the kinds of jobs from which they walked away and (as our earlier research showed) from which they often felt shut out? Does returning to work offer them a chance to rebound, if perhaps not catch up entirely with the men (and women) who've worked continuously? What losses, if any, do they incur in their restarted careers—and what possible gains?

We find that women successfully return to work, but they don't resume their former careers. Instead their reentry requires a protracted period of questing and career reinvention. With a premium placed on their roles as caregivers and status keepers in upper-middle-class families, women value flexibility and meaning and turn their backs on their former careers in order to fashion new solutions to the work-family bind: freelancing and radical redirection to jobs in female-dominated fields that they formerly eschewed. While these women, unlike most, are able and willing to bear the costs of these significant accommodations—notably, retraining, lower earnings, and loss of pathways to leadership—we show that they in fact have limited options in returning to professional workplaces little changed from those they left behind. As a result, the very women who are best positioned (and indeed expected) to surmount barriers and close gender gaps instead pursue career-family strategies that work for them *individually,* but that ultimately exacerbate and increase gender inequality *overall.* This is the Catch-22 of opting out and opting back in. Women going it alone can't break this cycle. We advocate policies to change this dynamic and to support women's retention and reentry—policies that will help not only privileged professional women like the ones we study but all women (and men) trying to combine work and family.

BACK TO THE FUTURE

Our understanding of these issues requires that we take a long view on women's lives—a movie rather than a snapshot. In our earlier research on career interruption among highly qualified and experienced professional women (most of whom, like the women in Silicon Valley, were graduates of elite, highly selective schools), we challenged the prevailing understanding of opting out.[6] Not only was it not as widespread as suggested by the popular media's hyperbolic headlines, but also it was not entirely optional or—as often depicted—about a return to traditional gender roles and values. For the vast majority of women who quit professional careers and were now "stay-at-home mothers," the decision to leave their careers and head home was highly conflicted and constrained. It was a function less of choice or preference than of a long-hour work culture and husbands who were largely absent on the home front; this combination created a high-intensity double bind that made it impossible for women to work and parent. This same work culture stigmatized flexible work options that would enable women—especially women who could entertain the option to quit—to continue to do both.

Our previous research, in addition to revealing the real reasons women exchanged careers for motherhood (at least for some sustained period), also shed light on their current lives at home and on their future plans. The large majority of these stay-at-home moms intended to return to work. A critical question, which our earlier study could not address, is whether these women—and highly qualified and credentialed women like them who opt out—are able to realize their intentions and transition back to work. By virtue of their human capital (e.g., credentials, work experience) and social capital (e.g., class privilege, good networks), some observers are optimistic about opt-out women's prospects for reentry.[7] Others are less sanguine. Citing the rapid skill obsolescence inherent in high-knowledge professional fields as well as potential ageism, they predict that women will be disadvantaged by their time out of the labor force, their prior history in and of itself a possible red flag signaling shaky work commitment.[8] That this fear is well founded is borne out by the results of a recent study of employers' evaluations of the résumés of prospective job applicants. Otherwise well- and equally qualified applicants for a professional job who had opted out of the labor force to take care of family fared significantly worse in their hiring prospects than did applicants whose employment break was occasioned by job loss or those who were continuously employed. Employers took opting out as a violation of ideal-worker norms and prima facie evidence of lower work commitment, deservingness, and reliability.[9]

The limited research on professional women's reentry finds that the majority want to resume careers (as we found), but, consistent with the second hypothesis, they have trouble doing so and often settle for jobs far below their qualifications and capabilities.[10] These studies also find that women undergo a substantial shift in their work orientation after a break, often redirecting away from former employers and professions.[11] Together, these results suggest that reentry is a time of considerable and protracted turbulence and flux. Yet while past research begins to shed light on basic outcomes associated with reentry, it is silent about the *process*. So, too, is our previous study, which looked primarily backward to explore the anatomy of women's decision-making around exiting careers. The study on which this book is based picks up where the last one left off, following the same group of women through the overlapping peak career and family-building years, taking them from their thirties and forties into their forties and fifties. This long-term longitudinal approach allows us to unspool women's lives from the fateful decision to opt out to understand not only its antecedents but the process and motivations underlying the challenging and complex decision to resume working (or not), which is often accompanied by the equally complicated and little-understood decision to change fields. Only by understanding the entire process—*and* its consequences—can we evaluate fully the privileges and perils of opting out.

WHY IT MATTERS

The women in that auditorium in Silicon Valley probably never thought they'd be there. Certainly, the women we studied never thought they'd be full-time, at-home moms. Their lives—up until the time they quit—were ones of achievement: they either had broken the glass ceiling or were poised to do so. Women like them, women of accomplishment and privilege, are "supposed" to be doing what their elite alma maters prepared them for—be leaders in their chosen fields.[12] Fifty years after the feminist revolution, we know how that's going for women, and the answer is "not well." Women face a leadership gap and a more quantifiable earnings gap. It's increasingly clear that highly gendered and costly strategies to accommodate career and motherhood—such as the euphemistically dubbed opting out—which disproportionately penalize women play a central role in creating and maintaining pernicious and persistent gender gaps. Opting out is perhaps the most visible and extreme manifestation of the "leaky pipeline," the metaphor for the process by which women go missing from the pool of talent earmarked for promotion and top leadership positions. Insights into the implications of career interruptions and discontinuous work histories are critical to understanding persistent gender gaps in leadership, authority, and earnings in the professions in which women now make up the majority share—51 percent—of employment.[13]

THE LEADERSHIP GAP

High-profile women leaders like Sheryl Sandberg, COO of Facebook, and Anne-Marie Slaughter, former State Department policy chief and Woodrow Wilson School dean and current foundation head, have used the power of their platforms to bring the issue of women's leadership to the forefront of public attention. Indeed, for scholars like us who have worked on these and related issues for decades, women's leadership and gender inequality are enjoying an unprecedented moment. Their two best-selling and highly talked-about books—Sandberg's *Lean In* and Slaughter's *Unfinished Business*—draw attention to the paucity of women like themselves at the top and identify obstacles to women's ascension, key to which is career and family conflict.[14] Sandberg adopts a motivational approach, drawing on personal experience to encourage women to build successful careers, to "lean in" rather than opt out, advising them not to quit before quitting, in a nod to the importance of ambition and career persistence. Slaughter, adopting a broader, more policy-oriented perspective, sees the gendered organization of paid work and unpaid caregiving, such as child care, as the root problem and argues for societal and policy solutions that more highly value caregiving work and better integrate it with paid employment.

Both books are by and large about high-achieving, college-educated professional women. Both have been critiqued for this focus, but they focus on these women for essentially the same reasons we do. First, women face a leadership crisis, or, more aptly, leadership faces a woman crisis. Second, while leadership is exercised across all levels of education, income, and class, it is still predominantly defined as residing in certain key positions that wield power and influence—CEO, judge, president, dean, manager, partner. There is a long history in the social sciences, particularly sociology, of studying privileged groups as a way of understanding the topside dynamics of inequality. While arguably unfair (and we would argue that it is), in an unequal or stratified society like ours the route to leadership is remarkably narrow. It often requires traveling a well-defined path, starting with degrees from widely recognized academic institutions that feed into employment in equally prestigious organizations that are themselves feeders upward. Therefore, by virtue of their class backgrounds, elite educational credentials, and early employment histories, the women we study are well poised for these top-level positions. We focus on them, not despite their privilege, but because of their privilege, to understand why women aren't attaining positions of leadership more rapidly in core arenas of society. While these highly educated professional women represent a privileged minority, if even they are stymied in their leadership trajectories, what does this say about the limits to women's access to power and influence within our society in general?

To illustrate how high-level leadership is generally obtained in the US, Sheryl Sandberg's journey to Facebook COO is perhaps better known than most but otherwise typical: undergraduate degree from a highly selective college (Harvard) and professional degree from an equally selective business school (Harvard Business School), followed by jobs at prestigious employers like Google, from which she was recruited to the number two job at Facebook. Hers is a textbook case of ascension to leadership, unusual only because she's a woman.

Just how unusual is shown in figure 1. Fifty years after women began entering graduate and professional schools in large(ish) numbers, they have failed to make it to the top. Despite holding just over half of all professional and managerial jobs, women are still only 27 percent of executive officers, 11 percent of top earners, and 5 percent of Fortune 500 CEOs. In Sandberg's field, high tech, women hold 9 percent of management positions. They fare better in law, where they are 45 percent of associates, 25 percent of nonequity partners, and 18 percent of equity partners, and in medicine, where they constitute 34 percent of all physicians and surgeons though still only 22 percent of medical school full

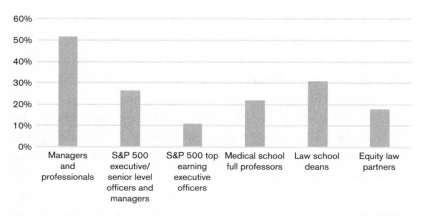

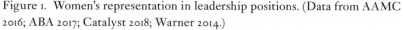

Figure 1. Women's representation in leadership positions. (Data from AAMC 2016; ABA 2017; Catalyst 2018; Warner 2014.)

professors and 16 percent of deans. Even in fields where women have long been active, such as health and social welfare, leadership is male. Women are 78 percent of the labor force in these fields but only 15 percent of top leadership. While these numbers are low, they used to be lower; however, at the current pace of change, it is estimated that women won't reach gender parity in leadership until 2085.[15]

STALLED PROGRESS ON THE ROAD TO PAY PARITY

Not only are women lagging on leadership, they are also hitting the wall when it comes to closing the pay gap. Current estimates suggest it won't close until 2058.[16] The pay gap, typically reported as the ratio of female-to-male earnings, is probably the most commonly cited and extensively studied indicator of gender (in)equality. It also lends itself to measurement and parsing more readily than leadership, although the two go hand in hand—upward career mobility on the path to leadership is accompanied by earnings growth. Progress in closing the gap has slowed considerably since the 1980s, and especially since 2000—the dawn of a new millennium, but not particularly auspicious for women. In 2010, various estimates show the ratio of women's to men's earnings (among prime-age, full-time, full-year workers) to be in the 80 percent range, little budged from where it stood in 2000.[17] Recent research shows that career interruption is a big part of this story.

Harvard economist Claudia Goldin has extensively studied college-educated women's career and family behavior, focusing on women graduates, like ours, of elite graduate and professional schools. Her research and other studies of high-achieving, college-educated professional women repeatedly find that women start out and stay equal with their male counterparts through their twenties. Somewhat counterintuitively, *"The difference in earnings by sex greatly increases during the first several decades of working life."*[18] Thus, at the early and important career launch stage, the pay gap is almost nonexistent, at or near parity, typically showing women earning 90 percent or more of what men earn. But the gap widens considerably, to 70 percent and more, as women hit their thirties and forties—and motherhood.[19] Not even taking into account the high-demand parenting in fashion today, just finding time to see your children is tough when you're working fifty-plus-hour weeks. This is when the so-called pipeline to advancement and pay raises starts leaking as women like those we study opt out by taking time out from employment altogether—or by deploying other strategies such as downshifting to a less demanding job—however reluctantly and last resort.

For graduates of an elite MBA program (University of Chicago's Booth School), Goldin reports that just under 20 percent of women graduates from 1990 to 2006 were not working and that about a quarter of those working were part-timers, both accommodations linked to motherhood. For graduates of a leading law school (University of Michigan), from 1982 to 1991, she also finds a motherhood effect on employment. Fifteen years out of law school, 21 percent of mothers were out of the labor force.

The penalty for taking time out of the labor market is especially high in the traditionally male-dominated professional and managerial fields such as finance and law that women have been entering in relatively large numbers since the 1970s. Among Harvard College undergraduates of the 1990s, fifteen years after the degree, Goldin reports that an eighteen-month hiatus in employment "was associated with a decrease in earnings of 41 percent for those with an MBA, 29 percent for those with a JD or PhD, and 15 percent for those with an MD."[20] In findings that echo our earlier study, she writes that "certain occupations impose heavy penalties on employees who want fewer hours and more flexible employment. The lower remuneration can result in shifts to an entirely different occupation or to a different position within an occupational hierarchy or *to being out of the labor force altogether*" (italics added).[21]

Time out of the labor force, occasioned by motherhood for women (but not fatherhood for men, most of whom work continuously without interruption) has played a bigger role in maintaining the still large, and seemingly persistent, gender earnings gap, eclipsing other factors—labor force participation, hours worked, education, and occupation—as women have increasingly started to look and act like men with regard to paid work. Goldin estimates, for example, that for the MBA graduates she studied, ten to sixteen years out, the earnings ratio is 55 percent: career interruptions and associated differences in job experience account for fully one-third of the gap, with two-thirds of this effect due to taking *any* time out, irrespective of length.

Research by another leading scholar of gender inequality, sociologist Paula England, further underscores that labor force experience or lack thereof plays an equally critical role in explaining the motherhood penalty, the difference between what mothers and otherwise similar women who are childless earn. The good news is that, to a greater extent than the gender wage gap, the motherhood penalty has declined. Among highly educated professionals like the ones we study, mothers earned 3 percent less than women without children in 2010, down from 19 percent in 1980.[22] Comparing workers across different points in the skill-wage continuum, however, England finds that women in the highest skill-wage category, that is, professionals and managers, despite having the most work experience (and least interruption), experience the highest penalty. This is because, as Goldin also found, returns to experience are so high in their fields that taking any time out is costly. For this group (and the others as well), "Half or more of the motherhood penalty results from losing experience or tenure."[23]

Long hours and overwork (paired with the ongoing expectation that women bear the brunt of family caregiving) also profoundly shape the gender wage gap. Looking at gender gap trends from 1979 to 2009, Cha and Weeden show that "the increasing prevalence of 'overwork' (defined as working 50 hours or more per week)" and the rising return to overwork, which favor men's earnings, account for the slowdown over the 1990s and 2000s in closing the gender pay gap.[24] The effect of overwork was so large it offset other earnings-equalizing influences such as women's increased education and labor force experience. It was also most pronounced among professionals and managers.

The foregoing research helps us quantify the sources and cost of career interruption as it affects women's earnings and the pay gap. Our research, with its in-depth qualitative focus, sheds light on how women come to make decisions that have such profound implications for their own lives and for women's status generally. Understanding career interruption—time out followed by reentry—is critical to understanding one of the key drivers of gender inequality and can suggest ways to mitigate it.

CORRECTING MEDIA NARRATIVES

As important as media coverage has been in bringing newfound visibility to gender inequality, the media portrayal of opting out is in need of correction. Opting out was largely a media creation, born as it was from a single highly influential article.[25] Our research and that of others have challenged the media characterization of women's decisions to interrupt careers as reflecting preference, but books and articles continue to recycle this narrative, often trivializing the women portrayed (e.g., as Park Avenue primates or ten-year nappers).[26]

Continuing media attention also has the effect of exaggerating the extent of opting out, giving the impression that every woman is doing it. While a significant share of college-educated women are—from 20 percent at any given time to 30 to 40 percent over the longer course of work lives—opting out is used by a minority of professional women, albeit with major implications. By hewing to a choice narrative and giving opting out outsize coverage, the media have the potential to reinforce damaging stereotypes. These ubiquitous stereotypes are throwbacks to the era of separate spheres and have the potential to normalize a strategy whose full implications—including downsides—are not yet fully understood.

While it's difficult to trace a direct connection between media coverage and behavior, it's noteworthy that millennials, the youngest generation of women now entering the workforce, who came of age in the opting-out era (after the 2003 coining of the term and subsequent attention to this phenomenon), appear to anticipate taking a career break in considerably greater numbers than gen Xers and baby boomers. A recent *New York Times* article ran under the headline "More Than Their Mothers, Young Women Plan Career Pauses,"[27] citing evidence from a number of studies. One, with which we were involved, was a survey of Harvard Business School alumni; it found that 37 percent of millennial women planned to interrupt their career for family, compared to 28 percent of gen X women and 17 percent of baby boomers.[28] While this trend might be seen to reflect a healthy shift in priorities and lessons learned from the struggles of earlier generations, not all millennials are sanguine about it. One of our twenty-something students reported that many of her friends were indeed planning to opt out, but she worried about the advisability of this strategy and bemoaned that something so potentially risky was now being seen "as a solution, not a problem." We share her worries, which is another reason to learn more about the long-term consequences of taking a career break. Unless there are radical changes in work, this strategy seems certain to exact a toll in earnings and advancement. Are there offsetting benefits? For young women who may be poised to adopt this strategy, our research can help them understand the trade-offs and make decisions with their eyes wide open.

Media characterizations also have the potential to, if not shape anew, reinforce existing stereotypes about professional women, work, and family. We've long known about gender bias in hiring, but a recent rigorously designed experimental study demonstrates that gender bias is more pronounced for upper-middle-class women than others.[29] Large law firms are less likely to hire women than men, and more likely to hire female applicants of lower class background rather than higher. Interestingly, while men get an extra (albeit unearned) boost from their elite class status, women do not, because, as the authors explain, "They face a competing, negative stereotype that portrays them as less committed to full-time, intensive careers."[30] Upper-middle-class women are not only seen as less career committed than their male counterparts but also rated as less committed than professional women from less affluent or educationally elite backgrounds. Media attention to an uncorrected, uncritical opting-out narrative—with its story line of women returning home to re-create the traditional male-breadwinner, 1950s-style family—perpetuates the stereotype that elite women are flight risks by choice when the reality is quite different. There is some evidence that married mothers from more elite academic backgrounds may be somewhat more likely to opt out,[31] but their rates of labor force participation, high by absolute or relative standards, belie a lack of commitment. Moreover, our previous research shows that their decision to leave paid employment is less about commitment than about the long hours and intractable work demands they face as primary caregivers. A better understanding of the full truth about opting out, looking beyond the one-time act of quitting and exploring its aftermath, can shed light on the reality of women's work commitment and further undermine, if not shatter, the myths that undergird sexist bias in hiring and promotion.

ABOUT THIS STUDY

To explore these issues, we needed not only to understand why women opted out—the key research question of our previous study—but to find out what happened next. We knew from our earlier research, for example, that the majority of women wanted to return to work—a demonstration, it should be noted, of ongoing work commitment among women who have otherwise been characterized as lacking it. But did they follow through? And were they successful in their efforts? Our original study gave us the perfect springboard to address these questions, but could we locate the women who'd shared their life stories so generously years earlier? Fortunately, the answer is yes. The follow-up findings, coupled with the results from the original study, enable exploration of the full sweep of women's work and family lives over the course of their prime work and child-rearing years.

The fifty-four women we initially interviewed were a privileged group. Although the media portrayal of opting out is deficient in many respects, it is accurate in identifying it as a phenomenon of affluence.[32] In fact, the typical stay-at-home mother is not a high-earning professional but a less well-educated and low-income woman.[33] She is home because of limited and precarious employment opportunities and inadequate and costly child care, in contrast to affluent women who are home because of long hours and because their husbands' earnings make quitting a viable solution to work-family conflict. As we use the term, therefore, *opting out* is not synonymous with being out of the labor force to take care of children or staying at home per se. Instead, along with leading work-family scholars Heather Boushey and Joan Williams, we distinguish opting out as a strategy to reduce work-family conflict that is used by the upper-middle class—typically construed as college educated and beyond, working in professional or managerial jobs. It is a specific response to the universal problem of work-family conflict that all women face—occasioned by the mismatch between the increasing presence of women in the workforce and the unchanging structure of work built around the traditional family—but that they address in different ways. Women from other backgrounds develop different strategies to integrate work and family, based on their own class, family configurations, and resources, and the features of the jobs available to them.[34] A common strategy among the working and middle classes, for example, is for parents to work alternate shifts, often dubbed "tag-team parenting." Low-income workers, vulnerable to irregular schedules, inadequate hours, and job loss, cycle in and out of the labor force, working when they can or need to around family demands, in low-wage jobs for which there is little or no reward to continuity of employment. That opting out is identified with the upper-middle class is further supported by research based on a nationally representative sample showing that married mothers who graduated from elite institutions with highly competitive admissions were slightly more likely to quit their careers than graduates of less selective schools (with labor force participation rates of 68 versus 76 percent, respectively).[35]

To recruit upper-middle-class professional women, we used referral or "snowball" sampling, drawing primarily from informal networks of undergraduate alumnae at four colleges or universities that are among the most highly selective in the country. We sought out women who had left careers as professionals and managers and were full-time, stay-at-home mothers. Formerly highly paid professionals, and married to men similarly situated, these were women who, at least theoretically, had some amount of discretion about whether to continue in their careers or quit. Half had earned advanced degrees. Among them were doctors, lawyers, scientists, bankers, management consultants, marketing and nonprofit executives, editors, and teachers. About half had worked in male-dominated professions such as law, business, and medicine; approximately one-third in mixed-gender fields such as publishing; and the remainder in female-dominated professions such as teaching. They were also geographically diverse, living in large metropolitan areas such as New York and Chicago in regions across the US. Our sample was largely white, reflecting the reality that opting out is a racially specific strategy for addressing work and family conflict. Historically women of color in the US have not had the same economic opportunity as their more privileged white counterparts to evolve an exclusively domestic role. Therefore, it is still a cultural exception, rather than a historical tradition, for women of color, and particularly black women, to choose to stay at home, even when and if the economic opportunity to do so is available; black mothers tend to be more egalitarian, view working more favorably, and work longer.[36] While our sample reflects this reality, it does include some ethnic and religious diversity, containing women of Hispanic and Jewish backgrounds.

At the time of our initial interview, women ranged in age from thirty-three to fifty-six, with a median age of forty-one. Most had two children, on average seven years old; they had worked a median of ten years prior to quitting, typically midcareer, and had been at home, out of the labor force, for five years on average. At the initial interview, we focused on gathering their background and demographic information along with family and work histories from college to the time of interview. We were especially interested in learning about their reasons for quitting their jobs and how they'd gone about doing it, but also wanted to understand their lives at home and their future plans for returning to work.

The challenge of tracking everyone down approximately ten years later was considerable. We describe these efforts and our study methodology more fully in the Appendix. For the follow-up, we were able to locate and secure participation from a full 80 percent (or forty-three) of the original interviewees. On key demographic characteristics, the follow-up sample matched the original sample remarkably closely, being virtually identical with regard to age, number of children, possession of an advanced degree, and number of years out of the labor force at time of initial contact.

For the follow-up study, we again used an in-depth life history interview approach, supplemented by a detailed yearly work-family chronology completed by the interviewee. In addition to updated background and demographic information, including work and family histories since our last interview, we focused particularly on whether women had attempted to return to work, and their decision-making around reentry as well as their experience of it. As before, we also explored their future plans. The in-depth nature of these interviews enabled us to glean information about the context of women's decision-making and to explore what work-family scholar Ellen Kossek has characterized as its "cross-level dynamics" spanning household, job, and organization.[37] Women were once again incredibly generous in sharing their lives with us, giving us a window into an ongoing process of reflection and reinvention. To help keep track of the women in the follow-up, who are referred to throughout the book, we provide a list of all of them in the Appendix, along with some descriptive background information about each.

A PREVIEW OF WHAT WE FOUND

Reflecting on what we'd learned about women in our first study, we wrote: "Their stories are not over.... Most were still in the process of re-invention, looking ahead to the future with a sense of agency tempered by trepidation and doubt about their ability to work again."[38] About a decade later, these women's lives continued to be characterized by reinvention and flux. While they were not without "trepidation and doubt," it turned out that most of the women in the follow-up—virtually all who had wanted to plus some who had been unsure or even disinclined—were able to reenter the workforce. The process of reentry was both easier and harder—and more complicated—than the women themselves could have anticipated, and key aspects of it have been missed or overlooked by previous research and the media. In common with previous research, we find reentry tied to reinvention, but we are able to illuminate how women come to make what turn out to be sur-prisingly radical turnabouts in their professional lives. The dynamics of opting back in mirror the forced-choice opt-out dynamic that pushed women out of the workforce in the first place. Thus, while opting out—a strategy born out of a lack of options in the workplace—doesn't preclude eventual return to employment, women continue to bear trade-offs and losses—as well as some gains—as they seek family-accommodating and meaningful work. We detail these strategies to show how professional women find themselves in what we call a "paradox of privilege," which shapes their initial decision to opt out and undergirds and constrains their reentry, while at the same time obscuring the existence of constraints.

THE PARADOX OF PRIVILEGE

We define *paradox of privilege* to mean the phenomenon whereby the gender-based interests of high-achieving women—for professional accomplishment, gender egalitarianism, and economic independence—are at odds with their class interests, which place a high premium on full-time caregiving as a means of class transmission within the family. Backstopping husbands' careers and being hands-on mothers take on increasing urgency to ensure that families maintain status in an era of widespread economic insecurity and status precarity.[39] The paradox of privilege describes a dynamic inherent in opting out and its aftermath in which the class (as well as race and heteronormative) interests of professional women (at least the most affluent and well-educated ones) work against their gender interests in various ways and at different points across the life course, ultimately reinforcing their subordination at home and in the workplace. In this way, opting out consolidates class and male privilege (and the intersecting advantages of race and heteronormativity) among the elite.

As a life course process, the paradox manifests itself in two stages. In the first, its dynamics are nascent. Highly educated upper-middle-class women are groomed to gravitate to high-status elite jobs consistent with their class. Such jobs, however initially welcoming of women like them, remain structured around the strongest ideal-worker norms (read "male-breadwinner assumptions") and require long hours and total commitment. Class also grooms educated women to marry men like themselves.

Until women become mothers, they are able to remain competitive with men in their demanding jobs and to maintain egalitarian marriages. With motherhood, however, these scenarios are disrupted by a potent combination. Because of their education, training, and experience (so-called "human capital"), their extensive networks of well-placed family, friends, and colleagues (social capital), and their savvy and sophistication (cultural capital), women of their class become not only caregivers but status keepers. This dynamic is a product of extraordinary pressures on them to mother intensively in a historical moment characterized by economic insecurity. At the same time, *despite* their human, social, and cultural capital, they are unable to refashion their jobs in ways that would support continuing in their careers and so watch as their husbands' career outcomes—buoyed by patriarchal privilege—eclipse their own. Thus, evincing paradox, successful marriage (class interest) cancels out—or at least complicates—women's career persistence and success (gender interest).

In the second stage, the dynamics of the paradox of privilege are more fully manifested. Once women are out of the labor force, their class privilege works to further undermine their gender-egalitarian aspirations by (1) keeping them out of work for a longer time, seduced by the patriarchal bargain of privileged domesticity and the status maintenance imperative of their upper-middle-class form of intensive mothering and community involvement; and (2) eroding their incentive to return to elite careers while giving them the freedom to pursue work that is less lucrative but more meaningful to them. In yet another demonstration of paradox, the acceleration of child-rearing demands hits hardest the very group prepared to realize the loftiest career heights. Women who were well poised to scale the gendered ramparts of elite male-dominated fields in their youth are stymied and deflected from these male enclaves upon motherhood; constrained by class-based parenting standards and the hostile climate of professional jobs, many either return to traditionally female jobs on reentry or work contingently on the perimeters of former professions.

QUESTIONS AND ANSWERS

Our findings raise a set of larger questions: Are women experiencing a kind of one-two punch talent drain—first at initial opt-out and again at reentry? Is redirection after a career break (including contract and freelance work) a fully optimized choice, a proactive and generative reinvention, or a default strategy that sells women short, underutilizes their talents, and erodes their productivity? The kind of workplace flexibility available in the current economy may come at a high price, a price paid largely by women while serving the interests of employers, who gain considerably from being able to recruit highly qualified working mothers on a contingent basis. Are employers taking advantage of ongoing labor market trends in ways that further bifurcate the labor market and intensify the work-family divide, and with it gender inequality?

The book is organized as follows. The next chapter introduces six women who are emblematic of the larger group of high-achieving women we studied. Their lives exemplify the paths taken by women to realize the next steps after opting out, and we use them to personify the recurring themes and common patterns we uncovered for the larger sample. The chapter also reviews the key findings of our prior study and summarizes subsequent research, some inspired by our previous study, that corroborates and lends further credibility to our findings and generalizes them to broader populations. Chapter 2 focuses on women's lives at home to reveal the strengthening pull of what we label "the seduction of privileged domesticity." The next three chapters reveal the long and winding road back to work. Chapter 3 looks at the early and tentative "family-first" stage; chapters 4 and 5 at the consolidating, "career relaunch" phase in which women figure out what they want to do when they grow up. Chapter 6 focuses on a range of outcomes—primarily objective, but subjective ones too—to provide an evaluation of the costs and benefits of the return-to-work strategies women deploy and, we hope, to inform the decisions of those contemplating a similar break. This chapter also looks at the exceptions—the women who did not (and as we find, never tried to) return to work—to understand the factors that turn a career hiatus into a likely career end. In the concluding chapter, we reflect further on the paradox of privilege facing high-achieving women and how the study's key findings illuminate—or challenge—current debates about professional women, work, and family. We identify key policies to support women's work-life aspirations, guided by the larger goal of informing the ongoing conversation about gender inequality at work and at home.

The women we study are not without regrets, but when we talked with them the second time they felt, by and large, that they'd lived happily ever after. Their lives are not fairy tales, however, although they may seem that way. Given that they are resourceful women with considerable resources, it's not surprising perhaps that theirs are (mostly) success stories. But is this success all that it appears to be? Their accomplishments on returning to work stand in stark contrast to what they could have been, and their long road back to work reminds us of their time and talent lost. Juxtaposing their individual success stories against the persistence of gender inequality and yawning gender gaps reveals the limits of private solutions to public problems. But to look ahead to solutions, we have to look back, so let's turn to the beginning to understand who these women were and how they fashioned work and family lives that found them in a place they never envisioned they'd be—at home.

ONE

Great Expectations

EXEMPLARY LIVES

The Marketing Executive

Kate Hadley, thirty-nine and the mother of three when we first interviewed her nine years earlier, had been a coxswain. Not just a coxswain, but captain of the women's crew team and the first woman to be elected president of her Ivy League university's rowing club, which included the men's and women's teams. "The coxswain," she told me, "is the person who literally sits in the boat and bosses people around and gives commands, calls strategy, motivates them." Perhaps thinking that she was sounding a little boastful, Kate self-deprecatingly added that she was "the unathletic one." The coxswain is the brain, not the brawn of the team—the strategist: "You're smart, you can think on your feet, and you don't weigh too much because they're pulling you, you're dead weight." As dead weight, Kate explained, coxswains were not regarded as captain material, and she seemed prouder of having been elected captain as a coxswain than club president as a woman. Both were unprecedented achievements.[1]

As we talked in the family room of her suburban Chicago home at that first interview, it was easy to envision Kate as a collegiate athlete. Tanned and trim, wearing a T-shirt, cotton skirt, and fashionable but functional sandals, she was articulate and reflective as she talked about her life growing up, a life she recognized was privileged and accomplished. The daughter of an international businessman, Kate described her mother as "a classic example of a corporate wife." Kate was accepted early decision and graduated from her Ivy League college in the late 1980s. With the benefit of several summer internships, she established herself quickly at a leading research and consulting firm. After about two years there, she was expected to get her MBA, but Kate was not yet ready for that. Instead, she launched a job search in Europe, landing a marketing job with a major brand-name company. Two years into this job, Kate felt the time was right for the MBA, "because I wouldn't want to be turned down for a job ever because I didn't have it and someone else did." Accepted by several leading schools, she decided to attend her father's alma mater, Wharton, one of the premier business schools in the country.

After earning her MBA, Kate switched firms, taking a job at another major consumer brands company that offered her the possibility of returning home to the US. Clearly identified as a high flyer, Kate moved steadily upward, at one point easily sidestepping a transfer to another part of the country in order to stay at headquarters and closer to Nick, her soon-to-be husband, and quickly becoming the marketing manager of the company's leading brand—the "mother brand," as she called it in her marketing lingo. When she was newly married and wanted to move to Latin America in order to pursue a career opportunity for her husband, Kate was able to leverage her expertise and transfer laterally overseas, ultimately getting a promotion to marketing director just before having her first baby.

Kate continued to work after her baby was born but cut back to 80 percent time, reasoning that this "would be a good way to still be in the game and in the fast track and keep up my networks and reputation, but that it would also afford me a slice of normality or a little bit of balance." While her boss granted this request, she noted that he found it "astonishing." Given the long distances entailed in traveling in Latin America, Kate estimated that she was on the road two to three weeks a month. Despite the grueling schedule, Kate had a second child eighteen months after the first. Passed over for a promotion in favor of someone junior to her, Kate "suspected it had something to do with me having my second baby and they thought I wanted to go slower and blah, blah, blah." Shortly thereafter, prompted by her husband's decision to return to the States for his career, the family moved back. Failing to line up a new job, and with family pressures mounting, including a third pregnancy, Kate quit. Looking back on her decision, she took satisfaction from how long she *had* been able to juggle career and family, musing, "I probably in some ways lasted longer than maybe some people thought I would in terms of working until my second child was one."

At our first interview, Kate had been home for three years. During that time, she'd been surprised and flattered to find that she was receiving offers to consult—offers she turned down, "distracted" by everything going on at home with three children and two dogs, plus a husband who'd taken on a demanding new job with constant international travel. As the crew coxswain, Kate had been the only person in the boat looking forward, but doing so now filled her with uncertainty. Back then, as Kate thought about her future, she wasn't sure she wanted to return to work "so I can become vice president of marketing by the time I'm fifty"—an aspiration in keeping with her elite MBA pedigree. Rather, Kate sought meaningful engagement, "to set a good example for my daughters." Still, she wanted to return to the corporate world, which she liked (unlike many others) because "there's a lot of security" and recognition, "where people knew the name of the company." She struggled, however, with a "lack of confidence because I've been out so long [only three years]." And she worried that a corporate job wouldn't give her the flexibility she needed, noting that she'd been reading about "just how tough it is for corporations to be flexible." Kate planned to return at some point, emphatically declaring, "I don't consider myself part of the opt-out revolution." When and how she'd return were open questions; Kate felt pressures to return soon but "hadn't done anything on it." This uncharacteristic indecision was "a sign," she thought, that she wasn't ready.

The CPA

The daughter of a police officer and a mother who had "never worked," Diane Childs was forty-one and the mother of two children when we first talked with her eleven years before. She was slender with short-cropped brown hair and a crisp, no-nonsense demeanor that was reflected in the immaculate uncluttered setting of her living room, where we shared a cup of tea. Diane had grown up in the big northeastern city where she still lived, and had stayed close to home for college, choosing a local university that was affordable and accessible, and a major (accounting) that was practical. She "mulled around in liberal arts for maybe a year or so" before going into the business program, a move prompted by the realization that "I'm going to have to find a job when I get out, pay off school loans, things like that." Graduating in the early 1980s, a time, she recalled, when "there was a big push for women," Diane jumped at the opportunities opening up in her field. Recruited right out of college, she went to work for a major accounting firm. Although she recognized that this job gave her invaluable experience, Diane "didn't love it." She recalled that the partners "made good salaries, but all looked like they were fifteen years older than they really were." Taking them as negative role models, and now a CPA, Diane decided not to pursue the traditional accountant's career path to partner and after three years moved instead to a job at a national real estate investment company. Here she learned the ropes of the real estate and construction industries and found a work environment more in keeping with her style and values. After three years, Diane transitioned seamlessly to a job where she was responsible for pulling together financing for a company that developed affordable housing. She worked long hours and liked it, despite her realization that relative to the for-profit world, the nonprofit side was stretched thin—short-staffed and underresourced, with salaries that were "not pretty." The fast pace of dealmaking and doing good appealed to her, and she derived great satisfaction and "fun" from what she was doing. Five years into this job, Diane had her first child, followed three years later by another. She switched to a part-time schedule—but it wasn't the solution she'd hoped for. She was asked to take on more work without additional pay and with no prospects for promotion. After twelve years in the position (seven of them working part-time with children), Diane quit and had been home one year at our initial interview.

Diane also planned to resume working, but since she had already eschewed the corporate world for the nonprofit sector, the former held no appeal. She was clear that she wanted to work on a freelance or self-employed basis, using her accounting skills, and, like many women, she timed her reentry to her children's milestones. Her youngest had just entered kindergarten. At our first interview, she projected going back to work when he was in middle school, about seven years away. In the meantime, Diane hoped to do something "to remain employable" but hadn't "really figured it out."

The Consultant

Blonde and fit, Elizabeth Brand met us at the door of her imposing suburban house for our first meeting. For the next two hours, with a quiet intensity Elizabeth detailed her remarkable career and the reasons why she had ultimately left it. Age forty when we first talked, she had one child with another on the way. Growing up in the South, with an engineer father and older brothers who also pursued scientific and technical careers, Elizabeth followed in their footsteps, not in her stay-at-home mother's. Liking math and science, she "tended to gravitate where guys did," one of only three women in the engineering program at the prestigious university from which she graduated. Quickly finding work in her field, she took a job with a multinational energy company, doing everything "from designing parts of pipelines to developing pipe specifications for a new plant that was going be built." Elizabeth's talents were soon recognized, and after only a year and a half she was offered "a really terrific opportunity" to work at a factory "that had a lot of issues." Located in a remote part of Idaho, a region of the country she had never even visited, this job gave her "nuts and bolts experience" at a very young age. Elizabeth was not only young, she was female, and she described the situation facing her as she started her new job: "I used to kid that I was the only professional woman in the whole town of twenty thousand people. Because anyone who ended up doing that left that town or the state." Despite trepidation from the plant's workers, who had heard that "there is a woman coming from California, and she's going to tell us how to run our plant," Elizabeth was able to win them over, and looked back on the job fondly: "It was a great learning experience. I learned a whole lot from the operators and the maintenance people.... So, on a personal level and a professional level, it was a tremendous growth experience."

Although she loved her job and the athletic, outdoorsy lifestyle of the Rocky Mountains, Elizabeth decided to apply to business school. Recognizing that her engineering background and unusual work experience would distinguish her, Elizabeth recalled (realistically, not boastfully), "Because I had a unique application, it was really easy to get in. I applied to, I think, MIT, Wharton, and Harvard, and got into all three, and decided to go to MIT because I thought it just seemed to be the right fit." Elizabeth once again found herself in a male-dominated world, one with "a lot of very conservative, particularly economically conservative, individuals." She took a lot of finance and technology classes and landed a summer internship with a leading management consulting firm, eventually joining them upon getting her MBA. In what she characterized as the "up or out" world of consulting, Elizabeth quickly moved up, from consultant to vice president in only seven years. Throughout her career, she worked on a variety of projects, many of them international in scope, in a range of industries, and made partner at age thirty-four. In the billable-hour world of consulting, fifty-plus-hour weeks and heavy travel were the norm. Two years after making partner, Elizabeth had her first child. Concerned that her extended periods of international travel and long hours would affect her ability to bond with her son, she took maternity leave and never returned. She had been home two years at the time of our first interview and, after undergoing a series of fertility treatments, was pregnant with her second child.

At our first interview, Elizabeth's plans to work again were distant and vague, but she was sure they wouldn't entail consulting. She wondered aloud whether, instead of quitting, she could have "found a halfway point ... and maybe gone into a different job?" For the time being, she envisioned going back to work in "six, eight, ten years," when her children were "fully in school," and hoped to do something "more academic, maybe more on the philanthropic side of things." She knew that great opportunities would not arise "without doing a tremendous amount of legwork," something for which she had no time.

The Editor

Nan Driscoll, forty-six at our initial meeting and the mother of three, had grown up in suburban New Jersey and, now living in an affluent suburb of New York City, styled herself "a second-generation suburbanite." She had short curly brown hair and large horn-rimmed glasses that gave her an appropriately bookish look. Having majored in English literature at a small Jesuit college in upstate New York, she was "uncertain of what I wanted to do. I knew I didn't want to teach, but I knew that I wanted to live in New York City." Narrowing her options to publishing and social work, she surveyed job ads to conclude she could earn a little more in an entry-level job in publishing—enough to "feasibly support myself and get a studio apartment." Her first job came easily, though disappointment quickly ensued: her boss "explained my entire job [sorting invoices] to me in eight or nine minutes."

Nan hung in, and "after about six months, I talked to the head of the business department and told him what I really wanted to do, the editorial side of things," in case something came up. Something did, and Nan soon found herself a managing editor, working more on the administrative side, which she described as "a fabulous learning experience." From here, wanting to "really edit," she became an associate editor, then sen-ior editor before leaving the company after six years for a larger, more prestigious publishing house. In her five years with this firm, she contin-ued to rise through the ranks, finally becoming editor-in-chief of the children's book division. Company priorities changed, however, moving away from children's books. "Feeling as though I wasn't getting any-where," Nan jumped ship to a small firm that specialized in book pack-aging, putting together children and juvenile book series for the imprint of well-known publishers. Nan loved the job, finding unexpected enjoy-ment in the business side, and was quickly promoted to editor-in-chief—"an opportunity I felt as though I could not pass up"—but a challenge now that she was married and trying to get pregnant.

Even in an industry she described as "filled with women," she was the first at her company to have a child, "so I worked out my own little maternity situation." Her boss was supportive of her efforts to craft a baby-friendly flexible schedule, but Nan had reservations, feeling that "it was much harder to be as effective as I had been." When the company, like so many in the publishing industry during the late 1980s, began experiencing financial pressures, the owner instructed Nan to lay off a single mother when he "saw [her] coming in three days a week and thought that she wasn't carrying her weight." Nan quit instead, explain-ing that she "was very lucky" because her husband, a corporate lawyer, earned good money. She reflected back proudly on that decision, noting that she had "left as vice president and editor-in-chief . . . with only the owner on top of me," having "achieved everything I wanted to achieve."

At the time of our first interview, Nan had been a stay-at-home mom for ten years and had worked for fifteen. Back then, she too was unsure about whether she'd return to work. Like so many women, she took pride in her past accomplishments, having had "a marvelous, marvelous career." Unlike most other women, however, she regarded her former career as a closed chapter: "I've been there, and I've done that. It was great, and it's a part of my life." Now, she said, she didn't "need a career" because she'd had one: "I have a second career, and it's my children, it's my family." Nan had decided not to return to work "for the time being. We're lucky in that we don't need to financially, so therefore [the questions are] do I want to do it and how would I arrange it?" Influencing her thinking was her belief that "it's more important to be there for my [children] now and in the next few years than it was when [they were] in kindergarten and first grade." She cited the "mind-boggling logistics" of chauffeuring "from three o'clock to seven o'clock every night with three kids, various lessons," and occasional sick days. In the unspecified future, Nan could envision working, but only if the job was nearby and didn't entail a commute to the city. She was clear then that she wouldn't return to publishing and that she was open to working in a "totally different field, as long as the hours are right, and it was interesting, somewhat challenging, and I felt as though I could learn something by doing it, or perform some sort of needed function."

The Trader

Meg Romano was forty-one and had three children at our first interview. Tanned and dark-haired, Meg was animated and expansive as we talked on her screened porch on a warm spring day in her charming suburban home. During her childhood outside New York City, Meg's "primary influence" was her mother, a summa cum laude graduate of Mount Holyoke who graduated college in 1958, when, according to Meg, "women just got married and had kids." Meg's mother did not work herself until she had to, when Meg's father, a banker, lost a series of jobs as a result of the collapse of the savings and loan industry during the 1970s.

After Meg graduated from college not knowing what she wanted to do, her mother pointed her toward Wall Street. Calling on a family contact, Meg found work as a clerk on the floor of the New York Stock Exchange, and "The rest, as they say, is history. That was 1982, and that was the first leg of this major twenty-year bull market that we've had. And so it was very exciting." She moved up rapidly, first by "schmoozing" her way into a better job at a bigger firm, where she was taken under the wing of a senior trader who soon realized how little she knew. "So basically," Meg recalled with gratitude, "he demoted me" so she could learn the ropes of this high-stakes field. Within the year, she "got a lucky break" and another promotion. After about three years, however, she "knew that this wasn't where I was going to make my career" and moved to the (relatively) quieter institutional trading desk. After two years, she was offered the job of head trader, an offer her mentors counseled her she could not refuse because it would not only afford her "exposure to all of Wall Street" but double her salary. "So they said to me, 'You know, for a woman of your age'—and at the time I was all of twenty-six years old—'this is a great opportunity.'"

Meg met her husband on the exchange, and when he wanted to return to Philadelphia, his hometown, to go to law school, she moved willingly. When the job she had originally lined up disappeared in the crash of 1987, Meg found another one in what was then a small firm but today is one of the largest investment funds in the country. Meg's fortunes prospered with the company's. Along the way she had three children and was able to move between working part-time and full-time as the situation demanded. When her youngest child was diagnosed with a serious congenital medical problem, Meg took a leave of absence. Ready to return, she lined up a part-time position that would enable her to oversee the final stages of her son's treatment. At the last minute, after she had been eight years with the firm, the part-time option evaporated and she was told she would have to return full-time. She quit instead.

When we first talked, Meg had been home four years, after a twenty-year career. She was more confident than most at these initial interviews, both about her ability to return to work and about her intention to remain in the same field, finance. As was typical, Meg voiced no regrets about her decision ("There's been none of that"), but, perhaps reflecting her background in finance, she was one of the few women who explicitly worried about "how are we going to swing retirement and three college educations, and at some point I'm going to have to translate some of that worry into actually actively making more money." She was secure that "the same traits that I had that made me as successful as I was in the first place are going to carry me forward in the next thing." She "[kept] her foot in the door of the industry and talking to people" through "some evening entertaining and attending industry functions." As for her professional licenses, "I've maintained all that. In the back of my head I'm doing everything that I need to do to step back into it." But the longer Meg stayed home, the longer she equivocated. She planned to return at some point but was unsure when, remarking with disillusionment that she had "finally gotten to the point that I felt like it was a myth that you could have it all."

The Scientist

When we first interviewed her, Denise Hortas was forty-five and the mother of two children, ages eleven and fourteen. Denise was voluble and enthusiastic. Growing up on Long Island, where "they had very good public schools," she was an outstanding student who excelled at writing and math and knew in high school that she wanted to pursue science: "I thought that I wanted to be a physician, and I knew that I liked biology." Finishing college in three and a half years, she immediately married her boyfriend (still her husband). Both she and her husband went on for PhDs, she in the sciences, he in humanities. Denise finished in six years, but her husband changed course to attend law school on the West Coast. With her sterling credentials she landed a postdoc at the same institution. During the last year of her postdoc, Denise had her first child: "And unlike all my previous years in science, where I came home for dinner and then went back to the lab, I just worked from ten to six, infuriating my mentor." "It was not an easy thing," she reflected, "but there was no question in my mind that I was not going to be [a big-time academic] researcher." She "realized in graduate school that—having been at two extremely good research universities—I did not have the best hands for research.... I did not love the doing of research, and I didn't like the very narrow focus of the actual research, but I loved the broader sense of being at the university and making the connections."

Living in the heart of Silicon Valley, where "there were a lot of opportunities to go to work for industry," Denise quickly found a job in the pharmaceutical industry conducting clinical trials to bring new drugs to market. She was upfront with her new boss about wanting to work what she called "normal hours," and her boss, the CEO and a woman she described as "a pretty significant figure in the pharmaceutical industry," supported her. Denise worked for this company through the birth of her second child, modifying her schedule from "normal hours" to part-time, then ramping up to full-time again. She rose rapidly up the ranks and marveled about "how much opportunity there was [at her firm], and when I was ready to take it, I would have it." Eager to advance still further, she arranged to meet with the company's new CEO, her supportive female boss having been pushed out in a merger. When she expressed her desire to ultimately become a vice president, her new boss replied, "You're not going to want to do that." Denise took that to mean "You're committed to other things." She came away from this meeting discouraged—and angry—feeling that she "now had a boss who had pigeonholed me" and that "there was this barrier raised in my face for the first time."

Denise quit, again with no regrets, and had been home only a year when we interviewed her for the first time. She was already starting to take on some consulting work in her field, pharmaceutical research, which she thought she'd do for "the next couple of years, because it suits what I'd like to do with my children." Her daughter, she noted, would be home only for another three and a half years and her son off to college in seven, at which point "I will be back in the workforce full-time. But . . . I may not be doing pharmaceutical development work. I may be a teacher or something." Although unsure of which field she'd pursue—teaching or continuing in pharmaceuticals—Denise was far more focused in her thinking about the future than most women at the time of initial interview. She was also more confident that she would be able to return to the workforce on her own terms, a function of her credentials, seniority in her field, and deep network of contacts.

REACHING FOR THE STARS

Kate and the other women profiled in this chapter and throughout the book are stars. Most of them graduated from a leading, highly selective college or university and earned a graduate or professional degree, and all previously pursued successful careers. Full-time mothers when we first talked with them, they may have returned home from different starting points, but their early lives were remarkably similar. Most came from middle- or upper-middle-class homes that bestowed distinct advantages that helped pave the way for them, especially through access to higher education.[2] They grew up in traditional families, their fathers working and their mothers at home, as was typical of women of their class and generation. Transitioning from youth to adulthood and school to work, their lives proceeded almost seamlessly, with little disjuncture or disruption. High-achieving and coming of age in an era in which young women, especially of their class, were encouraged and expected to reach for the stars, these women—each in her own way— did. They related the stories of their earlier lives with candor and enthusiasm, revealing their strengths and their weaknesses, which they had often transcended. Denise's recognition, while doing a postdoc, that she didn't have good hands for research might have daunted, if not defeated, many in her position, yet Denise coupled this recognition with another—that she *was* good at making connections. Strikingly, women's early education and career-building efforts were highly focused, and their movements from one stage to another were relatively frictionless and always upward. These were smart women, whose privilege, savvy, and intelligence had paved the way to top schools that were, in turn, a springboard to top jobs. Although they were not boastful, what resonates throughout their accounts is confidence and an accompanying sense of real accomplishment.

As women became mothers, however, many encountered friction and uncertainty of direction for the first time in their lives. No longer golden girls, they found their competence and commitment questioned, and their confidence ebbed as they felt the unaccustomed sting of stigma and stalled careers.

WHY WOMEN REALLY QUIT

The common understanding disseminated by the popular media is that women like these quit for family. At first glance, they do, because in opting out they turn to full-time motherhood. But our previous research revealed the shortcomings of this explanation—*full-time motherhood is what they do when they quit, not why they quit*.[3] First, these women, with few exceptions, had never intended to devote themselves exclusively to raising a family. The vast majority (90 percent) had seen as their early and long-standing life goal the combination of career and family. Moreover, they pursued their careers with diligence, the average woman having worked ten years prior to quitting. Second, motherhood per se was not typically a trigger to quit, since the majority had worked well past their second child. Third, further challenging the usual maternalist construction, many had quit when their children were older, at least school age, not when they were babies and toddlers, and had found the unanticipated transition to stay-at-home motherhood very hard. Fourth, while women told their bosses and coworkers they were quitting for family, this was a face-saving, burn-no-bridges cover story. As sociologist Sarah Damaske finds, women of all backgrounds, whether they're talking about why they work or don't work, always frame rationales about work as "for the family,"[4] a gender-role consistent narrative that covers all bases and meets with social approval (which is why "leaving for family" explanations cannot be taken at face value).

The true reasons women quit were rooted in real conflict about the nature of the working conditions of the careers they left behind. Women's decisions to quit were multifaceted. They cited jobs, children, and husbands, but it was work, not family, that dominated their narratives. Nine out of ten gave work-related reasons. Workplace pushes operated in tandem with family pulls—especially today's high-demand mothering standards, and husbands who were often "missing in action" on the home front. Close attention to their stories reveals that opting out was a default option, pursued when others had failed and typically with reluctance and regret. The price of success for these women was being in what many called "all-or-nothing jobs," characterized by long hours and relentless demands. While this was slightly more pronounced in the high-status, historically male-dominated professions like business and law, it was a fact of life in mixed-gender fields like publishing and marketing too—all of which saw a speedup in hours at just the historical moment—starting in the late 1970s and beyond—when more and more women were entering them.[5] Long hours—on the order of fifty to sixty or more per week—was the single most commonly cited reason women couldn't make work work. And while they most often talked about long hours in the immediate context of their own jobs, their husbands worked at a similar pace, making them unavailable at home.[6] Husbands' earning edge (reflecting the well-known gender pay gap) also sheltered them from home front responsibilities and privileged their careers over those of their wives (although even when wives outearned their husbands, his career was still expected to take precedence—a gender dynamic often glossed as a matter of "personality" or individual preference). This synergy of long hours and dual-career marriages in the context of husbands' privileged absence from domestic responsibilities was often what created a "break point" for women in their ability to continue their careers.

A related reason for quitting, rooted in the hold of the contemporary overwork culture characteristic of today's professional and managerial jobs, was the failure of efforts such as reduced hours, telecommuting, or other forms of flexibility to relieve the time bind. Two-thirds of women in the study were able to make some kind of alternative work arrangement before quitting, typically working part-time (though about 10 percent of those who asked were turned down—more often, these were younger, less experienced women in their thirties). Not surprisingly, given the tyranny of the ideal-worker norm, which demands complete commitment to job without family or other personal distractions, women found their innovative efforts to work part-time or job-share short-lived and doomed to failure.

These women discovered as working mothers—typically the only ones requesting or using alternative work arrangements—that in their firms "part-time professional" was an oxymoron. As part-timers, women had the significant responsibilities of their jobs taken away, lowering their status but more importantly to them limiting their contribution and impact. They saw their "part-time" hours creep up to full-time without commensurate pay; lost any chance for promotion; and knew they were just one new manager away from seeing their hard-won flexibility denied. Women also felt keenly the *stigma* attached to their efforts to challenge the long-hour culture. Statements linking work status and/ or motherhood status to stigma (so-called "stigma statements") were widespread, voiced by 76 percent of women in our first study, the average woman making three.[7] Christine Thomas, a marketing executive at a major software company, invoked the notion of stigmata (the marks of stigma) when she remarked, "When you job-share [in this company], you have 'MOMMY' stamped in huge letters on your head." Blair Riley, an associate at an elite law firm, was able to arrange to work part-time but hid it from her immediate colleagues. She likened working part-time to illness: "It's something like a cold. It'll pass or you leave." Women often internalized this stigma as a sign of their own failure, which further undermined the success of these efforts and weakened their attachment to their jobs and careers.

THE MOTHERHOOD BAR

The speedup in professional and executive careers creates a culture of overwork. In tandem with the choke hold of the ideal-worker (read "male worker") model, this culture undermines the viability of flexible work arrangements to create what we call a de facto motherhood bar. In the past, mothers were legally prohibited from working, even as teachers, the most female of professions. Today, women are recruited to enter traditionally male fields such as law and business, and while no one forces them to leave, the conditions of work—especially in the top firms—make it very difficult to remain for those who are (or want to become) mothers. The new motherhood bar functions, via overwork and hostility to workplace flexibility, to undercut working mothers' retention while promoting interruption and intermittency, which become normalized.

THE CHOICE GAP

While these women recounted stories of unrelenting workplace pressures and the failure of their best efforts to develop coping strategies, they rarely voiced feelings of victimization or discrimination. Having internalized the norms of their professions, few felt the sting of bias or prejudice, despite having experienced the motherhood penalty firsthand. Their affluence, their understanding of the privilege of their position, their professed perfectionism, and their strong sense of personal agency led them to adopt the narrative of choice. References to "choice" studded their interviews, phrases like "active choice" and "professional choice" appearing in 70 percent of them. Women were often emphatic that any penalty they encountered on the job was the consequence of their own actions and preferences. They frequently construed their decision to quit their careers as "feminist," invoking third-wave feminism as being all about individual choice (in contrast to second-wave feminism, with its focus on structural gender equality). The thirty-somethings in the sample were twice as likely as the forty-somethings to use choice rhetoric frequently. Typical was thirty-four-year-old Melissa Wyatt, a fund-raiser who quit after going from a full- to a part-time job: "I would characterize myself as a feminist. And I like the fact that women today have choices. And I think that's so critical."

This disjuncture between the reality of the pressures—and lack of options—and the rhetoric of choice in which women frame their decisions to quit is what we call the choice gap. Behaviorally, it can be seen in the difference—or gap—between what women would like to do, persist in their careers, versus what they actually do, leave them. Choice rhetoric, in its focus on individual preferences, obscures the powerful institutional barriers women—even highly capable and privileged women—face. Perhaps the ultimate example of choice rhetoric is the characterization of these women's actions—in which they suspend or terminate careers they care about and have made considerable investments in—as opting out. Our analysis revealed that women in prestigious, powerful, and lucrative professions had, in fact, limited options to continue in these high-demand careers once they became mothers. Their affluence afforded them the option of leaving the workforce, but this "choice," our research revealed, was not a preference but an all-or-nothing decision necessitated by the all-or-nothing nature of their work.

THE EVIDENCE MOUNTS

Our central finding, that high-achieving women's decision to interrupt or suspend careers is strongly shaped by the conditions of work (in synergy with ongoing inequality in the gendered division of care work in the home), is corroborated by a large and growing body of subsequent research on opting out.[8] A recurring theme in the research literature is the key role played by a work culture attuned to an ideal male model, which penalizes flexibility and, by extension, female professionals who seek it. A study of three top professions in which women have made considerable inroads (law, medicine, and business), for example, found women's opt-out rates highest in business, followed by law, and lowest in medicine. This differential was attributed to the longer hours and inflexibility of work in the first two fields, medicine having become more flexible with the move away from the private practice model to larger group practices such as HMOs.[9] Another study of high-achieving women similarly attributed the decision to quit careers to work or organizational factors including inflexibility, discrimination, and lack of advancement opportunities.[10] Echoing the efforts of the women we studied, women who quit would have preferred to keep working had they been able to work flexibly with reduced (read "reasonable") hours. A study of women in banking likewise found that women left because of a combination of masculine workplace cultures and inflexible workplaces, especially an expectation of long hours and constant availability. On return from maternity leave, women reported seeing their responsibilities reduced, their status downgraded, or their positions eliminated—similar to what we found when women switched to part-time, often concomitantly with their return from parental leave.[11] Yet another study concluded that women, especially professional women, were being "pushed out" of the workplace upon becoming mothers. Their research found that women in flexible jobs before motherhood were more likely to remain in the workforce.[12] Research also finds that women in organizations that were more supportive of work-family balance experienced less stigma around pregnancy and motherhood. These women were also less likely to leave the workplace after giving birth.[13]

Our major finding—the effect of long hours or overwork, specifically— is increasingly well documented. Sociologist Youngjoo Cha, analyzing a nationally representative data set, demonstrates that mothers (but *not* men or childless women) who work fifty hours or more per week are more likely to leave male-dominated occupations, either by moving to jobs in non-male-dominated occupations or by exiting the labor force. Confirming what we found—that long hours and motherhood don't mix—among women who work long hours, mothers are 52 percent more likely to leave than women without children. Part-timers, both men and women, are also more likely to exit male-dominated jobs, jobs that hew strictly to ideal-worker norms and hence penalize part-time work, as we observed. Looking only at labor force exits (opting out), Cha finds that the overwork effect is greater for mothers in male-dominated occupations, who are three times more likely to exit the labor force than mothers in other fields. Men who overwork, like the husbands of the women we interviewed, are *less* likely to exit. Because the overwork effect is present only for mothers in male-dominated jobs, Cha concludes, as we do, that "pressure from the workplace plays an important role" in understanding women's exits both from male-dominated jobs and from the workplace itself.[14]

The influence of husbands' long hours on women's decisions to quit has also been documented in subsequent research. One study found that women whose husbands overworked (putting in fifty or more hours per week) were more likely than women whose husbands worked regular hours to leave the workforce.[15] Another study by Youngjoo Cha found the same thing, with the likelihood of quitting if one's husband worked long hours even greater among women with children, further underscoring the nexus of long hours and persistent cultural assumptions about women as primary caregivers.[16]

Many women in our study reduced their hours before taking the decision to quit, thereby reducing their contribution to total household earnings. Research finds that women whose earnings make up a smaller household share are more likely to leave careers. We construed husbands' higher earnings as a support that made staying home possible— more of a reason for husbands' decision to continue working than an immediate reason for women's quitting. Nonetheless, women frequently invoked their lower earning power, especially to explain why their husbands could not contemplate quitting (and they could), a critical rationalization that gave precedence to their husbands' careers.

LOOKING AHEAD: DISTANT DREAMS

When we first interviewed the women in our study, they were full-time, at-home mothers. Not only had they had to confront the unanticipated end of careers they'd long planned on pursuing, they had to adjust to the new and unknown world of full-time motherhood, which had never figured in the life plans of the vast majority. The transition to the world of being "at home" was as profound and challenging as the transition out of the world of work. Women came to embrace their lives as stay-at-home moms, yet few gave up on the prospect of resuming work. Looking ahead, women did not voice their usual confidence. Like the women in the auditorium at the career returners conference, they were concerned that their prospects for returning to work were diminished by their time at home.

WHITHER DREAMS?

At our initial interview, the prospect of working again was, for virtually all women, a distant dream. Once women were absorbed in the busyness of everyday lives as full-time, at-home mothers, their thoughts about a return to work were soft in focus and remote. When they could articulate specific goals, these were often more about what they did *not* want to do, reflecting a lingering rejection of their former careers.

Women whose lives had flowed unerringly now found themselves adrift and uncertain given the options open to them. Chief among their wants were (1) flexibility, which translated concretely into part-time work, and (2) meaning. For both, they would have to look far afield from their past careers, exacerbating the sense of rudderlessness created by the crisis of confidence over the gaps in their résumés. As we discovered when we followed them up years later, and as we'll see in the next chapters, time at home presented challenges—and seductions—that deterred a few women from working ever again, but it also presented unanticipated opportunities. Most did return to work, but often in ways they hadn't anticipated when we first talked with them. Neither we nor they could have foreseen the "lack of confidence because I've been out so long" journey ahead.

TWO

The Siren Call of Privileged Domesticity

DRIFTING TOWARD PRIVILEGED DOMESTICITY

After the birth of her third child, Meg Romano only reluctantly left her job as a financial trader when promise of a part-time position failed to materialize. The thought of quitting seemed positively frightening to Meg, who, like many other women in our study, avowed that her identity felt inextricably tied to her professional accomplishments. However, once she was home, and over time, Meg's perspective was transformed. Four years after stepping out of her career at age thirty-seven, with children ages four, eight, and nine at the time of our first interview, she saw how much the routines of daily life were filled with opportunities to enhance her children's development: "[Children] don't come to you and say, 'Mom, I really need to talk to you about something important that happened at school.' They tell you it when you're driving them to piano lessons, and from the back of the car comes this little voice, 'Mom, what do you think about this?' In some ways I think it's easier for them to talk to the back of your head." Meg continued to explain that these unprompted conversations allowed for "a lot of moral guidance and developmental guidance that I'm doing for my children on the fly that, if I weren't here and accessible to them, someone else would either be doing it or missing the cues that … they want to talk."

In tandem with her evolving attitude about the importance of being home, Meg's plans for returning to work changed. At first, she remained determined to go back to her former employer, saying, "I always felt like I would be going back, that that door was wide open." But by forty-one (at the time of our first interview), she declared that she was "in a completely different place." She was now content to put her career on hold for a much longer period: "My daughter is turning ten in October. She'll only be with me eight more years and she'll be going to college. And my other daughter will be behind her and then my son. I will be fifty. I'll have twenty more years to work if that's what I want to do." By our second interview, Meg was fifty-one. With her children almost launched, she had returned to work just two years earlier, after almost nine years at home full-time.[1] Although she was exuberant about her new career as a development officer in a small educational nonprofit, her trajectory had certainly veered far from its original course.

As her story illustrates, once women made the wrenching decision to quit their jobs, they often and unexpectedly spent many years out of the labor force. About one in five women had not gone back to work by the follow-up interview, and they had no immediate plans to do so. But among the rest, the total amount of time women had spent at home full-time by the time of our follow-up interview averaged ten years. Importantly, a significant portion of reentry women did not stay out of the labor force *continuously,* but rather dipped briefly in and out of very part-time jobs, while heavily prioritizing their family responsibilities (a pattern that will be discussed further in the next chapter). This larger postquit pattern is rather striking given where these women started. As described in chapter 1, our participants were ambitious and accomplished and almost without exception had risen rapidly in their fields. Many had continued working beyond their first child; they had resigned only reluctantly. So how do we explain the typically yawning postquit hiatuses?

Having been effectively shut out of their characteristically inflexible, long-hour workplaces, these women were reluctant to return to them quickly because their need for family flexibility was ongoing. However, another deeper and more surprising dynamic was at play here. Once home, these women experienced a surprising drift to what we identify as "privileged domesticity." Over time, their new lives as at-home mothers created a heightened involvement in mothering, community volunteer work, and traditional household roles, in which, informally speaking, they "baked the bread" while their husbands earned it. This gradually deepening investment in domesticity (with its *Mad Men*–era division of family labor) was strongly shaped by these women's family affluence, while also serving to promote it. This occurred for two reasons closely related to our participants' economic and social privilege: (1) their growing consciousness of their key role as homemakers and status keepers in enhancing the class-based success and well-being of their families, especially their children; and (2) a discovery of the pleasures afforded by domesticity in a context of economic affluence. The latter dynamic related to their ability (as a household) to pay others to do some of the more unpleasant aspects of homemaking, such as housework, and to focus more instead on its meaningful and enjoyable features, such as intensive mothering, community work, and expanded leisure time. Over time this drift to privileged domesticity was seductively rewarding in many ways, but it also heightened women's dependency and subordination within the family, and it made a full and timely return to work harder and less likely.

FOR THE GOOD OF THE FAMILY: CULTIVATING FAMILY FORTUNES

As we saw with Meg, once home, women became much more acutely attuned and responsive to the daily rhythms, routines, and needs of family members—particularly those of their children, but also those of their husbands, and sometimes their aging parents. Having cut short their own rising careers to better manage family, our participants rechanneled their drive, energy, and considerable talents into ensuring that their husbands and children attained the highest levels of success in career and school, what we call "status keeping" to distinguish it from caregiving and housekeeping per se. This process over time also embedded them ever more firmly into highly specialized, traditional gender roles. Whether or not they were directly aware of it, women's newfound ability to provide intensified "backstage support" as full-time mothers and wives helped them to realize a characteristically upper-middle-class strategy for optimizing family economic and social advantage.[2]

Leveraging "His" Career

Before they had children, women described having relatively egalitarian marriages with their husbands, with whom they often shared the same or similar educational and career credentials. However, with the arrival of children, things often became more "traditional" with respect to housework and child care. These women, in common with virtually all women, assumed the lion's share of responsibility for domestic work, including the care of children and elderly parents, as well as overseeing the countless duties of running a household. Because of the nature of their highly demanding, long-hour jobs, husbands' lack of availability to help out with family responsibilities could obscure their unwillingness to do so. Either way, the effect of husbands' absence in family life weighed heavily on women's decisions to quit (and initially to scale back), because it often fell on them not only to pick up the slack but also to create a sense of "family." Here, Rachel Berman, a warm and dynamic redhead who had formerly worked on Wall Street, reflects on how her husband's new position influenced her decision to stay home: "My husband had taken a job three months earlier with another investment bank, and we knew his life was going to go to hell, because he was in the mergers and acquisitions department of [a high-profile firm that] was in the paper today.... So we knew that his life would be nonstop travel ... and we decided that somebody should be home to be more attentive to the kids, because now we had a second child." Although women's jobs often made similar demands on them, they tended to defer to their husband's career as primary and perceive theirs as secondary (especially when their earnings were lower, but even when this was not the case). This finding echoes other research showing that the transition to parenthood signals a moment of deepening gender inequality within marriages, when traditional ideas about gender roles come to the fore and men's careers are tacitly given primacy.[3] This pattern, which has been described by sociologists as "the hegemony of the male career," may be most pronounced in marriages among the upper and upper-middle class, because husbands' unusually high earning power legitimates their exemption from household labor.[4]

As the foregoing discussion suggests, the drift to domesticity was a marital dynamic that had already been set in motion for some mothers before they had fully left work. However, many women indicated that once they were home, their husband's dependence on them to parent and perform other household tasks only grew. Some women observed that their husbands simply stopped helping out with household chores that came to be seen as their domain since they were now at home full-time. Undoubtedly, these largely unspoken dynamics were only heightened by women's loss of economic bargaining power once home. Lauren Quattrone described herself and her husband as "joint decision-makers" prior to exiting her career as a lawyer with their first child: "Before we had children, when we were both working, it just didn't seem like life was that complicated then. We shared things pretty equally. And then definitely when I stopped working most of the household responsibilities shifted to me. You know, his job was to go to work, and my job was to do everything else."

The gender inequality embedded in these traditional arrangements often only emerged after a certain amount of interviewer probing but was rarely described with a tone of overt resentment. However, there was evidence that some couples, particularly husbands, may have tried to mask or sugarcoat these dynamics. For instance, Melissa Wyatt, forty-one years old at the time of our first interview, described her venture capitalist husband as "always" using a business metaphor—one evoking neutrality and equity—to refer to the very traditional household division of labor that developed after Melissa left her job as a non-profit administrator after their first baby: "He's revenue and I'm operations." Perhaps recognizing this phrase for the euphemism that it was, Melissa herself began deploying it for her own ends: "And I always say to him, 'Well, sometimes operations needs a little help.'"

As a full-time presence at home, women enabled their husbands to become more of a "full-time" (meaning 24-7) presence at work. In an era when very long work hours (or "overwork," as it is called by economists) are increasingly the norm among highly educated professional and managerial workers, women's dedicated backstage support clearly enabled husbands to recharge and supercharge their careers.[5] Nathalie Everett, formerly a marketing manager in a high-tech industry, described how her full-time homemaking status now enabled her husband "to fully leverage his time [and] be more successful ... just because he has 100 percent of his time to be able to focus on his job." Although helping to "leverage" their husbands' careers did not drive women's decision to leave their own jobs, over time couples came to increasingly recognize the economic and domestic benefits of this strategy. Lisa Bernard, a soft-spoken woman in her early sixties by the second interview, described the evolution of her separate-spheres marriage as a kind of "feedback loop." As she had scaled back on her career as a health care executive, eventually quitting, her husband had increasingly scaled up his. For instance, since she quit, he had held a deanship and eventually had acquired an extra faculty appointment at a separate school within the prestigious research university where he worked. She continued, "I think we did [this] without really saying it. As he got busier, that made the fact that I had more time and flexibility more important."

Some women confided that at times the "value added" from their full-time presence at home and their husband's clear preference for this kind of arrangement had prevented them from resuming their careers. Melissa Wyatt had offered to return to work during a period of instability in her husband's job. However, according to Melissa, her husband hadn't even considered this a serious option, and said: "Are you kidding? I couldn't do what I do if we both had to be on a work schedule. I mean, we couldn't balance one more schedule, one more.... What you do is incredibly helpful so that I can focus 100 percent on work, and do a good job, and know that things are taken care of at home. So, I wouldn't trade that for a nonprofit salary." Notice here the implicit calculus in her husband's response. Melissa's relatively low earnings potential in the nonprofit world is compared against her far greater perceived value in the home—*creating family* and helping to maximize his lucrative (but long-hours) career in finance. Other husbands made this same calculation, viewing a full-time wife as a win-win for them—enhancing both their work *and* family lives.

Women themselves often made a similar kind of calculation. Typically, their own jobs, and not their husband's, were placed on the "costs" side of the ledger and were viewed as necessarily expendable "for the greater good of the family." Diane Childs, the former CPA, said: "I did an analysis of 'Here's what I bring in, here's what goes out the door for the child care and whatnot,' and at the end of the day, for the stress we had as a family, it was nothing, it just wasn't financially worth it."

Sociologists who study work and the economy have described a growing prevalence of long work hours in professional and managerial occupations over the last few decades, as well as a steep hourly wage bonus or premium associated with "overwork" (a premium that is particularly high in the traditionally male-dominated professions). The causes of these trends have been linked with growing class inequality in American society. They include large structural shifts in the economy plus the proliferation of winner-takes-all or tournament-style compensation systems in elite professions (e.g., "up or out" promotion ladders in law, academia, and certain sales and business contexts). These systems handsomely reward overwork and penalize those who will not or cannot comply.[6] Regardless of their origins, opting out and then staying out appears to be a rational strategy for upper-middle-class families (whose members work in the increasingly competitive higher echelons of the professions). It is an approach that maximizes the earning capacity of the breadwinning spouse without sacrificing family life. But opting out is also a highly gendered strategy that advances husbands' careers at the expense of those of their wives.

Not Your Mother's Homemaker: Children, School, and Concerted Cultivation

June Cleaver from the 1950s television sitcom *Leave it to Beaver* may have spent much of her time keeping a spotless home and cooking elaborate meals for her family, but the women we interviewed had a different focus. It was their role as mothers, not housewives, that was of paramount and driving concern to them, and in particular their responsibility for producing academically successful and "well-rounded" children. As we will see, these women were decidedly not "just housewives"; rather, they were choreographers of their children's extracurricular activities, their children's academic coaches and advocates, and domestic planners for the entire family. Women often spent large amounts of time chauffeuring children from one after-school activity to another, helping out in their elementary school classrooms or with daily homework, closely tracking their social and emotional milestones, engaging them in various enriched educational and cultural activities, and generally overseeing their growth and development as individuals and "citizens of the world." Once the women were home, their heightened involvement in every facet of their children's lives played a leading role in their drift to domesticity.

As it turns out, lofty expectations about what constitutes good mothering are not just the province of high-achieving mothers on a career break; rather, they represent a dominant contemporary cultural model of mothering in the US, which sociologist Sharon Hays has described as the "ideology of intensive mothering." This model of parenting is "child-centered, expert-guided, emotionally absorbing" and "advises mothers to expend a tremendous amount of time, energy, and money in raising their children."[7] As mentioned, these ideals are not limited to the upper or upper-middle class, but sociologists have found that women in this demographic may be more acutely attuned to the message of intensive mothering (mindful as they are of expert advice). They are also better able to put its stringent ideals into practice because of their greater resources—educational, financial, and otherwise.

Indeed, according to one important study, social class seems to matter greatly when it comes to how parenting is actually practiced. Sociologist Annette Lareau found that compared to their poor and working-class counterparts, middle- and upper-middle-class parents (primarily the mothers) in her study practiced a much more resource- and labor-intensive form of child-rearing that she called "concerted cultivation."[8] As the name suggests, this parenting style focuses on fostering the talents of children through a hectic pace of organized activities and extensive attention to and advocacy on behalf of their children's developmental needs. Lareau found that even as "concerted cultivation" created anxiety and a frantic way of life for middle-class families, it also conferred a wide array of social advantages to children as they transitioned to adulthood. These benefits included greater confidence and skill in navigating and succeeding in the key arenas of school and work (arenas that already heavily reflected middle-class values and standards). Importantly her research, which has been confirmed by others, suggests that "concerted cultivation" as a parenting style is a central feature of upper-middle-class women's status-keeping role and a key contributor to the transmission and maintenance of class privilege among these families.[9]

By virtue of their class, professional women, regardless of whether they are employed outside the home, engage in practices of "concerted cultivation." Indeed, wanting to be more engaged in their children's academic and social development, especially as they grew older, was an important factor in some women's original decision to leave the workforce. Denise Hortas stayed in her highly demanding position as a pharmaceutical executive until her children were nine and twelve, but around this time in her kids' development, her attitude changed:

> I just felt that with the kids being in seventh grade and fourth grade, they were kind of getting to that age where … the babysitter does not cut it.… When they're littler, they need people to be nice to them, and feed them, and take care of them, and smile at them … But frankly, as they got older … and started asking—you know, that ride home from school when they ask you amazing questions and it's important how you answer that question— it has to do more with your *values*, and before they were asking, "When am I gonna have a cookie?"

As Denise illustrates, the importance of imparting *their* "values" (not the nanny's) was a common refrain among women as their children grew older. The word *values* came up so often that we came to understand it as a kind of code word to describe women's tacit understanding of the social advantage and status they could confer by virtue of their distinctively class-privileged parental influence—their tastes, preferences, educational dispositions, and so forth.

However once women were home, mothering—now a full-time job—was further intensified for them. They commonly reported having developed strong feelings and beliefs about the importance of full-time parenting that *increased in intensity*. As we saw with Meg, many women who experienced this intensification were those for whom leaving work had not been primarily precipitated by a strong maternal pull, making the emergence of these feelings all the more striking.

IVY LEAGUE BOUND   Women's intensified mothering was informed in particular by a desire to help their children academically. Most of these women had excelled in school, which undoubtedly greatly strengthened their motivation and perceived obligation to nurture their children intellectually and provide them with the maximum academic advantage. Many also enjoyed this process, as Kate Hadley remarked drolly: "My big joke right now is, I thought I graduated from sixth grade already because I did it myself; I've now done it with Kira. And last night I was helping Elise with an essay, and, you know, I just really enjoy being involved with their day-to-day lives."

This drive to be a critical part of their children's schooling also played a key role in delaying many women's reentry to the workforce and/or lengthening their overall time out of paid employment. Elizabeth Brand, whose first interview was dominated by details about her former career as a management consultant at a top firm, had transferred much of her intellectual drive and enthusiasm to intensive engagement with her children's schooling by the time of her follow-up interview. Home for nine years by then, Elizabeth said she had no immediate plans to return to work because "There's a lot of value [my children] get from their engagement with me that they wouldn't be able to have if I was working." Rachel Berman, the former Wall Street trader with an MBA from an elite business school, disclosed in our first interview that a return to work was not in her immediate future. Rachel was concerned about her nine-year-old daughter's apparent lack of internal drive to do her homework independently. Echoing Denise Hortas's comment "The babysitter does not cut it," Rachel explained: "My sitter can't sit down with my nine-year-old and do a math assignment. So if I weren't home in the afternoon to assist, I don't think it would get done. And I think she would get frustrated, and I think then she would not do as well in school, and I think it snowballs...."

Once at home, women became keenly attuned to the minute details of their children's growth and academic performance. Any potential deviations from developmental norms or from their own expectations— no matter how minor—were seized upon as opportunities for intervention. Women were willing to go to great (and often time-consuming) lengths to advocate for their children and to address any perceived problems in their schooling. This included seeking expensive independent tests, therapies, consultants, and tutors to diagnose and ameliorate learning problems (that were sometimes not perceived as such by school officials); transferring children to boarding schools or other types of specialized private educational institutions to ensure that they received more individualized attention and/or enriched academic support; and, in a few limited cases, even home-schooling their children.

Two mothers engaged in a practice called "academic redshirting," which involves delaying the start of kindergarten or first grade by an entire year for children who will likely be among the youngest in their class. This is done in order to give children a developmental advantage over their classmates (or to avoid disadvantaging them), and it is a practice most common among white, affluent families.[10] In both these cases, the mothers wanted to redshirt their children to counteract perceived (minor) learning problems. One of the two mothers, Melissa Wyatt, complained that some parents used this practice in a dishonest way—to help their average child get to the top of the class. And she admitted that it exerted pressure on other parents to do so as well in order to keep their own children academically competitive.

At the other end of the educational trajectory, some women became fierce advocates for their children in the college admissions process—arguably the ultimate goal for many parents when it comes to supporting their children's academic development. To improve their children's chances of gaining admission to elite colleges, particularly the Ivy League, these mothers became highly involved in managing their children's application process. Any problems that arose, such as flagging motivation or less-than-stellar grades and test scores, were aggressively addressed through specialized college counseling and tutoring services.

Blair Riley, formerly a lawyer at a top firm and an Ivy League graduate herself, admitted to placing a lot of pressure on her daughter Erin, an only child, to gain admission to an Ivy, saying, "I was a little neurotic on the subject." Although her daughter was talented and creative in the visual arts, Blair worried that Erin would not be competitive enough given her less than absolutely perfect grades and her lack of a distinctive career focus. Her fears were confirmed when her daughter's guidance counselor at the prestigious boarding school she attended delivered the crushing recommendation that Erin apply *only* to a group of colleges that Blair had never heard of before, and not to any Ivy Leagues. "I was disappointed, but she was disappointed largely because she knew that it mattered to me and Sam [her husband], and we'd both gone to [Ivy League college], and his father had taught at [same Ivy League college], and his brother, I mean—it's just very weighted, to say the least."

Determined to prove the guidance counselor wrong, Blair embarked on a rigorous campaign to ensure her daughter's admission to a top college, preferably the one that she and her husband themselves had attended. Describing the process of coaching Erin in the college admissions process, she remarked: "I have to confess, I went over and over and over her essays with her. Nothing went in that I hadn't seen and that her father hadn't seen, and we called upon all the academics we knew too." The all-consuming effort did pay off as Erin was admitted both to her parents' prestigious alma mater and to another Ivy League school, one that she particularly favored and ultimately chose to attend.

EXTRA EXTRACURRICULARS   A crucial element of "concerted cultivation" among today's affluent parents is involving children from the earliest ages in extensive organized activities. These activities may at times be an enjoyable source of recreation for children, but they have a much more serious goal from the perspective of parents. By encouraging involvement in a wide array of extracurricular activities, parents hope to identify and nurture special talents and abilities. More implicitly, parents recognize that these activities help position children to acquire the social skills, attitudes, and temperaments (what social scientists call "social capital") that they will need to succeed at the highest levels in school and professional life.[11] Women were well aware of the important role they played, as stay-at-home mothers, through their near-constant availability to chauffeur children to far-flung (sometimes out-of-state) sporting events, practices, club meetings, and competitions.

Many women's extensive involvement in their children's extracurricular activities—especially heavy during the elementary and middle school years—consumed as many hours as a part-time job. Kate Hadley detailed a dizzying array of enrichment activities that each of her three daughters (aged ten to fourteen) participated in, consisting of a total of six to eight separate weekly commitments for each child. Notably, some of these activities required an intensity of time, commitment, planning, ability, resources, and equipment more characteristic of professional-level activities. For instance, all three girls were members of an elite swim club that demanded five practices a week and occasional weekend swim meets. As well, all three girls were members of a rowing club, with the middle daughter so proficient that she was regularly competing at national-level competitions all over the country. Kate described this very time-consuming involvement in a good-natured way that minimized her own sacrifices: "Rowing is a very hands-on sport for parents, as the equipment is so bulky and extensive. I have a trailer that I attach to my Suburban in order to get their racing shells to different locations. When they row, it is pretty much an all-day activity: ready by 8:30 a.m. and off the water around 4:00 p.m. So there is a lot of waiting around, which makes for good reading and needlepoint time!" Notably, Kate, who was interested in returning to work on a part-time basis, had postponed initiating her job search to the fall, after her daughter's rigorous summer rowing season was over.

Bettina Mason, a lawyer who had been at home full-time for nineteen years, was less sanguine about the sacrifices she'd made. With her kids now grown, she recalled in a sardonic fashion the heavy schedule of driving demanded by her two daughters' quasi-professional involvement in soccer and tennis:

The more elite tennis club was twenty minutes away, and forty minutes total, and it didn't really make sense to wait for them because their lessons were two or three hours, three or four times a week. So yes I do ... remember feeling that I needed a microwave in my car. And a refrigerator.... I think at times you do feel a little bit like "Hmm, do they really know that I was a lawyer and I worked at a large law firm?" Because, really, what I feel like right now [laughs] is, I feel like a maid. Just, sometimes you will have those thoughts, but obviously this is a choice that I made—to do this.

Although unusual in its tone of complaint, Bettina's comment reveals an underlying reality—that women's increasing investment in their children's future career development could exact a steep cost on their own careers.

VOLUNTEERING AS INTENSIVE MOTHERING AND STATUS KEEPING

"I was a stay-at-home mom who didn't really stay at home much," said Frances Ingalls, a former public school teacher who had spent much of her twenty-one years outside the paid workforce busily engaged in an alternative unpaid career as a volunteer in her community. Over the years, Frances had become deeply involved in various nonprofit groups devoted to women's rights issues, acting in various leading capacities such as board director, fund-raiser, and even founder of one of these groups. She typically devoted about ten to twenty hours a week to these activities.

In her striking commitment to volunteer work, Frances was both highly typical and atypical of the patterns we observed. Like many other women, Frances became engaged in multiple volunteer activities in her community soon after leaving her career as a way of replacing some of what was now felt to be missing in her life at home—connection with others, mental stimulation, and a sense of purpose and accomplishment. Like other women, she was willing to invest large amounts of her time and skill in these activities and to become involved at high, even professional levels.

But in one significant way, Frances was somewhat exceptional. Most women we interviewed were involved in volunteer activities almost exclusively geared toward enhancing the quality of their own community and family life. Few of them, like Frances, donated their time and skills to philanthropic endeavors or political and social causes that created benefits beyond their local community or social sphere. In this sense, the high levels of volunteering that women did once home can be seen as an extension and further intensification of their mothering and status-keeping roles, dedicated as these unpaid activities largely were to the concerted cultivation of their children's social and academic capital. Significantly, women's increasing involvement in volunteer work tended to draw them deeper into domesticity and away from the paid labor force, even as it expanded their activities beyond the home.

Although the volunteer roles they occupied were varied and numerous—class mother, PTA president, Sunday school teacher, science fair organizer, school fund-raiser, Scout troop leader, chairman of the school or church board, and so on—the focus of many, and by far the most popular volunteer involvement, was in their children's schools. Volunteer work in schools helped to bring them into closer orbit with their children's world outside the home—the classroom, the playground, their children's friends and parents, aspects of their children's lives in which they were eager to become full participants. This work also enhanced their influence with varied school officials from teachers to administrators. After detailing an involved list of school-related volunteer activities, Donna Haley made explicit an important motivation for her heavy involvement (one that was likely more tacitly understood by other women): "But the thing I've found very useful about all the volunteer things that I've done at the various schools is that it really helps you to build a bridge ... to the 'movers and the shakers' [in the community]."

As Donna's comment above suggests, women were well aware of the way in which their involvement in these high-level volunteer activities enhanced their own profile and influence in their communities and their children's schools. Patricia Lambert, a former marketing executive, had achieved successively higher and more prestigious trustee positions on the boards of her children's private high schools (and subsequently on the boards of the two elite colleges her children were attending). She talked in particularly rapturous terms about the status and sense of accomplishment that she derived from her work: "I would say that was probably the best example of my feeling engaged and worthwhile and really using all the skills and intellectual skills, personal skills, all the kind of leadership things I enjoy and think I do pretty well. The board there is a very high-performing, very highly educated, really dynamic board, and it has a very active role in the governance of the school.... It's a really terrific board. So I chaired the strategic plan committee there twice. It was a real hotbed of activity and very, very rewarding for me."

In particular, many women were drawn to educational fund-raising— either within their children's schools or within local education foundations (organizations that raise funds to enrich programming within a local school district). Often women saw this activity as a direct means to use their high-level business and professional skills to enlarge or enhance the resources of their children's schools. Meg Romano became heavily involved in her school district's education foundation. She eventually became a head officer of fund-raising, and in the midst of the Great Recession managed to raise over $2 million on behalf of her children's public school—funds that were used to enhance the school library, completely upgrade classroom technology, and bring in authors and artists to enrich the curriculum. Although her children ribbed her occasionally about all the time she spent on her volunteer work, Meg recognized that they were "incredibly proud because they could see exactly what the benefit was right within their own classrooms."

The irony about these impressive volunteer fund-raising efforts is that they took place within public school districts or private schools that were already well funded, well resourced, and considered among the "best in class." For instance, Meg herself mentioned that her children's local high school—a beneficiary of her fund-raising efforts, and long considered part of an exceedingly strong suburban public school system—had recently been named among the top one hundred schools in the nation by a national news magazine. Therefore, these women's highly skilled efforts to "give back" primarily enriched the lives of their own already well-endowed families and communities (and heightened inequality between the haves and have-nots).

Some women were involved in volunteer efforts that were geared toward helping "the needy," but it was often done with the primary goal, not of charity for its own sake, but of educating their children about the wider world beyond their affluent suburban enclaves and instilling the "right" values. Women's volunteer involvement closely mirrored the ebb and flow of their children's school and extracurricular activities. Donna Haley likely spoke for many women when she admitted that her volunteer work was largely tied to her children's educational involvements and that "the minute the kids left those schools, I did not continue that activity at all."

GENERATIONAL SPEEDUP: MOTHERING ON OVERDRIVE   Even though all women we spoke with engaged in the intensive mothering practices of concerted cultivation, many were quite critical when they observed these same practices being enacted by other parents. They worried about the consequences of such highly involved parenting, commenting critically on their observations of "overscheduled" childhoods and intensely competitive pressures on children. Frances Ingalls was particularly pointed:

> One of my gripes is that parents are overstructuring their children's time. One thing that is very different than when we were children is that parents are very keen on giving their kids absolutely everything in terms of experience and material possessions. We live in an affluent area, so I think it is even more pronounced. But I have met tons of parents who have their kids go from one activity to another, to another, to another. They never have any downtime. That is a huge gripe.... These same people will have their

kids in ballet five days a week, because they're at the competitive level, at age six.... It's all about having that Olympic athlete. Our kids are going to be the best because we can provide it.

Nan Driscoll, who had worried aloud about her youngest daughter's apparent lack of interest in extracurricular activities, complained at a later point in the same interview about the unhealthy pressures that other mothers place on their children: "*All* my kids have come home with tales of what so-and-so's mom said to them. Like, 'She said that if he starts a club, given his SAT scores *and* his grades, if he starts a club he'll get into an Ivy League school.'"

Some women voiced resentment about the pressures they felt as the enforcers of such exacting standards. Sarah Bernheim, a thirty-nine-year-old former marketing executive who by the follow-up was still at home full-time with four young children, put it this way: "I think that parents today are stretched too thin, doing too much, and think that they need to *do* too much with the kids. They need to have them in *every* class.... They need to have them in *every* activity."

Several women noted that the new child-rearing pressures now almost *required* an opt-out parent (read mother), a point made by former nonprofit executive Melissa Wyatt: "I think parenting has become much more difficult, which is why I think a lot of parents have, the family has one parent stay home. It's a full-time job keeping track of their schedule and making a good environment for them."

Comments like these came up most often when we asked women to reflect on similarities and differences in child-rearing practices between their own and their parents' generation. Almost unanimously, women felt that there was far greater pressure on parents today to be intensively involved in every aspect of their children's lives. Just as there has been a "speedup" at work among professional and managerial workers over the last generation, research also points to a "speedup" in parenting and an intensification of the ideals of mothering, particularly among the affluent. These ideals may leave mothers like Bettina Mason—the lawyer who had stayed at home full-time for most of her two children's child and teen years—feeling "inadequate as a mom, if I didn't have the time to devote that I did." Reflecting this pattern, time use surveys find that mothers now spend roughly 30 percent more time per week on child care than mothers did in the 1960s.[12]

More specifically, research on contemporary child-rearing strategies among the professional and managerial classes has suggested that intensified parenting ideals and practices may be a response to a changing and more precarious economic climate—one in which upper-middle-class parents are now far less certain of their children's ability to reproduce their privileged class position.[13] For instance, sociologist Marianne Cooper studied how families from varied social class backgrounds are coping with rising economic insecurity. She found that upper-middle-class parents were acutely aware (much more so than their working-class counterparts) of the increasingly competitive nature of the globalized economy, and that this "fueled their anxiety about how well their children would turn out and intensified their expectations of their children."[14] The affluent families in her study also tended to feature an overworked breadwinning father and a highly educated stay-at-home mother who specialized in fostering her children's academic and social development. This research, along with our own, suggests that opting out and the drift to domesticity may be a response to increasing status anxiety among upper-middle-class families and a doubled-down effort to maintain their class advantage.

EVERYBODY'S CAREGIVER   Once home, women often became the default caregivers not only for their children but also for their aging parents, their husband's aging parents, and other extended family members in need. For some women, this became yet another factor in lengthening their time out of the paid labor force. Husbands, siblings, and other extended family members seemed to assume that because women were already at home they had the time and inclination to take on primary responsibility for every kind of family health care and elder care issue. Women willingly shouldered this burden; indeed, some embraced it.

Mirra Lopez, formerly an engineer who had been at home for twelve years by the time of the follow-up interview, had become the point person in the care of her aging parents (whom she cared for eight to ten hours a week). With characteristic equanimity and graciousness, Mirra said, "I do take on more responsibility with my parents because again you fall into this trap of 'I have the time and I'm willing to do it.' So I don't like to even get my brothers involved because I say, 'I'll get it done.'"

Husbands' extreme work schedules and lack of parenting availability— the very dynamic that had pressured women off their own career tracks— also meant that they were not available to care for their aging parents; therefore women also often became the primary caretakers for their elderly in-laws. As Amanda Taylor put it: "We had some family health issues with [my husband's] parents. His mother had had a stroke, and there were just a lot of things. I was always the default family medical management person [laughs]."

Some women reported that elder care was a factor in keeping them from reentering the workforce even when children were almost or completely out of the house. Patricia Lambert, a slim, high-energy former marketing executive, was an empty nester by the time of the follow-up interview and had been out of the workforce for eighteen years. She described a sequence of serious health problems that her parents had suffered and that she had managed. These included her father's battle with an aggressive form of cancer that had eventually killed him and her eighty-five-year-old mother's two heart attacks. Although Patricia had toyed with the idea of getting back to paid work, she and her husband had agreed that it was "an important thing for me to have a life flexible enough to drop everything."

DISCOVERING THE PLEASURES OF
PRIVILEGED DOMESTICITY

Once they were at home, after initial ambivalence and much to their surprise, women discovered many pleasures and rewards linked to full-time mothering and community volunteer work. And this discovery increased their commitment to being home, deepening their drift to privileged domesticity.

Perhaps one of the single most pleasurable aspects of being home for women was having the time to breathe, slow down, and live life at a more leisurely pace. The slower pace permitted women to fully appreciate the intrinsic satisfactions of mothering. This reaction was most poignant among women whose work lives had been crushingly busy. Denise Hortas, who had once loved her job as a top-level pharmaceutical executive, had become increasingly burnt out as her company restructured and became "more and more corporate." What this meant, according to Denise, was that she was now expected to do "three jobs" instead of just one (with no extra pay). In the meantime, Denise began to feel that she and her husband (who worked long hours as a corporate lawyer) were missing out on the lives of their two early adolescent children. On the eve of her decision to quit, Denise realized: "I feel like we bought all of this stuff, but the one thing that we would both like to have, which is some time with our children, we really didn't have."

Echoing the reactions of many other women, Denise felt a kind of joyful release from the heavy weight of work demands. Women's appreciation of this added time to simply hang out with and delight in their kids was ongoing and tended not to diminish with time. Marina Isherwood, who was back at work by the follow-up interview after taking ten years out to raise her children in an affluent Silicon Valley town, did not regret her time out: "I am glad I was home when [the children] were in middle school and high school. It was probably mostly for myself.... I loved going to the basketball games and I loved going to the baseball games, loved going to the jazz band stuff. It was highly entertaining having them home. It was a combination of not missing anything that was fun and not missing anything that could have been potentially a problem."

Opting out now also opened up a space in women's lives to become involved in community volunteer work on a professional level, which many found deeply satisfying. In fact, they often succeeded in deriving levels of meaning, status, and enjoyment from their community work that were similar to, or even greater than, those they had experienced in their former careers. The pleasure and intrinsic family flexibility of volunteer work dampened women's incentive to reenter the paid labor force quickly. In fact, it motivated a few women to avoid paid employment even during the empty nest phase so that they could continue to prioritize family events, vacations, and visits with their adult children. Bettina Mason, who received "a great deal of satisfaction making a difference in other people's lives," also liked the flexibility that volunteer work gave her to regularly travel and attend her two daughters' college tennis matches in the Midwest and on the East Coast. This was why, she remarked, "I've chosen not to be paid because I would like to arrange my volunteer efforts in a way that I can do those things."

Beyond added time to enjoy their children and to become meaningfully engaged with their communities, women discovered additional pleasures they hadn't anticipated. Chief among these were expanded opportunities for leisure and self-development. Even before they quit, women's affluence had enabled a high quality of life. They lived in beautiful, well-appointed homes, situated typically in safe and leafy suburbs with good school systems and nearby parks, and with all the creature comforts of modern living. But now they actually had the time to relish the everyday pleasures—both physical and social—that surrounded them. These unexpected satisfactions eased their conflicted initial transition home, while ultimately and over time deepening their drift homewards.

Lauren Quattrone, an energetic woman with short blonde hair and the build of an athlete, had left a lucrative career in corporate law six years prior to our first interview. She denied feeling bitter about having given up her career to stay home with their two children, even while her husband's legal career thrived (she and her husband had met while attending the same prestigious law school). In fact, according to Lauren she was the lucky one: "I have to say in many ways I have a much nicer life than he does. He works really hard. If he can squeeze in a half an hour to go swimming every day, it's a big treat for him. I get to hike in the mountains for two hours and have lunch with my friends and do stuff for my community. I don't feel that I've gotten the shaft at all." Women's time at home enhanced their appreciation for "quality-of-life" issues such as these and, as we will see in upcoming chapters, often diminished their desire to return to the workforce either quickly or full-time. During a three-year break from her legal career, Donna Haley developed a drive to "always have a good quality of life": "Quality of life to me means having work but not letting work sort of take over some of the other things that [my husband and I] do. Because we like to be able to get on our boat and just go to [nearby state]. We're big sports fans. I like to be able to go to a [name of sports team] game. And I want to be able to control that. And I want to travel." Women also used their expanded leisure time to explore personal interests and new sides of themselves. They described taking up new activities and hobbies (or restarting old ones) like doing photography, learning to play musical instruments, learning a new language, taking classes on art and architecture, joining book clubs, and finally becoming serious about exercise. One woman, a former lawyer, even proudly confessed that she was writing a legal thriller.

The freedom to take extended and sometimes elaborate family vacations that could be easily scheduled in tandem with husbands' time off played a surprisingly strong role in disincentivizing a return to work for some of the most affluent women. This was the case for Melissa Wyatt, whose husband's financial success as a venture capitalist afforded him a high degree of control over his work schedule. At the follow-up interview, Melissa detailed four vacations totaling a month of travel that she and her family had taken in the previous three months. When asked whether she planned to return to paid work, Melissa sounded doubtful, in no small part because she believed a job would put a significant crimp in the family's frequent holiday plans.

For a few women, a desire to prioritize ample leisure time over paid work was related to aging and a desire to slow down and prepare for retirement, or even to take an early retirement. Brenda Dodd was one of them.

She had retired early from her reentry career at age fifty-nine because she and her husband realized "that our health is fleeting, so we are kind of taking advantage of every opportunity we can to travel right now."

SEDUCED BY PRIVILEGE?

By the follow-up interview, women's typically lengthy tenure outside the paid labor force (with periodic dips in and out on a very part-time basis) formed a truly startling contrast with their prequit work trajectories of rapid upward ascent. Viewed dispassionately, these women had become, at least for a significant time, the proverbial "stay-at-home wife"—the kind that some observed their bosses were married to, but that few of them had ever aspired to become.

Our interviews revealed that, beyond women's reluctance to return to inflexible jobs, the act of stepping out often initiated a seemingly inexorable drift into the world of privileged domesticity—a comfortable realm that beckoned women with its rewards and pleasures even as it subordinated them as dependents. In this light, one might view privileged domesticity as a kind of patriarchal bargain: a trade-off in which women are seduced by the pleasures of privileged homemaking into sacrificing their own interests as women (to achieve economic and social autonomy) for the class-based interests of their families.[15] However, given the constraining realities of the women's situation—the long hours, the inflexibility of their former occupations, and the perceived primacy of their husband's career—it is easy to understand how affluent domesticity appeared to be a rational and appealing choice. These dynamics also illustrate how, from a class standpoint, the seemingly old-fashioned phenomenon of traditional separate spheres may in fact operate as a strategy for privileged families to maximize their economic and social capital in an increasingly competitive, winner-take-all economy (even as it reinforces gender inequality within these families).

Alternatively, one may view women's drift away from former careers and into privileged domesticity as a kind of silent protest against the inhumanity of the all-or-nothing, long-hour work cultures they have abandoned. In this view, women's experiences at home reveal and make possible the opportunity for a healthier and more meaningful quality of life centered on family, community involvement, and self-exploration. Although the opportunity to do so may be a privileged one (albeit born of constraint—another paradox), it reveals the potential benefits of reimagining and taming work so that all employees have access to work-life balance that promotes health and well-being rather than burnout and opting out.

Despite substantial career interruptions, most women desire to and eventually do follow through on their intentions to reenter the paid workforce. However, as we will see in the next chapter, their time at home and the resulting changes they experience in their values and outlook have dramatic consequences for the "how," "what," and "when" of their work return and ensuing career trajectories.

THREE

Putting Family First:
The Slow Return

After a yearlong "family sabbatical," Denise Hortas was ready to go back to work. But instead of returning to her former position as pharmaceutical executive—a round-the-clock job that that had left her exhausted and unable to focus on her children—she decided to shift gears. Until her youngest child was in college, she vowed to accept only employment that would fit around the rhythms of family life. For Denise, the obvious means to this end was to work as a part-time consultant. Well respected in her field of biotechnology, she was fully confident that she would have no trouble drumming up business. More importantly, Denise knew that if handled right, consulting would allow her to strictly limit her schedule to fit around her children's school days and vacations.

By the follow-up interview, Denise's well-laid plans had evidently been successful. Her work as a *very* part-time freelancer (and later as a middle school science teacher) had in equal measures allowed her to "step off the wheel to focus on my family," *and* to "keep her hand in" her profession. As soon as her children left for college, she had stepped back into her former career and was now vice president of a small pharmaceutical company.

With striking regularity, women sought work upon reentry that allowed them to heavily prioritize family life; and like Denise, they encountered surprisingly few barriers. However, few women were able to navigate their reentry trajectories *over the long term* with as much ease, continuity, or confidence as Denise.

Marina Isherwood, for instance, had quit her demanding job as the director of marketing in a medical group (where she had managed over $150 million in business, marketing, and promotion) so that she could become more involved in her school-aged children's lives. Like Denise, Marina returned to work as a very part-time consultant (ten to sixteen hours a week) in order to stay involved with her profession while focusing on family. However, freelance work was not quite as flexible as Marina had hoped. Client meetings sometimes required her to work beyond the hours of her children's school days, a compromise she learned over time that she was unwilling to make. After a few years of mounting frustration, Marina quit altogether, reasoning that "I couldn't meet [my clients'] needs, and my family's needs, and I decided that basically I was going to put my family's needs first." Underscoring the point, Marina mused, "You sort of draw that line, and everything else has to bounce up against it." Marina exited the labor force for another decade and returned to relaunch her former career only when her youngest child entered college.

JUMPING IN ONE FOOT AT A TIME

The phenomena of opting out and opting back in are often popularly depicted as all or nothing in nature. Like the heroines in fairy tales whose narratives always end with marriage, media stories about opt-out women often finish with women's blissful embrace of domesticity; this account implies that opting out is an end point in women's careers.[1] On the rarer occasions when the media do focus attention on professional women's reentry, it is often depicted as a herculean (and often thwarted) effort to plunge headlong from domesticity into a full-career relaunch.[2] Neither of these narratives is accurate, and our findings illustrate why.

First, despite the pleasures of privileged domesticity, most women always intended to and eventually did reenter the paid workforce. Fully four-fifths of our follow-up participants (thirty-four out of forty-three women) ultimately returned to paying jobs, mirroring the proportion who had expressed this intention during their first interview, when they were still at home. The length of time women spent outside the labor force between their initial career exit and their first reentry job varied greatly, from just a few months to eighteen years, but was an average of about six years. These findings reflect the empirical literature on professional women's career patterns, which has found that a large majority of women both desire to and eventually do reenter the work-force after a career break.[3]

Second, contrary to the media depiction of reentry, we found that most women did not try to spring back into the work world full steam ahead. In fact, reentry was typically a slow, sometimes halting process, most often occurring in two distinct phases: the "family-first" and the "career relaunch" periods. The media typically miss—and hence confound—these two phases, in which women's experiences are very different. Women reentered the workforce on a family-first basis once their youngest child had entered school full-time. With young school-aged children, women in this initial phase of reentry continued to be strongly invested in intensive mothering—particularly those activities that focused on their children's education and the transmission and maintenance of their family's class privilege. For this reason, they deliberately chose work characterized by very limited hours but expansive flexibility that would permit them to continue heavily prioritizing family life. The length of the family-first phase was variable, but it typically lasted about four years. It wasn't until their youngest child was beyond the elementary school years that most women attempted to more fully relaunch their careers.

About three-quarters of all women who reentered the workforce did so initially on a family-first basis, and they are the subject of this chapter. Chapter 4 describes the career relaunch period that occurred most commonly as the second phase in women's reentry process. In both periods, women's attitudes about work had been reshaped. A minority of women—about one in five—had not returned to work at the time of our follow-up and had no plans to do so; these women and their stories are discussed in chapter 6.

KEEPING A HAND IN

Chapter 1 detailed women's rapid career ascent prior to opting out, as well as their intense ambivalence about stepping off the career track. Most continued to have an unwavering expectation that at some point in the future they would revive their careers. However, their growing gender- and class-based investments in intensive mothering and community work were greatly heightened by their experience of privileged domesticity. Therefore, by the time women began to feel the itch to return to the workplace in some capacity, their desire was strongly tempered by a wish to place family life first, at least while their children were young. They sought work as a source of engagement, identity, meaning, and supplementary income; but their enthusiasm and commitment for it typically ended at three o'clock—the end of the school day.

Women's return to work in this phase was driven, not by a desire to relaunch their careers in any meaningful way, but rather by the wish to maintain a toehold in the world of work in preparation for a later and fuller return. Denise Hortas exemplifies this pattern. The projects she worked on as a very part-time (about fifteen hours a week) consultant tended to be quite circumscribed in scope and were less challenging and admittedly at times "unspeakably boring." Denise persisted because "I was doing it to keep my hand in, to keep up to date.... It was a way to keep connected with my former work community, which meant so much to me." For similar reasons, former trader Meg Romano seized a serendipitous opportunity to do some very limited freelance work in her field (just five hours a week) shortly after she quit. Although she felt far from ready to reenter fully with her youngest child still an infant, she recognized it as a chance to "keep my foot in the door of the industry." A few years later, she discontinued her involvement even in this limited line of work, as the occasional client meetings sometimes conflicted with her ability to pick up her son from preschool.

For women like Denise and Meg, "keeping a hand in" (even if just for a few years at a time), can be seen as a forward-facing strategy in anticipation of a future fuller return. However, for other women it represented more of a backwards-facing strategy that was primarily a means of coping with the loss of their former identities and the emotionally rocky transition to full-time homemaking. Some women managed this by seeking (or more reactively, seizing opportunities for) jobs with very limited demands. Typically, these were women who reentered within a year of their original quit, worked very limited hours for a few months or years, and then eventually quit working altogether as they became more immersed in their new lives at home. In our first interview, former teacher Felice Stewart described "feeling this void" shortly after her career exit, "like I need to work. I don't have a paycheck." For about a year she became involved in a network marketing scheme that involved selling cosmetics to her friends and family members for a few hours a week. The work provided a social outlet ("My sister was in it, and friends of mine were in it, and we had a great time") and a sense of industry and purpose. But her involvement "petered out" as these needs gradually came to be filled instead by her increasing involvement in volunteer work and in her children's lives.

A year after leaving her job as a law associate at a major firm, Lauren Quattrone also took up very part-time freelance work as a way of coping with her transition home. For two years she alternately taught a class at a local law school, graded bar exams, or wrote legal memorandums on a contract basis. She explained, ever so slightly tongue-in-cheek, that the work "gave me a reason to put a skirt on, comb my hair, and go downtown." After two years she had settled into her new life at home, and with a second child on the way she gave up paid employment altogether for another eighteen years.

For the most part, money was not a primary factor driving women back to work in this phase, but it played a contributing role. Typically, the money women earned was considered "supplementary" income. As Karen Gordon put it, her husband's full-time job (as a top executive in an engineering company) "pays the bills," and her part-time job (as a freelancing engineer) paid for the extras—a few added luxuries. Contributing to the household economy in this way and achieving some degree of financial autonomy (even if only to a marginal degree) was a source of gratification; it was therefore an important, though often implicit, motivation.

Although the exception, a few women were nudged back to work earlier than they preferred by husbands who wanted them to supplement family incomes during financially tight periods. This was the case for former editor Nan Driscoll, whose husband urged her to take a part-time job providing administrative support for a local youth sports league when her youngest child was seven years old. "I hated it, and it was my husband's idea," Nan grumbled, "but it brought in a little extra money." Thankfully for Nan, it was work she could do from home on a flexible schedule, and she was able to update some of her computer skills. As we will see in the next chapter, family finances played a more significant role in driving the timing of career relaunch.

EMBRACING THE GIG ECONOMY

Women's approach to reentry in the family-first phase was defined as much by what they chose *not* to do as by the strategies they actually employed to get back to work. Reflecting other research on this topic, women overwhelmingly (with only one exception) chose *not* to return to their former employers, knowing from experience that if they pursued this path they would almost certainly not find the flexibility they so highly prized.[4] In this phase, women were seeking to fit work around the edges of family life, and accordingly they sought jobs with limited hours and demands (typically no more than fifteen hours a week), as well as maximal scheduling control.

Our participants used two main strategies in order to accomplish these goals. The first and most popular tactic was to work very part-time as freelancers or consultants *in their former professions*. Close to three-fifths of all women made their reentry debut in this manner. Women were able to find consultant work in their former professions in a wide range of fields, including law, engineering, health care, finance, and marketing.

This was a popular strategy because freelance work paired career continuity (drawing on and keeping up-to-date former professional skill sets and networks) with maximal scheduling control and flexibility. The only exception to the latter benefit was when project work involved a lot of client contact (or fast-moving deadlines), as we saw in Marina Isherwood's narrative earlier in the chapter. Freelance work also typically permitted women to work from home. Furthermore, the project-based nature of freelancing often allowed women to take on as much or as little as they felt they could handle.

Denise Hortas describes how she was able to manage client expectations and use the circumscribed nature of project work to create a work schedule that fit her children's school calendar:

> I said, "I can work between nine or ten and two or three every day. And I can do some things in the evening, and I don't travel and I don't work during the summers. So if that's fine with you, and during those other ten months you have a project you need—oh, and I don't work during school vacations—but I'm happy to help." And everybody said, "Oh yeah, sure!" They had a lot of work for me, way more work than I could take on, I was very careful about not taking on too much.

As we will see, during the career relaunch phase, piecing together a full-time or more substantial part-time schedule could be tricky. But in the family-first phase, women's preference for limited work (with the security of their husband's breadwinner income) permitted them the freedom to turn down projects that didn't fit their family schedule.

The second tactic women used in this phase was to take largely contingent work *outside their former occupations*. These jobs were part-time nonprofessional or paraprofessional ones that permitted scheduling control because of very limited hours and contained demands. Women became office managers, Tupperware and Avon sales representatives, freelance paralegals, substitute teachers, on-call medical office assistants, and so on. Surprisingly, fully two-fifths of all women in the family-first phase initiated a return to work with this type of job. Unlike their former professions in law or business, in which part-time work was part-time in name only and often entailed full-time hours, these non- or paraprofessional jobs were less stressful, and their demands (both mental and emotional) were limited. Many of these jobs allowed women to work as many or as few hours as they desired. Even the on-call positions, such as substitute teaching, which involved less predictable hours, permitted women to turn down assignments that didn't fit their scheduling needs.

Both of these strategies had one thing in common: women's embrace of jobs in the contingent labor market—or, as it has been called, "the gig economy."[5] Despite the well-known disadvantages of contingent work—job insecurity, a characteristic lack of guaranteed employer benefits (e.g., health insurance, social security, disability, unemployment insurance, or retirement benefits), and little opportunity for traditional career development—women strongly gravitated to these jobs because of their high degree of flexibility. They knew from hard experience that they were unlikely to find family-friendly hours in the kinds of "good jobs"—professional and permanent employment—from which they had opted out. The permanent or primary labor market has historically provided workers, especially white-collar professionals, with higher-quality jobs featuring security, benefits, higher wages, and career advancement—the types of jobs that women had had prior to opting out. But these "good" jobs, designed with the outdated assumption of a male-breadwinner household, have rarely also offered high levels of family flexibility and the option of part-time hours.[6] Given the dearth of truly family-friendly jobs in the permanent sector, women gravitated by default to contingency despite its clear costs. Fortunately, women's economic privilege freed them to make the trade-off. All but one returned to work in the family-first phase on a contingent basis.

Other research has also found that professional women who opt out commonly opt back in again using part-time self-employment, home-based entrepreneurship, and other forms of contingent work to achieve greater family flexibility.[7] One researcher calls this strategy "opting in-between," observing that it is a tactic that allows these mothers to stay in the workforce on their own terms while their children are young.[8]

"THE WORKING WORLD STALKED ME!"

Less than six months after leaving her job as an associate at a prestigious law firm, Olivia Pastore, then in her early forties, decided to take a short course on midlife career transition at her alma mater. "I wasn't quite ready to go back to work, but it was fun being with my girlfriends for three Wednesday evenings," said Olivia, an energetic, warm, and confident woman who was a natural storyteller. At the end of the course, the instructor, who also happened to be a high-level administrator at the university, approached Olivia and offered her a job. It was to be a part-time, yearlong job-share as a law school career counselor. "That's how I got into law school career services—I always say, 'very serendipitously.' I never thought about doing that." Summing up her unexpectedly seamless passage back to work, Olivia exclaimed, "The working world stalked me!"

Newspaper and magazine articles tend to offer a grim prognosis of women's chances of returning to work with ease. A few recent headlines from some prominent media outlets evoke the flavor of this phenomenon: "Moms 'Opting In' to Work Find Doors Shut"; "After Years Off, Women Struggle to Revive Careers"; and "Off Ramp to On Ramp: It Can Be a Hard Journey."[9] Such media stories often portray women's reentry efforts as protracted or ending in failure or frustration as employers rebuff them for having passed their "sell by" date.[10] Or they focus on the uphill battle women face in grappling with dreaded questions about the gap in their CVs (as one recent newspaper headline suggests: "Should Women Explain Gaps in their Resume after Raising a Family?").[11] Judging from the women at the career relaunch seminar in our opening scene, these kinds of stories can trigger ample anxiety and concern in women like those we studied.

In stark contrast, we found that with very few exceptions, women's reentry in the family-first phase occurred easily and at times even effortlessly. Surprisingly, few women noted any barriers to returning to work in this phase; and job searches (when they occurred at all) typically took only a few weeks or months. So how did women get back to work with such ease?

First, a majority of women (three-fifths) in the family-first phase found jobs serendipitously, without even looking. While open to finding work, they did not proactively seek it. Instead, they were sought out by others, who recognized these former professionals turned at-home mothers as a potentially prime source of highly skilled temporary labor. Accordingly, very few women in the family-first phase sought jobs through the conventional route of trolling internet job sites or the classifieds, or formally applying for jobs. And perhaps because so few women actually conducted a formal job search in this phase, not one complained about the problem of the résumé gap.

Former colleagues, friends and family, and even people women encountered casually identified them as potential assets for short-term jobs that involved limited hours. This was true in the case of Olivia Pastore, who was spotted, talent scout–style, as a lawyer turned full-time mom who might be open to a limited-commitment gig, especially one that would permit dabbling in an alternative career. As the administrator who offered her the job undoubtedly recognized, a seasoned and credentialed career counselor would likely reject such a short-term, part-time job without benefits. However, somebody like Olivia might see it as an opportunity—as she did. The downside of this "opportunity" for Olivia became apparent at the end of the academic year when her job-share ended. While Olivia thought she had discovered a new vocation in career counseling and was getting rave reviews from her students, her boss refused her request to renew her part-time contract. Instead, her job was converted back into a full-time position. As this story illustrates, employers looking for staff who can conform to their "just-in-time" needs may look upon the pool of talented professional women like Olivia as a "reserve army of labor" ready to be tapped and potentially disposed of when their labor is no longer needed.[12]

Former colleagues occasionally checked in on the availability of participants to do contingent work in a pinch—part-time, project-based, or seasonal work. If women were ready to step back in, it became their first official reentry job. Brenda Dodd, formerly a medical technologist who had been at home for over ten years, got a distressed call from her girlfriend, a dentist, one day. Her friend asked Brenda whether she'd be willing to "come in and answer the phones" to replace an employee who was out sick. Brenda obliged, and very unexpectedly ended up becoming an on-call dental assistant for many years.

Volunteer experiences also created opportunities to reenter the workforce, even for women who hadn't been actively seeking a job. Martha Haas was unexpectedly offered a job at her children's private school where she had been volunteering. Martha had casually mentioned her former career in development to the headmistress at a school function, and a few weeks later, the headmistress offered her a part-time temporary job-share as a development officer. At first Martha refused. Although she had been contemplating a part-time return in the wake of her recent divorce, she wasn't ready to go back just yet. But eventually, Martha came around: "[The headmistress] told me that she had gone through a divorce when her kids were young, and she said, 'You need a project.' And I thought about that, and the tendency, especially when you're at home, to just overthink things.... I never would've thought about looking at this point in my life, but it's just been a wonderful period of growth for me."

Another reason that women's return to work in the family-first phase was relatively quick and easy was that a significant proportion of them returned as consultants in their former professions. Those seeking such freelance work tended to have been out for shorter periods of time, so they were able to successfully draw on their professional networks. Denise

Hortas captured the surprising ease of this process when she remarked, "So when I decided after a year that I was going to start consulting I just got in touch with everybody that I had worked with and said, 'I'm available.' And I immediately started working with about six different clients."

Finally, some women were amenable to setting a lower bar on the *type* of work they were willing to perform as long as the job featured a lot of flexibility—a compromise that hastened the reentry process. Karen Gordon, who returned to work as a freelance engineer, was surprised how quickly she was able to find work in her field that met her demand for very part-time hours (no more than two days a week). She concluded that "part of it was just really low expectations. I was like 'I will do anything!'"

THE HIDDEN PASSAGE

Our findings about women's ease of reentry at the initial family-first phase differ not only from popular media accounts but also from the social science research in this area. Although the research on workforce reentry among professional women who have opted out is relatively scant, it consistently finds that women struggle with a number of barriers. These obstacles include ageism, skill obsolescence, professional networks gone cold, the stigma of a résumé gap, and the lack of ability to find family-friendly positions.[13]

Our findings may differ from the survey research because these accounts appear to focus on the more challenging career relaunch phase of reentry and have overlooked its less ambitious prelude, the family-first phase. As we will see in the next chapter, women did experience some significant barriers to reentry, but generally not until they attempted to more fully restart their careers. Popular and social scientific accounts of the reentry process likely miss the family-first phase because women themselves may not consider the kinds of jobs they take on during this period—typically very part-time and temporary, and sometimes nonprofessional—as part of their official career trajectory.

Remember that participants tended to view these reentry jobs as casual engagements or placeholders. In other words, even though the family-first phase is marked by women's first ventures back into the workforce, it may be viewed by women themselves as merely an extension of their career break. It was common for participants to gloss over or even forget to mention jobs that they had held in the family-first phase as if they didn't "count," and to instead focus on their first serious efforts to recharge their careers. The in-depth and longitudinal nature of our interviews (which included a detailed employment history) allowed us to identify a phase of the reentry process that may function as a bridge between privileged domesticity and career relaunch, one that women themselves often fail to recognize as part of their journey back to work.

Nevertheless, it is still surprising that women were able to find jobs with such apparent effortlessness in this phase. This ease may be attributable to the synchrony between the types of jobs that they were seeking—nonstandard, very part-time, and highly flexible—and the rapid growth of the contingent labor market in recent decades, where most of these types of jobs can be found.[14] Because contingent jobs are increasingly plentiful, are female-dominated, require little employer commitment, and are less desirable to many workers than permanent jobs, hiring in this sector may be less competitive; and for the same reasons, traditional employment barriers for mothers in this labor market (e.g., the stigma of employment gaps, family responsibilities) may pose less of a problem.[15] In this context, it is not hard to see why our participants, with their considerable social capital and apparent willingness to work for lower pay and less security, were evidently viewed as highly desirable prospects by employers with temporary, circumscribed, or "just-in-time" labor needs.

A TIME OF FLUX

The whole period of reentry was a time of great job flux for many women during the family-first phase and—as we will see in the next chapter—the career relaunch phase as well. Most (about two-thirds) who returned to the labor force exited again entirely at least once after their initial reentry, sometimes for lengthy periods. Women typically held multiple jobs—an average of three—during the period between their initial reentry and the follow-up interview; and their first job was typically held for a relatively short time—just two or three years. However, the characteristic reasons for job instability were quite different in each of the two reentry phases.

As we have seen, in the family-first phase, job flux was related to women's prioritization of the demands of family over those of paid work and the temporary nature of the contingent jobs they took upon reentry. However, job flux was also sometimes related to women's dissatisfaction with the content of reentry work, which was often below their skill levels. After a few years of working in jobs experienced as boring or repetitive, some women were ready to quit altogether or to find other work. And if their children were older, sometimes job dissatisfaction with family-first-style jobs could be a catalyst for a career relaunch. Recall Nan Driscoll, who took a job as an administrative assistant for a neighborhood sports league to help out with family finances. Nan fundamentally disliked the work and found it tedious. Therefore, once her youngest child finished elementary school, Nan decided to quit in order to launch a whole new career in teaching.

This striking flux in women's labor force participation upon reentry reflects the theory and research on professional women's careers, which finds that while men tend to follow linear, continuous career paths, women's work trajectories tend to be nonlinear, disjointed, and interrupted by the demands of caregiving.[16] In Sylvia Hewlett's national study of highly qualified women, aged twenty-eight to fifty-five, she finds that a clear majority of these high-echelon women experience periods of career interruption and/or less than full-time, standard work, and hence "fail to conjure up the lock step patterns of traditional male careers."[17]

FAMILY FIRST ONLY

Although most reentry women eventually left the family-first phase and attempted to relaunch their careers, a significant minority had not done so by the time of the follow-up interview. These women had only ever reentered the workforce on a family-first basis. The majority of these women had younger children who were still at home, and they planned to make a fuller work debut once their children were older. In other words, these were women who were simply at an earlier phase in their work-family trajectories. However, a handful of "family-first-only" women had no plans ever to restart their careers. These women were older empty nesters (mostly in their sixties) who were more similar in profile to women who had never returned to the workforce at all (a group we discuss in chapter 6). Similar to this latter group, the older "family-first-only" women were more likely to say they had little or no financial need to work, and to have disavowed any interest in returning to work in the first interview.

WHAT'S NEXT?

As we have seen, despite years out of the workplace, most women persisted in their desire to return to work eventually. But this desire was in tension with the inflexible long-hour structure of women's former (and their husbands' current) elite careers and the ongoing pulls of privileged domesticity. As we saw in the previous chapter, opting out increased women's investment in family life quite dramatically over time. Once women opted out, their desire to intensively mother and the traditional division of household labor solidified and grew, functioning as a means of maximizing family class advantage. The latter dynamics, along with a lack of financial urgency, strongly tempered their drive to return to work quickly and fully. Their use of very part-time, stop-and-start contingent labor (mostly in their former professions or the paraprofessions) permitted them to maintain some connection to work while effectively extending the period of privileged domesticity. In effect, we can view women's slow and halting return to work in the family-first phase as a product of the very same class and gender dynamics that propelled their opting out and their ensuing drift into privileged domesticity.

Eventually, as their children age and become more independent, women's desire for autonomy and career fulfillment surfaces more completely. But as we will see in the next chapter, women's time at home has reshaped their vocational values and interests in ways that have profound and unexpected implications.

FOUR

Career Relaunch: Heeding the Call

Since stepping out of her career over a decade earlier, Meg Romano had occasionally dabbled with paid work. But once her two eldest children were on the cusp of entering college, Meg recalled feeling a pressing need for a new sense of purpose in her life.

> So I'm looking at the landscape of my life and I'm saying, well, all right, so what happens when my children go to college? Do I just play tennis and go to the club? That to me really holds very little appeal. And so I started thinking about going back to work and what that would look like. I spent some time with a career counselor, and you know, I'm fortunate. I'm in a financial position where I can take the time to say, "What is it I really want to do, and care about and am interested in?" I don't necessarily have to work—it's certainly helpful when you have two children in college at the same time—but it was more about "I want to work."

Meg had firmly decided not to return to her former lucrative career in finance, now thirteen years in her past. The unforgiving hours in her profession and her now outdated skills were a discouragement, but more importantly, Meg now no longer wanted to return. Instead, she had discovered an entirely new vocation through her years of time-intensive community volunteer efforts as an educational fund-raiser.

Through her new set of contacts in the world of education development, Meg eventually landed her dream job as a development officer in
a small educational nonprofit, an organization she had worked closely
with and admired over her years as a volunteer. With her youngest
child in his teens, a major appeal of the job was her ability to occasionally schedule her hours flexibly—a perk she had negotiated as a condi-
tion of accepting the full-time position. Although Meg Romano's path
to an entirely new career appeared seamless, in fact it was the outcome
of a decade-long, intensive, and largely deliberate process of developing
a new professional skill set and network through her deep immersion in
community volunteer work.

OPTING BACK IN (AGAIN)

A clear majority of our sample defied the media's grim prognosis about
their chances of achieving a career revival. Reflecting their long-
standing commitment to work, and despite often lengthy career interruptions, more than half (twenty-five out of forty-three women) ultimately went on to relaunch their careers by the time of the follow-up.[1]
For most, the "drive to revive" had evolved from a preliminary "family-
first" period of marginal paid employment (although about one-third of
women jumped back into work more fully without such a preparatory
period).

Career relaunch represented a major turning point for women. In
contrast to the family-first phase, in which work was not actively sought
out (and often was dropped if it impinged even slightly on family
demands), the career relaunch phase was marked by women's *proactive*
and *sustained* efforts, typically in anticipation of the empty nest. This
meant that instead of letting work come to them in a hit-or-miss fashion, women actively invested in networking, updating their résumés
and applying for jobs, seeking career counseling, and in some cases
acquiring new credentials. In fact, as we will see, the career relaunch
phase could be characterized as a period of *questing,* in which women

were engaged in a process of actively reviving or seeking out new professional commitments that could sustain their interest for the remaining ten to twenty years of their working lives until retirement. Women were also now willing and able to work substantially longer hours (typically about twenty-five to forty hours a week in the career relaunch phase versus five to fifteen hours a week in the family-first phase), which typically gave them access to more satisfying, higher-level professional opportunities.

By the time of relaunch, women had been off the career track for an average of ten years, although two-thirds of them had worked on a family-first basis during this period, usually for about three to four years. In the family-first phase, women were likely to be in their early forties with their youngest child having just entered primary school. By career relaunch, women were typically in their late forties, and their youngest child was on the verge of adolescence; their older children were typically in high school and/or were already enrolled in college. This was a moment when many women's intensive involvement in their children's schooling (and other efforts at status transmission and class maintenance) was diminishing, and they were beginning to look ahead to the empty nest.

LIKE A DUCK

On the surface, women's initial career relaunch appeared to be a relatively smooth process. But as with ducks swimming across a pond, their apparently smooth and graceful glide across the water belied vigorous effort, even turbulence, just below the surface. In this second, relaunch phase, some of the more negative aspects of the media depiction rang true, for as we will see, the process of career relaunch was often fraught and fundamentally challenging. Getting back to work per se was not hard, but fashioning a viable long-term career was. The combination of women's negative experiences in family-inflexible workplaces, their extended immersion in the world of privileged domesticity, and the process of aging itself created significant changes in their career orientations, such that most were now surer than ever that they did not want to return to their former employers. Just as they had undergone a process of transformation in stepping out of the workforce and adapting to new lives at home, reviving their careers required yet another often protracted process of adaptation and change. Although women fashioned a variety of strategies, each one presented its own set of problems. In fact, the process of opting back in again was inherently challenging because, to one extent or another, it impelled women to vocationally reinvent themselves.

So how did women navigate the process of career relaunch? When and why did they ultimately commit to more fully restarting their careers? Did they do so on their own terms? And how easy or hard was it for women to finally renew their careers after so many years of limited or no involvement in paid work? These questions are at the heart of this book, and many of the answers crystallize in this second phase of the reentry process.

THE RIGHT TIME

After almost twenty years at home as a full-time mother and community volunteer, and with her youngest son headed for college, fifty-four-year-old former lawyer Lauren Quattrone finally returned to the workforce full-time. Musing on her decision to fully relaunch her career, Lauren articulated a sentiment shared by many women we interviewed: "I really felt like I needed something more structured to take the place of the world that I was losing by not having children at home." With a slight hint of self-deprecation, she added, "Certainly [the job] has given me another outlet for my time and energy—I'm just too busy to mope too much about missing them."

Lauren's comments capture an important theme echoed in the relaunch narratives of many of the women we interviewed. That is, the timing of women's career relaunch was often connected to important developmental milestones in their children's lives—markers that signaled their children's growing maturity and readiness for college, and correspondingly their own lessening involvement in intensive mothering and community volunteer work (both of which centered on enhancing their children's social and educational capital). Effectively, as they prepared their older children to launch into the wider world outside the protected spaces of home and community, many women were readying to do the same themselves.

For Lauren and some other relaunching women, the catalyst was the classic empty nest—when their youngest child was in the final years of high school or had just entered college—a period that marked a great diminishment in their role in the process of concerted cultivation and status keeping. Overall this was a time when there was little remaining doubt that their purpose as full-time arbiters of their children's social and educational development was rapidly coming to an end (or had already done so), as Marina Isherwood's comment suggests: "I decided to go back when my youngest child was in his senior year of high school. Sure, I had been very involved in their schools. I supported their life, so by the time they got to be driving in their junior year of high school they really didn't need me for transportation. But I was still engaged in a lot of school things. When I saw that drawing to an end, and [was] kind of getting tired of it too, the question was, 'Well, what's next?'" Recalling the moment that had propelled her to restart her career, former attorney Olivia Pastore, then forty-eight years old, said, "My son had graduated from high school the year before, and ... our daughter was a high school junior about to be a senior, and it felt like ... the era of 24-7 hands-on parenting was approaching its end."

Another popular moment for women to relaunch was when their youngest child was in middle school. Some women observed that there was a big shift toward independence during the middle school years when preadolescents begin to "focus on their friends and [pull away] from the family." Simultaneously, this postelementary school period was viewed as a time when the demands for parental volunteer involvement in children's school activities declined markedly, leaving some women feeling somewhat bereft of purpose and social engagement. This was the case for Nan Driscoll, who launched her new career as a special education instructor when her youngest daughter was thirteen years old and her two older daughters were in college. Nan's career relaunch was spurred in part by her desire to renew the active social life she felt she was losing as her children aged: "Your social life tends to revolve around other people you're doing your volunteer work with or the parents of the friends of your kids. But as soon as your kids are old enough to get to where they want to go to on their own, by the time they hit high school there's just much less automatic interaction at the adult level."

"ONE MORE RUN": IN SEARCH OF MEANING

Now that their children were older, relaunch women felt strongly that they had one more chance to develop a meaningful second career; and they were energized. Christine Thomas, confident and intense, had become a consultant in her former field of marketing by the follow-up interview and had been meeting regularly with a professional women's support network for many years. She had observed this type of renewed enthusiasm for work in the empty nest period both in her own life and in the lives of the women in her group (who, like her, were all in their early to midfifties): "It's interesting that we have a different perspective once all our kids leave home. We all feel like we have one stint left in us where we can really put a lot of energy in, even full-time. Work-life balance is not quite as much an issue for us anymore.... 'We have one more run' is what we say." As Christine's comment suggests, with added time on their hands, these highly educated and talented women wanted to work; they were not satisfied with simply keeping a clean house, playing tennis and going to the club, or otherwise retiring into obscurity as their privileged counterparts in previous generations might have done. However, most women who returned to work were not primarily motivated by money. In this phase of mid- to late midlife, husbands had entered the peak earning years of their elite professions; and while the costs of college for their children loomed large, typically women's contributions to the family economy via paid employment were viewed as helpful but still largely discretionary. Instead, women relaunched their careers primarily because they enjoyed work. And in the wake of, or in anticipation of the empty nest, they sought from work a renewed sense of *purpose, identity,* and *fulfillment.*

Women's desire for meaningful work—typically with a social purpose—often led them to pursue jobs in the nonprofit sector that were related to, or a direct extension of, the kind of philanthropic work they had been doing as volunteers for many years. Lauren Quattrone, who restarted her career after two decades as a full-time homemaker, had immersed herself in senior-level board work, first in her children's schools and then in her church. Lauren was thrilled when she applied for and got the position of executive director of a religious nonprofit group—an organization her church had worked with closely over the years, whose mission was to fund community groups addressing issues of poverty. But her decision to take the job also meant turning her back on the far more lucrative prospect of returning to her former profession as a corporate attorney. When asked why she had made this choice, she replied: "I wanted to do something more meaningful. I thought doing nonprofit work would give me that meaning that I know doesn't necessarily come from a firm practicing law. I mean it *can* in certain kinds of law but not in the kind I have any experience doing." In recognition of how affluence had influenced her career choice, Lauren added, "I've been lucky that I don't *have* to make a lot of money for my family to live well, so that makes these decisions easier."

Similarly, Meg Romano's efforts were strongly guided by her desire to do work about which she could feel passionate. Like Lauren, Meg had effectively prioritized meaning over money and status. She had done so not only by turning away from the corporate sector in favor of nonprofit development work but also by deliberately choosing to pursue a position in the less prestigious arena of small educational nonprofits rather than the more elite world of higher education. Meg had spent time networking with development professionals at a local Ivy League university, but she ultimately realized that she did not feel sufficiently passionate about this world to pursue it further:

> I didn't like asking for money just because the game of development inter-ested me. If I was going to ask people for money I had to believe strongly in the cause. So I was doing a lot of informational interviewing at [Ivy League University] and their various groups, and I walked away feeling like "Oh, I have no affiliation with [Ivy League University], I didn't go there." It's not that I didn't believe in what they were doing, but I couldn't talk about it with the same passion that I could speak about what we do with [small non-profit education foundation where she volunteered]. And so then I started thinking about, in what other spaces and places could I have that level of passion?

The yearning for a career with a purpose may have been thrown into even sharper relief for women like Meg and Lauren who were clearly cognizant of just how optional work was for them. Their class privilege freed them to pursue jobs in less lucrative fields but also set the bar higher for choosing work that promised meaning and fulfillment.

Related to the pursuit of meaning was women's search to rekindle and affirm their former identities as career women—a part of them-selves that had been lost (or at least submerged) during the years of privileged domesticity. Kate Hadley put it most explicitly when she remarked that a primary reason she had returned to work was that "I wanted to get my working identity back.... I wanted to get that identity of working and contributing to a bigger purpose." Although Kate was one of the few women who returned to a semblance of her former pro-fession in the corporate sector, the sense of purpose she sought in relaunching her career had to do with a desire for her talents to be rec-ognized and meaningfully deployed in spheres beyond the domestic. Former attorney Olivia Pastore also followed this pattern of desiring to renew her career as part of an identity quest. When asked whether she had ever considered *not* returning to work, she said, "I take pride in myself as a smart working person; that's always been an important part of my identity."

Beyond seeking meaning and identity, women also sought a sense of sheer enjoyment from work. Emily Mitchell, a former customer service supervisor in a major insurance company, decided to restart her career after close to two decades as a full-time homemaker. She had spent many years as a dedicated volunteer in her children's schools and at a local domestic violence agency and had ultimately become "burned out and tired of volunteering." Once Emily's youngest child was almost ready to launch, she felt a strong push to pursue work that would provide a "sense of fulfillment," as well as enough remuneration to permit her to contribute to his college education (the latter being an important but secondary motivation).

In a pattern that was typical of relaunch women, Emily cycled through a few different jobs before finding one that seemed like just the right fit. She quit her first job, a part-time administrative assistant position in a small insurance agency (her former industry), because of a sense that the job was not drawing on her full professional skill set. Next, she tried her hand as a part-time community coordinator at a local nonprofit agency, a position she had previously performed on a volunteer basis. To her surprise, this line of work didn't feel like the right fit either, and she eventually quit:

> What I found was ... the work was a little depressing. It wasn't fun. And not that it should be. But I think that I was at a point in my life where, if I'm going to go back to work—having taken time off to raise my kids, which is hard work, and then doing a lot of volunteering, which is great, and sometimes thankless, really—my driving force was, what do I want to do for *me*? At this point in my life, what would make me want to go to work every day? What would make me have that sense of fulfillment? What would be enjoyable and also provide me with a little bit of income?

Because many women, like Emily, were not primarily motivated by money, they could be highly selective in their job search: in other words, the work had to feel worthwhile enough for them to pursue or persist with it. Eventually, Emily started a small but successful clothing store in the business district of her community. Although the shop was not yet particularly profitable, it more than satisfied Emily's desire to find a satisfying vocation that drew on both her business savvy and her lifelong love of fashion.

MONEY DOES MATTER

For about a third of relaunch women, money did play a significant role in their motivation to return to work. However, financial considerations drove the *timing* of relaunch for these women rather than the desire to relaunch itself (with only one exception, as we will see), typically propelling them back to work earlier than they were expecting. The primary triggering event for a financially motivated relaunch was the loss of (or significant reduction in) a husband's income; and this occurred for several reasons, including a husband's job loss, his initiation of a business start-up, or his death.

Kate Hadley's husband, a successful financier, decided to launch his own private equity fund. "So as he was preparing and getting all the legal documents ready and figuring out his business plan, he said, 'It would take a lot of pressure off me if you were earning money again.'" With the youngest of her children still in nursery school, Kate reflected, "I could've gone on for another five years." But with the prospect of little or no household income for several years as the business gained traction, as well as the loss of family health insurance and other benefits, Kate felt "the need to contribute and reduce the stress" on her husband. In this sense, Kate and a few other women like her acted as a "reserve army of labor" for the household, stepping into the labor force (and sometimes out again) as needed, providing a cushion against financial risk for their husbands' sometimes volatile business ventures.[2]

A husband's bout with unemployment could also be a spur to relaunch for some women. Given that the Great Recession of 2008 occurred within the time frame of our follow-up period and that it hit male workers particularly hard (the "mancession," as it has been called), it should not be surprising that we heard a number of stories about husbands who endured spells of lengthy and/or frequent unemployment.[3] Although the families in our study were typically affluent enough to comfortably manage without household income for a certain period, longer or frequent spells of unemployment placed increasing pressure on wives to seek paid work. This was the case for Jessica Beckman, whose husband, Martin, was a marketing executive in the high-tech industry. Since the Great Recession, Martin's sector of the industry had become increasingly volatile, and he had been laid off several times. Although Jessica hadn't been expecting to relaunch her career during this period, when a series of substantial part- and full-time freelance marketing consulting opportunities arose, she embraced the opportunity to stabilize the family's financial situation and contribute to her two teenage sons' impending college expenses.

Two women experienced the death of their husbands during the study follow-up period, and in each case this provided a financial catalyst to career relaunch. For a few years after her husband's death, Helena Norton preferred to work only marginal hours (as an admissions assistant at the private school where she had formerly been an educational administrator) as she and her three children recovered from the trauma. However, when her children were aged twelve through eighteen, she sought and found a more substantial part-time job in her former field, both because she needed the health insurance coverage (her husband's COBRA plan was about to expire) and in anticipation of the empty nest.

At age forty-six, Trudy West also relaunched her career—becoming a full-time teacher's aide—in the wake of her husband's death. However, unlike most women in our study, Trudy, a soft-spoken woman, had quit her former career in telecommunications without any plans or desire ever to return to work. By the follow-up interview, her preference for staying home had not changed. Her career relaunch was atypical in that it was motivated *exclusively* by financial factors and represented a significant deviation from her original long-term plans and preferences.

A handful of women (just three) effectively shared the breadwinning role with their husbands because their husbands were in less lucrative professions. These women (like most other American women) had *always* had a more sustained need to contribute to their household income; consequently their career breaks were shorter and their return to work was more strongly motivated by financial considerations. Olivia Pastore was one of these women. As we learned earlier, work was an important part of Olivia's identity—but money also played a key role: "In a practical regard, my husband's a lawyer, he's got a sole practice, neither of us has ever really made big bucks.... I mean, I've heard this from [other women], you know, 'We don't really need my income.' That's a statement you'll never hear from me, other than to say it's not true in my case."

A TEMPERED RELAUNCH

In the relaunch phase, most women were excited to rev up their careers. However, typically their enthusiasm remained tempered by an ongoing, strong preference for work that could be performed on a family-flexible and less-than-full-time basis (typically about twenty-five hours a week). Why this preference for substantial part-time work—instead of a full-time return? The vast majority of relaunching women still had children at home—recall that their youngest child was typically still in middle school or high school. Also, husbands were now in the prime of *their* careers, often occupying senior-level positions (e.g., CEOs, law partners, serving on boards of directors) that involved even greater demands and longer hours than before. Given these ongoing pressures in combination with their anticipation of the empty nest, most women were not looking for a hard-charging relaunch; nor did they want to remain in the "career-on-idle" mode. Rather, women who'd had a family-first orientation now sought an integration of work and family.

While some accented the family side of the equation, others emphasized the work side, depending on each woman's particular circumstances, preferences, age, and life stage.

Even though women's children were now typically considerably older, flexibility was still a predominant concern. Although Jessica Beckman was unusual in the economic imperative she felt to work full-time because of her husband's unstable employment, her actual preference to work part-time even in the relaunch phase was common. This preference was shaped by her desire to enjoy the added leisure time she had become accustomed to during her years at home ("I like having time to get coffee with friends, I like having time to work out"), but most of all so she could attend to the ongoing and (in her perception) increasingly unmet needs of her two teenage sons:

> My son is trying to get his driver's license and he needs to get a certain amount of practice hours in, and he hasn't been able to go out the last few days because my husband and I have had too much work. So I really don't like that. I find myself apologizing to them, and they go, "It's fine, Mom. Don't worry about it." And I know, but I hate it. It's stupid stuff. My son took a diagnostic SAT test, and I haven't gotten to take a look at the results to see where his strengths and weaknesses are for five days. My younger one needs his soccer kit, with the full uniform set. I haven't had time to figure out what size he needs. It doesn't need to be ordered yet, but normally I would have done that right away. I haven't had the chance to say to him, "We need to figure out what size you are" and take care of that. So I hate that. I've spent a long time keeping my family running smoothly and taking care of everyone's needs, and that was an affirmative choice I made.... So my ideal would be less than I'm working now, currently.

This kind of "concierge parenting" was common among women and often continued even after career relaunch.[4] It was a dynamic that helped to explain why many avoided going full throttle as they on-ramped their careers.

For many women, prioritizing family flexibility and part-time work in the relaunch phase effectively meant taking a demotion from the positions they had held prior to career interruption. Brooke Coakley relaunched her career as a hospital administrator at age fifty-one after almost five years at home. Her quit had been occasioned by a perfect storm of family events that included her husband's grave illness and her son's serious mental health issues. Brooke, who had held an executive-level position in a major hospital prior to stepping out—a job that had included extensive line-management responsibilities and extremely long hours—deliberately chose not to seek out a full-time or senior management–level position upon return. When her former boss and mentor, Jane Renfield, admitted to her apologetically that she did not know of any high-level openings in her field, Brooke responded, "Jane, I don't want a vice president position anyway. I'm not looking to take on all that workload." Elaborating further in our interview, Brooke said, "I had done that for so many years, I knew what it would entail." Instead, Brooke eventually found a contract position in the same hospital, but with no line-management responsibilities, and with a half-time sched-ule that allowed her to work from home occasionally. Although both her husband and her middle school–aged son were doing well by the time she returned, her time at home had resulted in a shift in her priorities.

> I guess what I experienced for the time that I was not working and trying to deal with [my son] and my husband [is that] I feel like I focus more of my attention on home life now, just because that's what I had to do for a long period of time, both to get [my son] through, to get him stable finally, and to support [my husband] through the challenges that he was having. And the sleepless nights that I had were for my family, they weren't for my job. And I know that's not the case for a lot of those VPs.

Brooke's case illustrates just how much women's years of intensive mothering during the opt-out period had fundamentally shifted their priorities over time, so that even upon career relaunch their appetite for family flexibility (at least while children were still at home) contin-ued to be considerable.

Starting back on a part-time basis was also a strategy some women used to cope with anxiety about relaunching their careers after so many years out of the workforce. Four women described intentionally pursuing less-than-full-time, lower-level positions because of their belief that their skills were rusty and less marketable, and their corresponding lack of confidence about jumping back in full steam ahead. Given their lengthy absence from the workforce, these women believed that in reviving their careers it would be best to "start small."

Despite the apparent preference for a part-time career relaunch, a substantial proportion of relaunching women (two-fifths) returned on a full-time basis. Notably, however, most of these women were well positioned to return full-time either because they were in the empty nest years and no longer needed family flexibility or because they had relaunched their careers as teachers, which permitted a full-time schedule that followed their children's school day. As this pattern suggests, women whose children were in college or beyond were more likely to take full-time work in their first relaunch job than women who had even just one child still living at home.

"BECOMING" ALL OVER AGAIN

As we have seen, in the career relaunch phase women were beginning to heed a stirring within to reconnect with parts of their identities that had largely lain dormant during both opt-out and family-first periods. Women recognized that they were on the cusp of a new life stage in which many of the family commitments that had firmly anchored their sense of identity for a decade or more were about to give way. They hungered for new sources of purpose and recognition, and like their former more youthful and unencumbered selves they were once again free to ask—or one might say, burdened by having to ask all over again—"What do I want to be when I grow up?"

Unlike their more traditional opt-out counterparts in previous generations who might also have peered beyond the empty nest wondering what was next, our women were in some ways better equipped to answer this question in a meaningful way, given the solid and successful professional lives they had developed before opting out. But as we will see in the next chapter, the process of career relaunch—which included, most pertinently, the search for answers to the existential question of career identity—would not be so easy.

FIVE

Questing and Reinvention

During her seventeen years out of the workforce, former publishing executive Nan Driscoll experienced a dramatic shift in her vocational interests. At our first interview several years after opting out, Nan was confident she would work again, but she was ready for a second career that would be slightly less demanding than her first. Teaching appealed both because she thought it might be rewarding and because it could be done flexibly. At age fifty-two, Nan began a four-year process of training for her new career as a special education teacher, first volunteering as a teacher's aide and then pursuing a master's degree in education.

By the time of the follow-up interview, now aged fifty-nine and with two of three children in college, Nan had been employed for several years in a nearby suburban school district. While she found her work immensely meaningful, Nan had been unable to obtain a full-time position as a special ed teacher with her own classroom. Instead, she was working part-time as a relatively low-paid classroom aide. Nan suspected that ageism and the "down" economy had played a role. But she remained sanguine, reminding herself of the upsides of having this "podunk" job, which included more time to read, go to the gym, play tennis, "make big stews on the weekends," and see her friends.

Not all women experienced this kind of frustration. However, like Nan's, many women's pathways to career relaunch involved a substantial period of questing, training, and career reinvention.

RELAUNCH EASE AND TURBULENCE

Chapter 4 focused on why and when women relaunched their careers; but how easy or difficult was it for them to actually restart and sustain their careers over time? What strategies did they use, and with what success? And what kinds of jobs did they seek?

Perhaps not surprisingly, a significant proportion of women (over a third) admitted that they had felt a keen lack of confidence in their ability to relaunch their careers after having been out of the workforce for so long, which echoes similar findings by other researchers.[1] These women's number one concern was that their skills would be perceived as outdated or obsolescent. This was a fear particularly for women who had formerly been in technical or rapidly changing fields. Former hospital VP Brooke Coakley shared this apprehension with her mentor and former boss, Jane Renfield, asking pointedly, "Am I a viable candidate in the marketplace? I haven't worked for five years. I mean, are people going to look at me and say, she's old hat? She's old news?" Helena Norton, who returned to her former career as an educational administrator after eighteen years (a period that included seven years of working very marginal hours for her former employer), remarked: "I didn't think anyone would even look at my résumé after only having limited part-time work for so many years."

As these comments suggest, women's concern about career relaunch often centered on the fear that they would no longer be competitive in the job market because of their lengthy employment gaps and rusty skills. Economists refer to this decline in job skills and knowledge as *human capital depreciation,* and it is widely acknowledged as a potential barrier to reemployment.[2] Likewise, an employee's *social capital*—the network of relationships with professional colleagues and associates that can be potentially beneficial in a job search—may decline during an employment break, posing additional barriers to reentry. However, with the notable exception of those in shrinking industries, few women complained of long or fruitless job searches. Surprisingly, given some women's distinct lack of confidence, as well as the popular media's bleak depiction of the struggle to opt back in, most of the women landed their first relaunch jobs with relative ease—usually within a few months to a year of starting their search. Why might this be so?

As we will see, women exhibited strong drive and were persistent in overcoming multiple barriers in their paths. They were highly proactive in searching for jobs, networking, scouring ads, and sending out résumés. But women's determination alone does not explain how they were able to overcome the potentially serious deficits they faced in starting new careers after lengthy career breaks. Rather, women's agency appeared to be strongly enabled by their class privilege. That is, by virtue of their affluence these women had the time, social contacts, and financial resources to actively reinvest in new careers during the lengthy period of privileged domesticity (as well as in the family-first phase in some cases). As we will see, this extended employment moratorium enabled them to engage in active self- and career exploration and to prepare for new fields by acquiring further educational credentials. Additionally, the fact that many were no longer trying to compete for the more unforgiving prestigious professional jobs they had left behind gave them an advantage. Even the women who were returning to former elite professions like law or hospital administration were typically seeking part-time, contingent positions in these fields that were less competitive.

However, standing back and looking at the arc of women's relaunch trajectories reveals that the process of restarting their careers was in fact challenging and protracted. It often took many years for women to explore and redefine their career identities, and then to prepare for and find jobs that met their highly selective standards. In fact, fully half of all career returnees had what might be described as a turbulent relaunch, as indicated by their experiences of marked job churn and even serial career redirection. From career relaunch to interview follow-up, about a third of the twenty-five returning women had *taken more than one job* (sequentially), an equal proportion had *exited the labor force altogether* at least once, and a fifth had *redirected their careers* more than once (moving from one unrelated profession to another).

Why was the career relaunch process frequently so long and turbulent? Most women were not returning to their careers as the same people who had left them behind, an average of a decade earlier; their basic orientation to work had changed. They faced the reality that they both could not and did not want to return to their prior employers and that they consequently had to find alternative career paths. Many women perceived that they *could not* return because they continued to prioritize family flexibility and knew from bitter experience that they would be unlikely to get it from their former workplaces. Too, as we have seen, many feared that the erosion of their professional knowledge and skills over time would be a barrier too hard to overcome, making it easier for them to contemplate starting over. But also, and almost to a woman, they *did not want to* return to previous employers. As we will see, their extended experience of privileged domesticity and the process of aging itself had fundamentally altered their values and interests.

REENTRY STRATEGIES

To address the barriers they faced to restarting their careers, women used one of three strategies: (1) *changing course,* or redirecting to entirely different careers; (2) *course correcting,* or pursuing freelance or contingent work in their former fields; or (3) *making a comeback,* which involved returning to their former professions but seeking out employers (almost never their former ones) who could accommodate their need for flexibility. Each strategy represented a different means of achieving work-family integration and to a lesser or greater extent reflected women's pursuit of vocational change.

As these strategies suggest, overwhelmingly women did not return to their former employers. Our findings on this score are consistent with a nationally representative study of highly qualified women who had taken a career break, which found that only 5 percent wished to return to their former employers.[3] Other researchers have also found that it is very common for women returning after a career break to go freelance or to redirect to entirely new professions, industries, or sectors of the workforce.[4] However, less is known about how and why women who opt out use career change as a strategy to relaunch their careers. This chapter describes the three strategies women deployed in returning to work, why these tactics were selected, and the challenges and opportunities they posed.

Strategy 1: Changing Course

Like Nan Driscoll, the former editor who relaunched her career as a teacher's aide, about two-fifths of all returning women executed a major career pivot upon their initial career reentry (this proportion rises to about a half if we include those who changed course at a later point in their relaunch trajectories). *Changing course* was the most popular career relaunch strategy, and the most emblematic of the processes of career questing and reinvention. It reflected women's desire for a career that was not only family flexible (unlike their previous professions) but also consistent with the deep changes in their vocational orientation that had occurred while they were home. Strikingly, the direction of change was almost uniformly a movement away from hard-driving careers in male-dominated and mixed-gender occupations in the corporate sector (i.e., finance, law, marketing, and the like) and into female-dominated occupations or otherwise philanthropic-oriented jobs in the nonprofit sector, particularly education. So, what occasioned such a dramatic change?

WORLDS OF CARING Various theorists of women's caregiving argue that the practice of motherhood and care has a profound impact on caregivers' values, thought, and orientation.[5] Similarly, we found that women's years of immersion in privileged domesticity often wrought deep changes in them that reshaped their career aspirations and plans. In particular, women's experiences of community volunteer work and intensive mothering grounded them in the values of care, connectivity, and altruism, values that increasingly felt at odds with their former experiences of the for-profit world.

Like Nan Driscoll, many women developed a vocational interest in education and teaching—the most popular avenues of course change—as an outgrowth of their involvement in their children's schools. Denise Hortas, the former pharmaceutical executive and PhD scientist, is also a striking example of this pattern. After years of extensive volunteer work in her children's schools, which included running the school's science fair and becoming a trustee and prominent member of the PTA, Denise became a middle school science teacher. Her years of involvement in the schools had led to a welcome self-discovery: "I found that working directly with children is such a joyful thing to be able to do. I adore it. I really value being able to do that."

Women's community volunteer work sometimes led them to new career paths that were equally altruistic in nature. Leah Evans felt like a "kid in a candy store" when she left her highly demanding career as a C-suite executive at a midsized hospital. Suddenly, she had the time and resources to explore her many interests in philanthropic causes. "I honestly did everything from NARAL to United Way to [environmental] conservation. I did a lot, jumped into a lot." But it was her experience as a board member at two different prestigious environmental and wildlife conservation nonprofits that created a profound shift in her career interests: "Of all the various volunteer things I was doing, I was most drawn in by the issues of conservation and environment issues. . . . So long story short, the volunteer work kind of led me to, 'Wow, this is really my passion, I really care about wildlife, I really care about animals, I really care about the environment.'" As a result, Leah returned to school to earn a master's degree in environmental science and relaunched her career as an executive at a conservation organization where she had volunteered.

Women's years of immersion in intensive mothering also could have an unexpected impact on their career choices. Former banking executive Amanda Taylor's curiosity about pursuing an entirely new career in epidemiology was piqued when she became involved in seeking care for her teen daughter's sports injury: "My daughter had shoulder trouble with swimming, and it's an epidemic in female swimmers, and I had this idea that perhaps it was associated with puberty and the hormones because that's when it happens usually with young women, when they're going through puberty ... and part of what I thought about was 'This may be something I want to do research in, and epidemiology would be a good place to start.'" When more medical crises ensued over the years (her father-in-law's stroke and her own mother's battle with various chronic illnesses), she became the default family medical manager. These everyday experiences of caring for her family's health, along with the added time to pursue coursework in the sciences at a local university, culminated in her decision to pursue a PhD and ultimately an academic career in the sciences.

NO GOING BACK   In evaluating future career possibilities, women's negative experiences in their former jobs often loomed large. Given their continued preference for part-time or otherwise flexible work, the long hours that had pushed them out of their former jobs to begin with played an important role in their decision to set their sights on alternative, more family-friendly careers. This was yet another reason why careers in the nonprofit realm, and particularly in teaching (in which the workday closely mirrored their children's school schedules), were especially appealing.

Women's disillusionment with their past careers, especially among those who had worked in the corporate realm, further reinforced their drift away from them. Some women experienced this disillusionment even before they had left their former jobs, in the form of a growing divergence between their values as mothers and primary caretakers and a corporate culture that they perceived as family unfriendly, overly profit oriented, male dominated, and even misogynistic. Meg Romano described feeling increasingly alienated in her virtually all-male workplace—the trading floor—once she became a mother. She felt she now had little in common with her colleagues who mostly were men with either stay-at-home wives or no children. Furthermore, the machismo and aggression required to remain competitive in her job felt increasingly at odds with her role as a mother: "I felt like Sybil; you know, I'm like trying to twist my head around to go from being, 'I'll scratch your eyes out over an eighth of a point,' to, you know, nurturing good mommy."

As they became more involved in community volunteering, some women found themselves increasingly drawn to what they perceived as the more mother-friendly and socially conscious work culture of the nonprofit world. This was the case for Leah Evans, the former hospital CEO turned environmental advocate; her immersion in the politically liberal environments of nonprofit community work was a catalyst for a significant shift in her perspective on her former career, such that she now "cringes" when she thinks about her former adherence to a corporate, profit-oriented mind-set.

TIME FOR A CHANGE   The process of aging and increasing maturity may have also reinforced women's shift toward "giving back." Theorists of aging and the life course from Carl Jung to Erik Erikson, as well as more contemporary life course scholars such as Doug McAdams, have described late midlife as a time of increased generativity—a stage of life when the desire to contribute to the welfare of others and to have a significant impact on the next generation is at its peak.[6] Related to this, researchers have found that a relatively small but increasing subset of older Americans are choosing to change careers in midlife and beyond in search of meaningful employment for the social good in fields such as education, health care, government, and nonprofits. Alternatively referred to as "second acts" or "encore careers," this dynamic is thought to reflect the growing need (and capacity) for Americans to work longer in the context of increased longevity and healthier aging, as well as the desire, associated with later midlife, to give back and have a positive social impact.[7]

Furthermore, recent research on women's career patterns over the life course suggests that career choices made by professional women in late midlife are more likely to be influenced by a search for authenticity and intrinsic meaning than at earlier stages. Studying professional women's career patterns over time, social scientists Mainiero and Sullivan have found that women's career values and motives shift at different life stages, roughly mirroring the arc of their work-family trajectories. The prototypical pattern is for professional women to move from an early-career focus on challenge and achievement, to a midcareer emphasis on work-life integration, to a late-career (corresponding to the empty nest period) focus on authenticity. According to Mainiero and Sullivan, this shift in professional women's priorities to work that feels truer to who they are appears to be driven by their increasing life maturity, self-knowledge, and freedom from family demands.[8]

Similarly, career relaunchers in general, but particularly the course changers, expressed a strong desire to find work that more closely reflected their core values and changing interests at this stage in their lives—their forties and fifties. As we saw in chapter 4, this was strongly reflected in their tendency to prioritize the intrinsic rewards of work—meaning, enjoyment, and social impact. Women's ability to prioritize fulfillment over pay is clearly, in significant part, a product of their class privilege. But comments by a number of women also suggest that this shift from an extrinsic to intrinsic orientation to work may have been a product of increasing maturity. Age and life experience appeared to permit greater self-awareness about work fit and preferences, as well as a greater self-confidence that was less contingent on external validation. Leah Evans, the former hospital CEO, described her prequit career as reflecting, in part, the values and interests of a younger, more approval-oriented self: "So I think if I had to do it all over again, you know, I got into health care because my father was a doctor and my mother was a fund-raiser for the hospital, it was like I was destined to be in health care.... I think I was much, much more focused on outward ministrations of success and to some extent being 'Oh, I'm a woman with an MBA, I have to achieve blah, blah, blah.' There was a whole lot of valuing that over other choices."

Some women's career change grew out of an increased urgency to follow their hearts in the face of a growing awareness of aging, loss, or a shrinking career horizon. In her late forties, Melanie Irwin survived a bout with cancer and then, shortly thereafter, the dissolution of her twenty-five-year marriage. On the eve of her fiftieth birthday, having faced her own mortality and now the possibility of being single for the rest of her life, she decided to "refuel my life." On a whim, she took up the hobby of horseback riding and eventually bought several horses. Then, shortly after her youngest child left for college, she opened up a horse riding stable and boarding facility in town. After having discovered her passion late in life, Melanie was clear that she would not return to her former career as a marketing executive in high tech, selling a product—computers—that she now realized had never been a keen interest of hers.

By its very nature, the experience of career relaunch after an extended period of opting out created a sharp break between past and present vocational selves. But although stepping out of their careers was not a life event that most women had ever planned for or expected, as Melanie's story suggests, such a career rupture (despite its obvious elements of loss) could become an opportunity for creative growth. That is, for some women it presented an opportunity to improvisationally stitch elements of old and new interests and skills into different careers more tailored to their changed identities.[9] But at what cost? And how did women navigate the vicissitudes of career redirection?

RISKY BUSINESS   Once it came time to relaunch her career, it took Nan Driscoll all of "about five minutes" to decide she did not want to return to her former field of publishing. Nan verbalized what many others clearly felt at this juncture: as fading remnants of a now seemingly unsalvageable past, their former careers held little appeal or promise. Although Nan knew she did not want to go back to publishing, finding and preparing for a new career was a much longer and more challenging process—with few guarantees of success. Nan took some comfort in the observation that, upon relaunch, many other talented opt-out women in her neighborhood had also rejected returning to their former professions and had then struggled mightily to reinvent themselves vocationally.

Changing course was not only the most common but also one of the most difficult relaunch strategies. Often women who used this strategy changed jobs, changed career strategies, or left and reentered the labor force after relaunch multiple times. Women who changed course at the outset of their career relaunch also took substantially longer to restart their careers than women using other strategies; that is, they typically relaunched their careers a full twelve years after stepping out—seven years longer than women who course-corrected, and four years longer than women who adopted a comeback strategy.

Why was changing course such an apparently unsettled and protracted process? Like starting up a new business, beginning a second career was essentially an entrepreneurial venture—a risky endeavor that involved considerable uncertainty, investment, trial and error, and vulnerability to failure.

REINVESTING, RECREDENTIALING   For most course changers, the training and preparation required to start over in brand-new fields required a significant investment—or "reinvestment" (given their prior career training and credentials). Acquiring a new educational credential was one of the most time-consuming and costly of all such investments; and not surprisingly, women who adopted a course-changing strategy were more likely than women using the other two strategies to do so. About half of all women who changed course at some point acquired at least one additional educational credential (such as a master's degree, a professional certification, or a PhD).

While some women sought advanced degrees primarily for credentialing, Amanda Taylor also used her coursework as an end in itself to help her explore and hone her career direction. Recall that Amanda's experiences as the family medical manager led her to first pursue a master's degree in biology. Amanda loved the coursework but discovered that she had some reservations about whether this was the right area of science for her. As a result, Amanda pursued a two-year postbaccalaureate science degree at an elite university in her city that allowed her to dabble in a variety of advanced courses in the basic sciences while also fulfilling various prerequisites she might need if she decided to pursue a science PhD. The following year she was able to complete an unpaid internship in a biochemistry laboratory at a nearby hospital, which confirmed her interest in research-oriented chemistry. Ultimately, Amanda's extensive investment in coursework, credentialing, and hands-on volunteer laboratory experience paid off; the following year she was admitted to a prestigious chemistry PhD program that happened to be her top choice.

Even if they did not invest in new credentials, many course-changing women paid their dues in other ways. For the majority, this involved years of volunteer work in their children's schools or local nonprofits. As we saw in chapter 2, this volunteer work could be so demanding and time intensive that it amounted to the equivalent of a substantial part-time job. For many women, volunteer involvement was a process that grew out of their desire to become more engaged in their community and their children's school lives. However, some women made significant volunteer investments in new areas as a strategy to experiment with their interest in (and to prepare for) new careers.

Additionally, changing careers could result in the need for a greater investment of time and energy once on the job, in order to get up to speed in a whole new field, as lawyer turned nonprofit executive Lauren Quattrone explains: "I would say there was a pretty big learning curve on a lot of issues—a lot of nonprofit management and program evaluation issues—things that I really had not done before. And that's still ongoing. I mostly spend Fridays reading literature in the field."

FROM TRIAL AND ERROR TO FLOUNDERING   A few women, like Meg Romano and Lauren Quattrone, seemed to sail right into their new careers. However, others spent years trying to define a new vocational path through trial and error and experimentation, moving through multiple jobs and/or educational experiences. Recall Emily Mitchell (discussed in chapter 4), who cycled through several different jobs and career strategies, finally finding her fit as a small business owner. Additionally, as we saw with Amanda, the process of educational credentialing could become a useful but time-consuming tool for experimenting with different vocational pathways.

Sometimes the process of trial and error led to a dead end. Lily Townsend's vocational experimentation began with a return to her former profession of corporate law. However, five years and several different law firms later, Lily realized that her prequit ambivalence had been confirmed. At this point she stepped out once again to reconsider her options. Recalling her love of language as an English literature major in college, Lily was drawn to the idea of a career in publishing. Accordingly, Lily spent time conducting informational interviews with fellow college alumnae in the publishing field, who warned her about contraction in the field and the profession's relatively poor pay. Undaunted, she continued to feel enthusiastic about pushing forward with her new aspiration, saying, "I thought it was time for me to enjoy what I was doing."

Over the next two years, Lily undertook the coursework necessary to receive several different professional certificates from a well-respected publishing program in her city (credentialing she was advised she would need in order to get her "foot in the door"), as well as doing extensive pro bono editorial work. At first, luck seemed to be on Lily's side. Relatively quickly, she was able to secure a job as a part-time freelance editor for a small company producing online educational material. However, dissatisfied with the job's increasingly administrative focus, Lily quit after about a year. Although Lily proceeded to mount a vigorous job search, as she dolefully reported, "Basically it's a black hole."

By the follow-up interview a full seven years after she had decided to leave the law, Lily had still not found ongoing paid employment in publishing. Instead, she was working a (very) part-time paid position as an office administrator. With the empty nest close at hand, Lily felt it was time to more vigorously revive her job-seeking efforts, but she was not at all hopeful about her prospects.

VULNERABILITY TO FAILURE While Lily's apparently dead-ended career trajectory was more the exception than the rule, it does highlight the fundamental vulnerability to failure that course-changing women faced. Like Lily, a significant minority of course changers had trouble either getting a job or sustaining work in their chosen field upon relaunch. This group of floundering course changers seemed to have in common the status they inhabited as *older novices* in professions with contracted labor markets. Course changers who entered such highly competitive job markets were particularly at risk because their maturity was a disadvantage in a field of mostly younger entry-level job seekers. The age bias toward younger workers was particularly pronounced in fields with lengthy pathways to promotion such as publishing and academia, in which younger workers were perceived to have a longer shelf life. Lily had known early on that publishing was a tight job market, but it was only later, during one of her publishing courses, that she learned about the field's strong ageism: "They get you right out of college for the most part at the very bottom and you have to work your way up. If you're older and you have had a previous career and you have some skills, there really isn't a clear place for you."

Amanda Taylor also faced the serious likelihood of age discrimination as an older entrant to the highly competitive (and shrinking) field of academic science. As she began her search for an academic position, she learned from her mentor and colleagues that she was facing an uphill battle as a mature job seeker (in her early fifties) in the context of an academic tenure track system that favors younger applicants. Faced with the possibility that she might not get a job in academia, Amanda was already exploring other options, but acknowledged that academia was the only route that would permit her to do what she most wanted to do—to pursue her own research agenda.

Women who changed course faced another vulnerability that became especially pronounced in a tight labor market; as newcomers to their fields or jobs they faced the phenomenon of "last hired, first fired." After earning her master's degree in education, former international sales manager Nathalie Everett had been enjoying her new job as a language teacher at a local public high school when the new administration decided to make cuts in the language arts program. As a new faculty member, Nathalie was "the low man on the totem pole" and was demoted to part-time. Desperate to earn a full-time income (her husband had recently been laid off because of recessionary pressures in his industry), Nathalie got recertified in two additional areas where she perceived the jobs would be more plentiful. But with major cuts to public school funding, Nathalie's job search efforts were in vain: "It literally was like throwing a stone into a pond. Nobody was responding anywhere."

Women who relaunched new careers as small business owners also faced a strong risk of failure. Several women started their own businesses in part because they believed that they would gain greater scheduling control. However, business start-ups are notoriously risky endeavors, and what is gained in scheduling control can be canceled out by the sheer time demands of establishing a successful venture. Former marketing executive Christine Thomas built a start-up women's leadership consulting business that folded just two years later. Ironically, her business—which aimed to assist Fortune 1000 companies in modernizing their work-family policies—required far more international travel than she had anticipated or could handle with three young children at home: "Here I was consulting to companies on flexible work policies and work-life balance issues and women leaving, and I sort of wasn't even drinking my own Kool-Aid."

Emily Mitchell and Melanie Irwin both started their own businesses as well, but as empty nesters they fared better than Christine with respect to the enormous time demands involved in a start-up. However, at the time of the follow-up, even several years after first having established their businesses, both were still struggling to break even financially and to learn the ropes of their new industries.

CONTINGENT LIVES, CONTINGENT CAREERS   Starting over in new fields meant some course-changing women were vulnerable to another source of job insecurity and turbulence. As we have seen, it was common for women to gravitate toward fields like teaching that were substantially lower paid than their former professions (albeit perceived as more meaningful and authentic). Unfortunately, such low-earning careers were particularly prone to being upended by an unexpected but sharp drop in family income. Denise Hortas loved her relaunch career as a full-time middle school science teacher, though she was earning a mere fraction of her former salary. However, when her husband, a corporate lawyer, decided to retire, Denise heeded his request to shore up the family income by returning to her lucrative former career. A similar dynamic occurred for Nathalie Everett, who eventually migrated out of her relaunch job as a high school language teacher and into the corporate world of textbook marketing. This abrupt switch to a more lucrative occupation was spurred in part by the precarity of her husband's employment during the recession. Thus the types of jobs—lower paid—that women were drawn to upon relaunch tended to reinforce the ongoing contingency of their careers on family demands, and in this case husbands' careers.

JOBS R US   Despite the lengthy and difficult nature of the career reinvention process, it was surprisingly easy for course changers to actually *obtain* jobs once they had set their sights on a particular path. One reason for this was that women's active engagement in community volunteer work during their extended employment moratorium often functioned as a veritable unpaid internship—providing women with job skills, experience, and key social connections in their prospective fields (even if most did not initially undertake these activities with the intention of preparing for new careers).

About half of all course changers were successfully able to leverage their volunteer experience to find jobs. Former health care executive Leah Evans's extensive philanthropic activities on the boards of several prestigious environmental and wildlife conservation nonprofits helped launch her new career as a nonprofit executive at one of these organizations. Before Leah had even finished her master's degree program in environmental science, a fellow board member alerted her to an executive job opening in the organization, which she got—likely because of her deep connections and lengthy volunteer experience in the area.

Women's affluence afforded them not only the time to develop their talents in new areas but also the resources. Acquiring added educational credentials can be expensive, not just time-consuming, but the cost of education did not appear to be a barrier. Furthermore, those course changers who built their own businesses were able to capitalize the typically steep start-up costs by using their own family assets, thus removing one of the most common barriers to entrepreneurship. For instance, Emily Mitchell was able to buy the small storefront property that eventually became the base for her small boutique by persuading her husband to finance it as a family real estate investment. Similarly, Melanie Irwin invested in her horseback riding business using the money from her divorce settlement.

In sum, although the process of discovering and preparing for a new career direction was often lengthy and fraught, once they had gone through it, women were surprisingly well positioned (with important exceptions) to find jobs in their chosen areas. A combination of course changers' class privilege and drive largely enabled them to re-create their human and social capital anew, often (though not always) making them competitive job applicants in their new fields.

Strategy 2: Correcting Course

Health care executive Lisa Bernard had been out of the workforce for less than a year when she decided to step back in again as a freelance consultant in her field. At first, and almost by default, Lisa looked for work as a health care consultant. She knew that project-based work in her area of specialization was plentiful and that working as a consultant would give her much more scheduling control than her previous hospital-based job—a job in which long hours were the norm, and meetings with doctors were regularly scheduled very early and very late in the day. However, Lisa still wasn't sure if consulting was merely a stopgap or a long-term career solution, so she sought the advice of a career counselor. She also had a few exploratory meetings with headhunters who were contacting her for jobs that were a step up from her former management role: "It was interesting because they would describe these jobs to me, which if I was taking the next logical step would have sounded wonderful, and I would have said, 'Oh, great, sign me up.' And I did interview for a couple of them. But as I would listen to them it was like, 'I don't want to be doing that any more. I don't want to jump back into what I just got out of in terms of the politics, and the hours, and the stress, and the total lack of flexibility.'"

Lisa's strategy of *course correcting*—pursuing freelance consulting or contract work in a former field—was a common one (adopted by almost a third of women returning to work). It permitted women to gain greater control and autonomy over their work schedules without having to abandon their former professions. Self-employment was attractive because it gave women the freedom to work from home, to schedule their own hours, and to be somewhat selective about taking on projects that meshed with their family responsibilities. Women who gravitated to this strategy tended to basically like the content of the work they had been doing in their former professions, and were in fields with more plentiful freelance opportunities. Of course, the appeal and viability of freelancing as a career option for course correctors were contingent on their privileged access to family health care benefits through spouses whose own jobs were well benefited.

Women who used a course-correcting strategy tended to have a stronger financial motivation to return to work. Accordingly, some may have gravitated to self-employment in their former fields as the quickest, most practical, and most accessible way of achieving a family-flexible career relaunch. In some cases, the strategy of course correcting permitted women who had disliked certain aspects of their former professions to adjust the content or structure of their work in ways that made it more appealing or satisfying. For instance, former senior editor Wendy Friedman discovered that stepping back into her profession as a freelancer permitted her to lose the "corporate" elements of her former job that she had disliked—the unrelenting workload, the meetings, and the administrative obligations—while retaining what she loved about the work: "I loved working with authors. And I've enjoyed the freelance stuff that I've done because I get to do the pure editorial work, as opposed to dealing with all this other stuff that can be a real chore."

EASY COME   The strategy of course correction was in many ways the easiest, most accessible, and stable of the three relaunch strategies. Overall, course correctors struggled less to find their first job and were less likely to have had turbulent career relaunch trajectories compared to course changers and those "making a comeback." Furthermore, the gap between quit and career relaunch was shortest for course correctors (typically just five years). The shorter trajectory may have been due to financial urgency, but it may also reflect the greater ease of course correction as a relaunch strategy.

It appears that course correctors had a fundamental advantage over their course-changing counterparts because as returnees to their former fields (albeit on a contingent basis) they could build on their pre-existing human and social capital. Also, because they had been out of the workforce for a shorter period of time and had often made active efforts to stay in touch with former colleagues, their occupational networks were relatively fresh. Former editor Wendy Friedman, out for less than a year, benefited from a still active network of contacts, as she recounts here:

> So this friend of mine who's a literary agent just said, "Do you want to do a little bit of work for me?" It was just reading a manuscript or helping shape

a proposal or re-writing, it was a small job.... You know, this agent is a friend of mine who I had worked with for years. So I said, "Sure! That would be fine!" ... I hadn't been out of the industry for very long. People were still being very nice, you know, and taking me out to lunch ... so it kind of just took off from there as a freelancer.

Although Wendy started her consulting career small (taking on only a few projects here and there) and in a serendipitous rather than proactive manner, her "family-first" beginning eventually transitioned more or less seamlessly into a relaunch phase, a period in which she became more deliberate and proactive about sustaining a substantial career as a freelance editor. Like Wendy, many course correctors had engaged in freelance work in their family-first phase, helping to smooth the way for an expedited career relaunch.

Yet another factor played a significant role in the ease with which course correctors were able to find jobs. As we saw in chapter 3, the generally less competitive nature of the contingent job market made it an easier reentry point for women, not just in the family-first period, but also in the career relaunch phase. After all, prospective employers may be more likely to take a chance on a worker who has been out of the field for a few years if the position is only short term and temporary. For this reason, some women (especially those who had been out of the workforce for a longer stretch) actually sought contract work as a deliberate strategy for overcoming the stigma of opting out and to gain an initial foothold in their former careers. Brooke Coakley, the former vice president of a major hospital division, used this tactic to get back into her field of health care management after an employment gap of five years—a gap she described as significant "in a business like health care, where payment systems are changing and new technology comes along, and a lot can change." Brooke was advised to avoid seeking jobs at the executive level (similar to the one she had left) at least initially and instead to seek contingent positions. Brooke drew heavily on her extensive network of former colleagues, including her former boss and mentor and her long-time associates from a professional women's health care management association. She was delighted to discover that recognition of her high-level skills and worth as a professional persisted, even after five years away: "Once I started reaching out to people, I found my colleagues, my professional friends, to be very supportive. I mean, they were, to a person, very encouraging. Gave me names, that sort of thing. So it was reaffirming." Brooke's two-pronged strategy of aggressive but targeted networking and openness to contract work paid off rather quickly. Within three months of starting her search, she was choosing between two job offers, both involving short-term project work in hospital management that accommodated her preference for a substantial part-time schedule.

EASY GO   However, the pitfall of course correcting as a strategy was its insecurity. By its very nature contingent work can be hard to sustain consistently over time; correspondingly, women commonly described experiencing strong ebbs and flows in their access to work, and difficulty achieving exactly the desired balance over time.

On the one hand there was the risk of too little work, an issue of greatest concern to those whose earnings were needed as an important share of household income. This was the case for Jessica Beckman, whose career relaunch as a freelance marketer was largely spurred by her husband's frequent bouts of unemployment in the wake of the Great Recession. Although Jessica was surprised by how seemingly easy it was to find project work (which former colleagues and associates sometimes offered her unsolicited), she found it hard to avoid gaps between the end of one project and the beginning of another. Projects could also end unexpectedly. With her husband's employment so precarious, the results financially could be serious. In one such case, Jessica had been hired as a marketing consultant for a project that suddenly ran into financial problems:

> Without warning me, they laid me off in November of last year, and we were out of money. Which sucks, it wasn't great timing. My husband had gone to work for a start-up. But he was drawing in a really small salary, like, really nominal. And you know, money can be really tight for start-ups. It

was a big blow when it ended. Not because it was my most favorite job ever, but you know, again, I worked from home, I set my own hours, and we needed the money.... So, again, a whole lot of ups and downs, which you will probably hear a lot of in this economy; and we realized that there is no such thing as job security at all anymore. So that ended very abruptly, and we faced the end of last year with no income. Like, the holidays coming in—nothing. Which really sucked.

Although the employment gap lasted only four months, the experience was unsettling, prompting Jessica to realize two things: that in freelancing "you can't really count on long-term prospects" and that she would have to spend more time on "business development" than she had realized.

On the other end of the continuum, some women complained that when freelance work rained it sometimes poured. Wendy Friedman, the freelance editor, described project-based work as a compromise between the gift of flexibility and the curse of "extreme unpredictability." She and her husband both freelanced out of their home, finding that while they both enjoyed very flexible schedules, "on a given weekend we could work many, many, many, many hours when everyone else is in the park or in the city at a movie, we're at home working. That's the trade-off." As this comment implies, in the career relaunch period women still enjoyed the flexibility of freelance work as they had in the family-first phase, but they were now less free to turn down projects requiring long hours if they wanted to sustain their careers as consultants.

Strategy 3: Making a Comeback

When Kate Hadley stepped out of her career as an international marketing manager at age thirty-seven, she never doubted she would return to her profession in the not-too-distant future. Although her employment had involved long hours and almost constant travel (one of the main reasons she had quit a year after the birth of her second child), she had loved her job. It was work that allowed her to feel she was making an impact in an area central to her company's global identity and brand.

As we know, Kate did return to work five years later, prompted by her husband's decision to quit his lucrative finance job and create his own start-up company. But emotionally, reentry wasn't easy for Kate. "I would say I had a lack of confidence just getting back into the workforce again because it wasn't like I had kept up on industry trends, so I was definitely intimidated walking in there."

Kate's trepidation went beyond the five-year gap on her résumé. With her youngest not yet in school full-time (and the other two still in elementary school), she was also concerned about the seemingly daunting task of finding a family-flexible job in her former competitive, fast-paced profession. Despite her doubts, Kate found something relatively quickly. The job, which drew on her marketing experience, was at a top consulting firm, and most importantly it offered flexibility. Because the position required no direct client contact, there was little travel, and she was permitted to work on her own schedule, and even from home sometimes. "I mean, it was all Blackberry and your computer, which, you know, I could sit in a taxi and dial up to whatever the network was, I could get my emails wherever I was."

Nevertheless, Kate discovered that the job still involved tight project deadlines. She found herself all too often having to open up her office laptop after dinner and work late into the night. After two years she reduced her hours to 80 percent time, explaining: "I just wanted a little more flexibility so that if I had to leave at two o' clock to watch [my child's] performance at school, I wouldn't feel guilty." But even this arrangement fell apart as Kate realized that the limits she tried to place on work could "disappear really fast. I wasn't good at controlling those boundaries." Four years after attempting to rev up her career, Kate quietly opted out again, and she was still at home when we interviewed her at follow-up.

Kate's story illustrates the third and final strategy that women used to relaunch their careers—one that we call *making a comeback*. It involved women returning to their former professions on a permanent (not a contingent) basis, deliberately seeking out employers who would accommodate their need for flexibility. Significantly, these employers were almost never their former bosses, who by their lights had already failed the flexibility litmus test. A third of career relaunchers were able to make a comeback in this fashion upon initial relaunch. As we can see from Kate's story, this was a strategy that could miscarry and leave women back where they had started.

WHY THEY CAME BACK Not surprisingly compared to the course changers, women who tried to make a comeback tended to experience more of a match between their current interests and values and their former professions. This was most clearly the case for women who returned to careers in education. These women continued to feel that their former professions were relevant, meaningful, and compelling to them (their experiences of privileged domesticity often having reinforced the very values and interests that had attracted them to teaching). Moreover, the female-dominated nature of the teaching profession and its child-centered scheduling permitted a full return after a long career gap with none of the stigma suffered by their counterparts in other fields. All three former educators who had relaunched careers by the time of the follow-up had done so by using the strategy of making a comeback.

Other comeback kids chose the more daunting path of attempting to return to careers in elite, largely male-dominated professions—occupational environments that had been hostile to them as working mothers. These women were strongly attached to their former careers, but their enthusiasm and motivation to return were strongly conditioned upon finding companies that would accommodate their ongoing need for flexibility. As we saw, Kate Hadley was passionate about her former career in international marketing but knew that if she returned to her former employer she would be committing herself to a lifestyle of constant travel. So she didn't even try. Instead, she sought out a track within consulting that, at least initially, appeared to offer the flexibility she needed.

Comeback kids returning to such hard-driving professions as law or business anticipated that finding part-time work would be like finding the proverbial needle in a haystack. Some were willing to make unexpected compromises. Bettina Mason was confident about wanting to return to her law career once her children were school-aged but was decidedly less confident about her ability to find a part-time job. A full year before she had planned to return (her youngest was still in half-day kindergarten), Bettina unexpectedly heard about an opening for a half-time position in her specialty area. It was located at a small firm only ten minutes from her house. "I really felt like I needed to nab it" was the way she described her reaction. Sensing that the odds would be against her if she held out for better timing, Bettina took the job.

Money was a motivating factor in the timing of return for over a third of all comeback kids. As we know, the changing fortunes of husbands, careers were almost always the immediate catalyst. Recall Denise Hortas's decision to cut short her honeymoon with middle school teaching in order to return to her former (far more lucrative) career as a pharmaceutical executive. The catalyst was her husband's impending retirement and her need to switch roles with him and become the family breadwinner:

> My husband decided that ... he had done corporate litigation for twenty-one years and he was really tired of it. He said, "You know, we're done. We saved for college, we're done with that. [Youngest son] is going off to college. I can't stand another minute of this. You say you're going back. Are you going back? Because if you do, I'll step off the wheel here and change what I'm doing." I figured that was only fair. I was having a wonderful time teaching, but it was very much my intention to come back to Pharma. So I did.

ON-RAMPING WITH EASE   Most comeback kids had little trouble in obtaining their first relaunch jobs, even when seeking family flexibility in their former male-dominated professions. This did not mean that women simply coasted into their jobs with little effort. To be sure, they were savvy in their strategies and determined in their efforts. Lily Townsend's use of a specialized employment agency is certainly one example of this. Although most women found their jobs using more conventional methods such as word-of-mouth networking, scouring job ads, and sending out résumés, they were typically vigorous and proactive.

But in addition to their drive, the comeback kids (like their course-changing and course-correcting counterparts) brought strong social and human capital to the table. As we have seen, these assets were a product of both their abilities and their class privilege, and they included sterling educational qualifications, specialized skill sets, experience working in reputable companies, and networks of former admiring colleagues. Although certainly this capital had depreciated over time depending on how long they had been out of the workforce, these women's working credentials still often placed them in an elite class even among professionals. Moreover, comeback kids were typically seeking family-friendly jobs, not positions at the highest levels of seniority—jobs for which they would have been far less competitive given their résumé gaps.

Kate Hadley, who scored a job at a top consulting firm soon after she began her job search, exemplifies some of these dynamics. Even though Kate had no experience with consulting and had been out of the workforce for almost five years, her specialized and high-level industry expertise in retail and consumer goods was unusual and relevant. Moreover, Kate had layers of advantage when it came to her social connections to the firm. An old college friend who had worked at the company provided the first contact, putting her in touch with the director of practice in her area (retail and consumer goods). Her father had had a lengthy career as a consultant at a similar company and had helped her to get an internship there in college. As further icing on the cake, during her interview Kate and the director had a good-natured laugh over their discovery that his wife socialized regularly with a good neighbor and friend of hers. As Kate herself summed it up: "It wasn't a risky thing for them to hire me.... I mean. I fit their mold!"

Denise Hortas also experienced a smooth transition into her former career as a pharmaceutical executive (although it was a little more seamless than the norm). Not only was she in a high-demand profession, but she was an unusually competitive candidate. She had sterling credentials (with a PhD from a top school) and a high level of professional success prior to her quit. Strategically, Denise had also kept in touch with her former female boss and mentor and had remained active in a professional association of women executives and scientists in the Pharma industry. According to Denise, hiring managers didn't seem to blink when she explained her time away from the industry: "I said I'd been a consultant for *x* number of years and I'd been a teacher of middle school science and math, teaching underserved kids for three years ... and here I have all these publications. And here I am, and I'm back! And it was like, 'When can you come in?'"

ROAD TO NOWHERE?   Women were often surprised by how relatively easy it was for them to find seemingly viable on-ramps back into their former professions. And for this reason, they were also often unprepared for the storm clouds brewing over the horizon. Many of the comeback kids had unstable career trajectories over time. The comeback women who initially chose to reenter male-dominated, or otherwise elite gender-mixed professions, largely accounted for this turbulence. Almost all of these women aborted their relaunch careers within five years of stepping back into them. Subsequently, they either did not return to work again (opting out a second time) or attempted to redirect their careers entirely, setting off a sometimes tumultuous process of career reinvention. Therefore, viewed from a longer-term perspective, the strategy of making a comeback to non-female-dominated occupations was often a winding, bumpy road that sometimes led nowhere.

What happened to make so many comeback kids head for the off-ramp again? In a word, many of the same dynamics that had derailed them in the first place. First and foremost was the problem of workplace flexibility. Comeback kids still had a strong ongoing desire for it, with at least one child typically still in elementary school (slightly younger than the norm for the rest of the relaunchers). Women negotiated hard with their employers for family-flexible schedules at the outset. Nevertheless, over time they often discovered that their carefully vetted arrangements fell apart or that employers were not as flexible as they had at first appeared. We saw this clearly with Kate Hadley, who initially thought she had found a relaunch job with the perfect balance, only to realize that its demands compromised too much of her ability to be present for her three school-aged children.

Bettina Mason was also a prime example of this dynamic. Bettina had returned to work a full year earlier than planned (her youngest child was not yet in school full-time) in order to seize a rare opportunity for a part-time job in the law. Bettina was elated to find that after five years away from her career she had not forgotten much and that former colleagues in the field still remembered her. "I felt this wonderful ego boost. It was wonderful in the beginning. I thought, 'This is great.'"

But after nine months the job expanded, and her initial half-time schedule turned into at least a three-quarters-time job, with occasional weekend work. "Other lawyers are all working full-time, and they're all expecting things.... People run down the hallway because they are under a lot of pressure to make deals, to meet deadlines. It was a very fast-paced environment." Bettina inserted wryly here that the other lawyers working full-time (and "expecting things") were almost all men with stay-at-home wives. Such a relentless pace left Bettina feeling that she "could not give [her employer] all that they needed" while maintaining a truly part-time schedule. Frustrated, she quit.

As they had the first time around, husbands played a tacit but still prominent role in women's decision to opt out again. If anything, at this point in their career and family trajectories some husbands were even less available to co-parent or to provide other help around the house. Those still in their prime career-building years had gotten used to the benefits of a stay-at-home wife and had adjusted (i.e., expanded) their own work schedule accordingly. For instance, Bettina Mason's husband was a trial lawyer with an "extremely, extremely demanding job." According to Bettina, her husband had voiced resentment and frustration with her decision to relaunch her career because "it was going to change his life also." This factor weighed strongly in her decision to opt out a second time because "there would be weeks at a stretch where he would never step foot in our house." When Bettina announced her decision to quit her part-time legal job a little less than a year after it had begun, her husband's mood was practically celebratory.

Kate Hadley had described herself as "very much the COO of the house" in our first interview ("[My husband] is not at all hands on with the children, how the household runs.... He just doesn't do any of that stuff"). By the second interview, she admitted that her status in this regard had changed little, even once she had returned to work again full-time. This intractable reality had informed not only her decision to opt out a second time but also the kind of work she would consider taking in the future, because "the way [my husband] works, he's not going to pick up the slack, so I still have to be the primary family organizer and overseer."

Apart from their struggles to find balance, the comeback kids who returned to careers in male-dominated or elite mixed-gender professions also struggled to find the right fit. Some learned through trial and error that their relaunch jobs were less in synch with their values and interests than they had first hoped for or assumed; and they soon found themselves in an active mode of career questing and job flux, much like their course-changing counterparts.

A LOW BAR FOR LEAVING   It is worth noting that a number of comeback kids, frustrated with their relaunch jobs, did not merely quit these positions to find others. Rather, they opted out of the labor force entirely for a second time. As we have seen, some felt burned by the insufficient flexibility they encountered all over again in their former professions. Others simply realized that the job or the profession was no longer a good enough fit. In these cases of opt-out redux, women's class privilege operated as a silent partner in their decision. They had little financial motivation to work, which meant that the bar for leaving was low and the bar for staying was relatively high—the work had to be highly satisfying, not just flexible.[10]

Bettina Mason had opted out of her legal career for a second time just a year before our first interview with her. At that point, she was already pretty sure that she would not return to the workforce again—ever. "We're in a situation where as long as my husband continues to do well," Bettina explained, "I will not be forced to have to earn money." In such a context of solid economic security (and a husband who had expressed resistance to her working), Bettina's thoughts about finding meaningful work in the future turned to philanthropy rather than the continued (possibly frustrating) pursuit of a career. As she put it, "I think that I will feel just as gratified in volunteering my legal time or doing something freelance or developing a new program that can be used in the schools." Indeed, thirteen years later, when we reinterviewed her, Bettina was still at home full-time (now with both children in college) pursuing an active combination of volunteer work and leisure pursuits.

Money too played a shadow but significant role in Kate Hadley's decision to opt out again. During the four years since she had returned to work, her husband's start-up hedge fund had launched and turned into a highly successful operation. Kate's income was dwarfed by her husband's. This freed her to leave an unsatisfying work situation and also took the steam out of her desire to revive her career again. By the follow-up interview, Kate had been at home full-time once again for two years. An executive search firm had recently approached her about a consulting job similar to the one she had left a few years earlier. But Kate found herself anxiously deliberating about taking the leap back into the workforce. She was strongly motivated to regain her career at some point in the not-too-distant future. However, given the lack of financial need, she felt sure it had to be just the right job: not just sufficiently flexible but also meaningful and enjoyable enough to warrant the sacrifice of her time away from her "tween-aged" children, who she felt still benefited significantly from her presence at home.

EXCEPTIONS TO THE RULE   A few women who started out in male-dominated professions were actually successful in relaunching *and* maintaining stable careers in their former fields. However, these women were exceptions that proved the rule about the substantial difficulty of *sustaining* a comeback in traditional elite careers. Denise Hortas was one such noteworthy case. By the time of the follow-up interview six years after she had stepped back into her former career, we learned that she not only had avoided the career attrition characteristic of those women making a comeback but had prospered. Within several years, she had advanced rapidly from a senior executive position just slightly below the one she had left upon opting out, to the number two position as vice president of the company. So what accounted for Denise's ability not only to sustain but to flourish in her comeback career?

Timing was everything in this case. Denise always knew she would return to the career she loved, but she wanted to do it when her children were older and she could better handle the all-consuming pressures of her profession. Her husband's retirement coincided with the empty nest years, giving Denise both the push and the pull she needed to return to her former lucrative but demanding occupation. With her children gone, Denise was now free to throw herself into advancing her career full-throttle, which she did.

Donna Haley was also able to return to her former profession as an attorney and to sustain a productive post-opt-out career. Unlike Denise, she was able to do so when her children were still quite young. The secret to Donna's long-term success as a returnee to an elite profession makes her another type of exception to the rule. By working in her husband's business in a corporate counsel role, she was able to make her own hours, work from home, and pick and choose projects, always balancing the needs of family with the needs of the family business. Even though Donna sometimes felt like she was just "an invisible hand in the business," she found the career path she had chosen rewarding and far more flexible, and therefore viable, than any of the alternatives in her profession. As she put it, "I have a great degree of control over what I do, when I do it, how I do it, and the way it gets done."

FORCED CHOICE OR PRIVILEGED CHOICE?

Unlike its popular portrayal, career relaunch after opting out was not just a single event but rather a lengthy, halting, and discontinuous process of career transition spanning many years. Furthermore, the difficulty women experienced in opting back in to work centered less on getting hired, as has been popularly depicted, and more on an intensive, sometimes frustrated quest for the "right" job. As we have seen, this quest almost always entailed vocational reinvention to one extent or another as women sought to restart careers that would reflect their changed identities and priorities. In fact, career reinvention can be viewed as the overarching approach that women used to return to work, regardless of which particular relaunch strategy they adopted. The ongoing contingency of women's careers in relation to the ever-shifting demands of family life only added to the flux and uncertainty of the career transition process.

Career reinvention can be understood as a proactive response as well as a realistic accommodation to the gendered constraints women faced in returning to their previous employers. These constraints were embedded in both the home and workplace, and they included the inflexible, long-hour nature of their former professions, the primacy of husbands' careers, and the class-driven intensification of mothering during privileged domesticity.

Adopting the tactic of career reinvention in the face of barriers to returning to their former professions, these women may also be seen as "entrepreneurs" of the life course.[11] Having deviated substantially from the traditional linear male career pathway by opting out, they each individually had to innovate their own pathways back into the workforce, with few institutionalized supports to help them do so. There were no obvious welcome mats awaiting women in their former professions, no preexisting family-flexible on-ramps. Nor was there a corresponding career playbook or life course map to collectively guide women through the major life status passage of career reentry after a major break. Therefore, like any entrepreneurial venture, the innovation they were attempting involved substantial creativity as well as risk, trial and error, and vulnerability to failure.

But importantly, their career innovation, while not supported by the culture, *was* strongly enabled by class privilege. Women's affluence provided them the financial freedom to explore, invest in, and pursue new career interests that arose from their immersion in the philanthropic, care-oriented culture of privileged domesticity. It also offered them the discretion to prioritize work that offered meaning and enjoyment over money, an enviable choice that few women (or men) of lesser means in society are able to enjoy. In effect, their class privilege provided the time, capital, and other resources needed to implement and realize their changed vocational values and interests. Thus career reinvention can be seen as both a *forced choice* and a *privileged choice* born of the paradox of privilege—the contradictory dynamics of women's gender subordination and their class privilege.

The previous few chapters have provided a close-up view—or to use a photographic metaphor, a zoom lens perspective—of women's gradual transition from privileged domesticity to career relaunch, a process characterized by a full range of trials, tribulations, and triumphs. But standing back and using a wide-angle lens, how do we assess the long-term consequences of opting out and opting back in? How do women's careers just before they stepped out of the workforce compare with where they end up over a decade later? Do the costs of their career reinventions outweigh the benefits, or vice versa? And how satisfied or dissatisfied are they with these changes? These are questions we turn to in the following chapter.

SIX

The Big Picture

A clear majority (over two-thirds) of women were currently back at work at the time of follow-up, most in the career relaunch phase. True to their original aspirations to eventually return to the workforce, they realized goals they'd set when we first interviewed them many years earlier. Kate Hadley used her marketing expertise first as a product manager in a consumer products company and then, after a career break, as an in-house consultant at a leading management consulting company. Diane Childs, a CPA, traded in a job as CFO of a housing nonprofit for freelance accounting. Elizabeth Brand, former partner at a management consulting firm, was still at home, not having yet attempted to return to work. Nan Driscoll transitioned from editor-in-chief to a teacher's aide. Meg Romano went from being on the trading desk of a large financial firm to being development officer for her local school foundation. Denise Hortas was the only woman who'd re-created and built on her previous career. After a stint trying her hand at teaching, she was now VP at a biotech pharmaceutical firm.

The foregoing chapters detail the two-stage *process* of women's return to work, including the often complex sequencing of jobs that occurs along the way. In contrast, this chapter takes stock of the *outcomes* of these and related decision-making processes by looking at features of the jobs and occupations women held at the time of the follow-up interview compared to the last job they held prior to opting out. At this juncture, women who have returned to work are at varying points in their journey: about a quarter are still in the family-first phase, but most—just over half—are in the relaunch phase. We also visit with the "nesters" to find out why they have not as yet returned to work and what their lives are like now, many years after having left the workforce. While these women's stories are not over, we assess women's outcomes—the bigger picture—by comparing their work lives before and after opting out. To do so, we focus on several key features of work that are commonly used by social scientists.

First, we look at the gender composition of the occupations women held before and after taking a career break. Women's entry into and integration of more male-dominated fields is regarded as an important indicator of gender equity. In addition, so-called occupational segregation is closely linked to, and explains a large portion of, the gender pay gap: otherwise similar occupations with a greater share of women workers are lower-paying than those whose workers are primarily men.

Second, we examine the pay and prestige of the occupations women held before and after opting out, which are critical measures of their economic and social standing. For both these analyses, we rely on detailed occupational data based on the entire US labor force.[1] Occupations represent broad groupings of similar kinds of work (e.g., lawyer, teacher), without reference to context. They are the aggregation of jobs, which are site or organization specific (e.g., lawyer at Debevoise & Plimpton, teacher at Mamaroneck High School). These analyses locate the experiences of the women we studied in the larger context of the American economy and occupational structure and, again, help to understand the big-picture implications of their decisions.

Finally, we analyze specific features of their *jobs* (which do take employer context or setting into account) to explore other features of their employment before and after a break. These tap the degree to which jobs are seen as "good"—relatively permanent, secure, and likely to carry benefits such as health insurance and pensions.[2] As we'll see, in all but one of these areas, opting out exacts a toll (and even the exception might be viewed as maintenance of a dubious status quo whereby women are accorded social standing but not its accouterments such as high pay). Less easy to quantify is the question: At what price? To answer this, we look at how women themselves assess their current jobs.[3]

RESEGREGATION AND FEMINIZATION OVER THE LIFE COURSE

The most radical and disruptive strategy by which women relaunched their careers—starting over in an entirely new field—was also the most common. The stories of Meg Romano and Nan Driscoll show the lengths to which women were willing to go to bring work back into their lives and the extent to which they had closed the book on their former careers, which had not met their needs before and continued to come up short. While at home, women discovered the appeal of caring work. This, coupled with the quest for greater meaning at midlife and the ongoing desire to find time for family, led them to explore historically "female" professions like teaching, options many had eschewed at the beginning of their work lives in order to pursue the then relatively new opportunities opening up in "male" professions like law and business.

The numbers tell the story. Take a look at figure 2, which is based on the thirty women who were working at the time of the second interview (i.e., omitting four women who had ever worked since first interview but weren't currently working). Before they quit, almost half (43 percent) of these high-achieving women, most of whom had graduated from highly selective colleges and universities, worked in male-dominated occupations (defined as those in which women made up one-third or less of the occupation's workers). In their current jobs, only one-quarter (27 percent) are in these fields. Instead, there's a roughly fourfold increase in the proportion of women returning to work via female-dominated jobs.

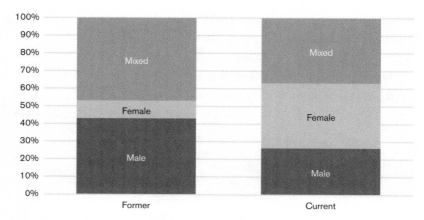

Figure 2. Gender composition of former and current jobs ($N = 30$).

These historically "female" jobs, which were held by only 10 percent of women before they opted out, now account for 37 percent on reentry. In an ironic throwback, women resegregate in hopes of finding what they couldn't in their former historically "male" professions.

Changing from a male- to female-gendered occupation was the most prevalent outcome, and the starkest change, but considering other types of occupational switches, a general pattern of "feminization" emerges. In addition to the most frequent male- to female-dominated switch, some women moved from a mixed-gender to a female-dominated occupation, as Nan Driscoll did when she left an editor-in-chief job in publishing for a teacher's aide job in the female-dominated world of elementary education. Others moved from a male-dominated to a mixed-gender occupation, as Amanda Taylor did when she left banking for a PhD and academic research career in the life sciences.

The next most common job change pattern, representing about one-fourth of all job changers, was staying within the mixed-gender category, as Diane Childs did when she switched from nonprofit executive to freelance accountant. Only three women moved to male-dominated jobs from mixed-gender or female jobs, and those who did were small business owners (more than two-thirds of whom, nationwide, are men), like Melanie Irwin, who went from computer marketing (integrated) to equestrian center entrepreneur (male).

Taken all together, resegregation from male- to female-dominated occupations reflects the most extreme form of feminization, but looking at the pattern of all changes across the life cycle shows not only movement into more feminine occupations but movement away from historically male to female jobs over the course of the family life cycle and motherhood. Notably, it's occurring among women who earlier in their lives were, if not pioneers, then early entrants in opening up or integrating the male professions, which they fled in opting out and continue to flee on returning to work. And for the same reasons: long hours, inflexibility, and a work climate antithetical to family, with a new one added—the growing desire for impact and meaning, a need that surfaced from their experiences as at-home mothers and that they don't see met in the types of occupations they left behind.

EXTRINSIC REWARDS

Earnings index a job's economic value, prestige its social standing. Social scientists regard both as important extrinsic rewards of work; people work for both livelihood *and* recognition and respect. These women's privilege, as we've seen, makes possible a high degree of discretion in the labor market. Most don't have to work for money. Their reentry is influenced more by the dual criteria of flexibility and meaning—intrinsic features of work—than by extrinsic. This emphasis on meaning and giving back is heightened by the fact that they are also aging, and are more likely to be contemplating legacy now than when they were younger.

Lost: A Pretty Penny

Women's moves to more female occupations have obvious implications for pay. Research repeatedly demonstrates that the more women in an occupation, the lower its pay, even or perhaps especially for occupations that are otherwise similar with respect to their qualifications and responsibilities. Accordingly, women who shift away from male-dominated to female-dominated fields take a big earnings hit (see figure 3, which is based on women who were working at the time of the follow-up interview). Before opting out, women worked in extremely high-earning occupations, which averaged a median of $111,635 for full-time, year-round female workers in those occupations. Many women's first job on reentering the workforce was a serendipitous "family-first" job followed by a purposeful "career relaunch" job. Accordingly, their initial reentry jobs were in lower-paying occupations, with median earnings of $54,985 (although note that most women were earning only a fraction of a full-time year-round salary upon reentry, as the majority worked part-time, and often very part-time, especially in the family-first phase), about half of median earnings in their previous occupations. Earnings prospects rebounded to relatively high levels (an occupational average of $71,075), as women found their footing, often changed jobs, and shifted to higher-paying occupations in the relaunch phase. However, relative to their earlier fields, women who changed fields landed in less lucrative occupations, the earnings of which, while relatively high by most standards, are still only about two-thirds the earnings of the occupations they held prior to exiting the workforce.

Maintaining the "Status" Status Quo

Occupational prestige or *status* (used interchangeably) refers to the public perception of a person's social standing based on their occupation rather than personal attributes.[4] Pay and prestige or social status are correlated, but not perfectly, because public perception of a job's social standing takes into account more than its pay. Qualifications, especially educational credentials such as advanced degrees, figure heavily in people's judgments about the prestige or status of given occupations, as

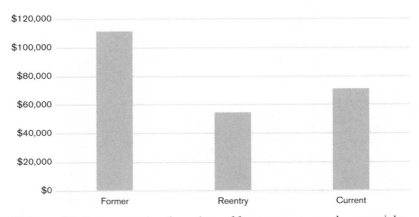

Figure 3. Median occupational earnings of former, reentry, and current jobs ($N = 30$).

does the authority wielded. Social judgments also tend to follow a blue-versus white-collar divide, with the result that, in general, women's occupations do not incur as large a prestige penalty as they do an earnings penalty.[5] Teaching, for example, which is high on education and authority and white collar, is perceived as relatively prestigious, but not high paying compared to male-dominated blue-collar trades. In fact, across the full occupational spectrum, there is no prestige gender gap, since women and men work in occupations that have, on average, the same level of prestige—what sociologist Paula England has labeled "a case of vacuous equality" because it reflects paternalistic benevolence and is symbolic rather than material.[6] Nonetheless, looking only at the professions, we do see a gender gap, whereby female-dominated professions such as teaching and social work are viewed as less prestigious—sociologists label them "semi-" or "quasi-professions"—than the so-called "classic professions" such as law and medicine, which have been historically dominated by men.

Sociologists have long studied occupational prestige as a global measure of an occupation's socially perceived worth, and they use a 100-point scale whereby higher scores reflect higher prestige. To the

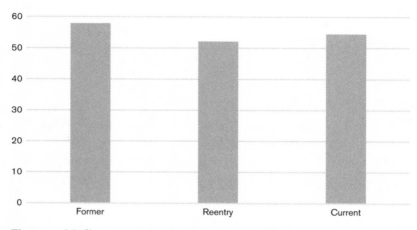

Figure 4. Median occupational prestige scores of former, reentry, and current jobs ($N = 30$).

extent that job changes entail a move from one occupation to another, the difference in occupational prestige score reflects social mobility across the class structure, either upward or downward. Some women did experience downward mobility. Nan Driscoll's change of occupation took her from a score of 59 for editor to 41 for teacher's aide. Meg Romano's change had little effect on her status, moving her from 52 to 53. Note, also, that because prestige scores attach to occupations, not jobs, they don't pick up changes in employer. Both Nan and Meg not only changed occupations but moved from leading national firms in their industries to their local school districts. Nor does prestige reflect whether a job is permanent or contingent. Course correctors like Diane Childs left permanent, secure jobs to freelance in the same occupations. These moves entail no change in their occupational status but might otherwise be viewed as a step down.

With these caveats, as shown in figure 4, women's job changes before and after opting out don't exact a meaningful prestige penalty insofar as those who do change occupation (and not all do) move predominantly into the white-collar female professions, occupations that are perceived as relatively prestigious. From before opting out (median prestige score of 58) to first occupation on reentry (median of 52) to current occupation (median of 55), prestige scores remain pretty stable, showing a rebound to almost prequit levels and none of the volatility— or the precipitous drop—associated with occupational earnings.

In reentering the workforce, women maintain the status quo, saving face—and maintaining social and cultural capital—while losing money. Moving to a new job whose occupational standing is equivalent to and consistent with their former careers, which at the same time meets their needs for flexibility and impact, is an added bonus of otherwise underpaid female-dominated jobs and offsets or cushions their financial downside. Thus these female occupations' relatively high prestige, insofar as they don't entail drastic downward social mobility, may be another part of their attraction, though no woman mentioned this explicitly as a motivation for going into them.

THE GIG ECONOMY

The second most common strategy for getting back to work was what we've called "course correction," staying in the same field or occupation but working on a freelance, consultant, or project basis—what's come to be known as "the gig economy."[7] This type of contingent employment has been growing rapidly since these women left the labor force, and they took advantage of the opportunities it opened up. Contingent employment is episodic and of limited duration, being built on a "just-in-time" or as-needed model for labor. Contingent jobs are without a formal or long-term employment contract, typically time or project limited, and without benefits such as health insurance. This class of jobs (and the larger gig economy) arose primarily to meet the needs of employers, allowing them to shed standing labor costs and provide hiring flexibility. But these jobs also offer flexibility to workers, which, as we've seen, is something returning women are looking for and not finding in permanent full-year, full-time professional jobs like the ones they left behind. Contingent jobs can maximize year-round flexibility and mesh with the rhythms of family, especially school and vacation schedules. Freelancing enabled women like Diane Childs, the CPA, to transition back relatively quickly to work, building on existing skills, expertise, and contacts. Similarly, Wendy Friedman, in an industry that's been at the forefront of the gig or freelance economy, was able to deploy her extensive editing experience to switch easily from a permanent job as a senior editor at a major publishing house to freelancing on book projects that came her way.

Figure 5 shows the extent to which women switched to contingent work from the jobs they left behind prior to opting out, when virtually all worked on a permanent basis (and enjoyed relative employment security and generous benefits that included paid parental leave). At the time of follow-up, currently about half are working contingently in project- or gig-based jobs that enable them to time their work over the course of the year around children and, to a lesser extent, husbands' schedules.[8] It should be noted that women who had relaunched their careers by the time of the second interview were doing significantly better on this score, with two-thirds working in permanent, noncontingent jobs, compared to their family-first counterparts, who were almost entirely contingent. If we assume that at least some of the family-first women will go on to relaunch careers, this predicts an upward trend in women's ability to secure more stable jobs over time, while also suggesting that even after relaunch they have lost ground on this important dimension of job quality, advancement potential, and security.

In addition to increasing the longer-term flexibility of their year-round work schedule by working contingently, women sought short-term flexibility by reducing their hours. By definition, women who were in the family-first phase at the follow-up interview were all working part-time, but in addition to that, almost half of the women who had relaunched their careers were also working on a part-time basis. Reflecting well-known trends, women in female jobs were more likely to work part-time, with two-thirds doing so. In contrast, in male-dominated jobs, which are more likely to hew to an ideal-worker, long-

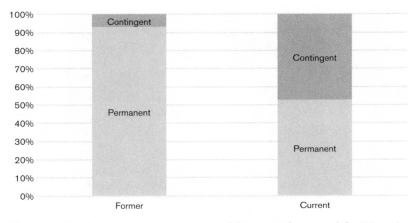

Figure 5. Contingent/permanent nature of former and current jobs ($N = 30$).

hour model of work, two-thirds worked full-time (with those in mixed-gender jobs equally split between part and full-time).

JOB SATISFACTION

Back at work because they want to work, not because they have to, and with the luxury of having been able to try out a variety of jobs to find the right fit, women knew their priorities and were clear-eyed about the trade-offs they were making. While objectively, especially with regard to pay, security, and benefits, their new jobs compared invidiously to their former ones, women were much more satisfied with work the second time around. While they loved their former careers and left them reluctantly, the long hours, demanding schedules, and stigma attached to seeming solutions like part-time work and job-sharing colored their perceptions of them. At the first interview, women most often indicated mixed feelings or moderate satisfaction, and fully two-thirds reported either low or moderate levels of satisfaction (see figure 6). Rating their current jobs, however, women are highly satisfied, two-thirds giving them the thumbs up.

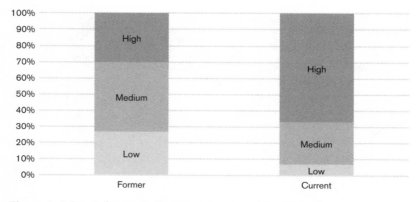

Figure 6. Job satisfaction in former and current jobs ($N = 30$).

Given the relatively high levels of satisfaction—about nine out of ten are moderately to highly satisfied—it's perhaps not surprising that women's degree of satisfaction is not linked to either pay (almost all having taken a major pay cut) or prestige (since most did not experience a drop in status). Nor is it linked to the particular strategy they used to reenter the workforce. Looking only at women who have moved into the career relaunch phase, course changers are as satisfied with their current work as course correctors or comeback kids. This suggests that there isn't a magic, one-size-fits-all path to successful career relaunch but rather a variety of paths back. When we look at the *change* in reported satisfaction between their former and current careers, however, as opposed to the absolute level of satisfaction with their current job, a slightly more complex picture emerges. Approximately three-quarters of both course changers and course correctors report an *increase* in satisfaction in their current jobs compared to their former jobs, and none reports a decrease in satisfaction. Comeback kids' experiences are more checkered, as we've seen, most notably with Kate Hadley, and only two-thirds (still a large majority) report increased satisfaction despite (or perhaps because of) the fact that, among all women, their current jobs are the most similar to the ones they left behind. Thus, while most women show increased satisfaction with their career relaunch jobs, women making the biggest changes in the circumstances of their employment, including major reinvention, register the biggest "bump up." Although they are not more satisfied than those who came back charting a more familiar course, relative to their starting points (i.e., their former careers), they evince a bigger gain, some of which may be the result of their lower levels of satisfaction with prequit jobs, but some of which may also be a function of the self-reflective process of reinvention and trial and error this group experienced in engineering their return.

THE GOOD AND THE NOT SO GOOD

Echoing their earlier thinking as they deliberated reentry and decided to pursue one or another path back to work, women repeatedly invoked flexibility and meaning—intrinsic rather than extrinsic features—in talking about what they liked about their current careers. "I have a ton of flexibility," said Nathalie Everett, thirty-nine, the former international marketing manager now working as a textbook sales consultant. Likewise, Christine Thomas, forty, the former senior marketing manager of IT now working as an independent digital media consultant, valued "mainly being flexible in terms of being able to attend important events," adding, "The clients I took on, some of them were targeting women, so I got to work on women's issues." Meg Romano, the former trader now working full-time as director of the foundation for her local public school, said: "I really believe in what we do and I see it with my three children." Martha Haas, forty-two, a former senior development officer at a major university who had been home twelve years and was now working as part-time development officer at her children's private day school, talked about rebuilding self-esteem, the erosion of which was one of the hardest hits for women who'd left their former careers and become, to the outside world, invisible stay-at-home moms: "It's been excellent for my self-confidence," Martha said. "To come in—and be so supported and see so many people like me—but to realize I really can contribute. . . . It's been kind of wonderful."

Despite their overall high rates of satisfaction, women were clear-eyed about what they'd given up. Women working as freelancers and consultants lamented the loss of workplace camaraderie. Christine Thomas spoke for many: "There is always sort of a sadness for the things that you've traded. And one of the things I feel like I've traded is a network of people that I loved working with that were very stimulating on a regular basis. I don't have peers any more. I don't have that and it makes me sad."

Another trade-off was noted by Karen Gordon, forty, a chemical engineer who formerly worked as a permanent employee, was home two years, and now worked as an independent contractor. While Karen was satisfied with her compensation, many women, especially those in female professions, were not. Her chief complaint was a common refrain among women working the gig economy: contract workers saw themselves sidelined to more marginal assignments. As Karen described it: "I do like the schedule.... Financially, it's lucrative. I don't always get, *obviously* [emphasis added], choice projects because I work part-time. And I am technically not an employee. I'm a contract employee.... So I sometimes get things that need to be done, but they're not glamorous. But I'm generally okay with that. You can't always have everything. You can't expect to have this schedule and then expect to be given high-priority needs, really hot projects. *That's just now how it works*" (emphasis added).

REMEMBER THE NESTERS—EMPTY OR NOT

Elizabeth Brand, now forty-seven, was still at home and in the years since our first interview had never gone back to work or even tried to. This was typical of the women in this group—about a fifth of our sample—who had been at-home moms continuously since we first spoke with them. They hadn't tried and failed to find a job; rather, they hadn't tried. Elizabeth had made partner at a highly prestigious management consulting firm at the young age of thirty-four, but after she had her first child, the time and travel demands of her job were such that she never returned from maternity leave, resigning instead. She was pregnant with her second child when we first met and subsequently had had a third. Her husband was still CEO of a beverage company, and as it had grown and prospered he had gotten even busier.

At our first interview, Elizabeth reflected on returning to work, and her reflections provide insight into why she—like so many other women—did not entertain going back to her former career: "I don't think I'll ever go back to the intensity of what I was doing before because management consulting is a pretty intense career. It's very fulfilling in a lot of ways, but it's stressful. And there's a lot of traveling, you're busy." Similarly, in looking ahead, she had priorities similar to those of other women who did subsequently return to work: "Like I said, just having [an] impact on the world is something that really means a lot to me. And I think I would have more time once the kids are fully in school, and all that. I could devote some amount of time. But I couldn't imagine devoting more than a third of a workweek to anything, maybe half-time."

At our second interview, Elizabeth's thinking about returning to work was little changed. Nearly a decade, and two children (ages four through ten) later, she was still uncertain about what she wanted to do, and the longer she'd been away from work, the more remote it became. Spending time with her kids was still a priority—strengthened over the course of her years at home—but returning was harder; Elizabeth described it as "a little daunting": "I don't even know how I would start or where I would go, because the path of doing that, I just don't even know.... Would anyone think that my experience ten years ago or nine years ago was still that viable, number one? Although I think I have a great set of skills that could help, I think that the things that would be open for me might not be the most attractive."

The perceived challenges of figuring out what she wanted to do and actually looking for a job were contrasted with the rewards of staying home—for now. Elizabeth had a rich volunteer life, and her family made clear they preferred her at home: "I think [my husband] probably prefers that I'm at home given how busy he is." Her kids were unambiguous: "I threaten my kids that I'm going to leave and go back to work, and they say, 'Nooooooooooooo! Noooooo! Don't do that, Mommy, don't do that!'" That returning to work was a "threat" speaks volumes about Elizabeth's current thinking about a real return to being a working mother.

At first glance, Elizabeth—and other women who had not yet returned to work—were not that different from women who had. If we compare the two groups when we first interviewed them, they were, in fact, similar on many key dimensions. Women who had been home continuously were, for example, no more likely (slightly less, in fact) to have preferred parental over paid care, they quit their jobs for the same reasons, and they evinced the same level of satisfaction with their former jobs as women who had returned. They were also equally likely to plan to return to work at initial interview, and, as Elizabeth's comments indicate, they were looking for the same things in a job, including being open to exploring new fields. This still-at-home minority was distinguished by three features: (1) they were more likely to have formerly worked in male-dominated professions, (2) they lacked confidence, and (3) they were more affluent than their returning counterparts (their husbands disproportionately worked in the most lucrative of elite occupations, such as high finance).

Two-thirds of nesters—those women who have not yet returned to the workforce—had previously worked in male-dominated occupations, compared to only half of the entire sample. Nesters, old and young, were also less confident about returning to work when we first talked with them than the women who had returned. These two characteristics—prequit careers in predominantly male occupations and lack of confidence in the ability to relaunch a career in the future—were directly connected to each other. In almost every case, as we see with Elizabeth, this lack of confidence was tied to the realization that they couldn't or didn't want to return to their former careers in predominantly male professions and were going to have to start over from scratch, unsure about what new careers to take up and how. In our initial study, when we first observed this uncharacteristic uncertainty among an otherwise accomplished and confident group, we labeled the phenomenon "another Ophelia moment," likening it to what psychologist Mary Pipher called the crisis of confidence and loss of identity among adolescent girls. It turns out that the "Ophelia" effect is not fleeting, but for these women, long-standing and persistent, apparent years later.[9] In another instance of privilege creating paradox, this Ophelia moment was often heightened by nesters' particularly high levels of affluence, which could undermine their motivation to push through the daunting barriers to career reinvention.

At an age when women are taking stock of their lives and, with regard to work, contemplating what will probably be their last act, the women in this group were still searching and finding no easy answers. Typical was Rachel Berman, fifty-six at our follow-up interview. With an MBA from a top-tier business school, Rachel had had a rough time at her last job, which she'd left twenty-one years ago. Employed by a leading investment banking firm, she'd encountered a rigid ("You can't do finance part-time"), macho, and misogynistic environment where her career was mommy-tracked. Only five years out of the labor force at the time of our first interview, she was uncertain about going back but was clear that if she did, it wouldn't be to finance. Sixteen years later, she declared full-time parenting "still fabulous, and it's exciting to watch the kids grow and mature and develop," but she is more ambivalent about everything to do with work, including resuming her career.

As we settled down for our follow-up interview in the living room of her home in the hills of Silicon Valley, her twenty-something daughter, visiting, but otherwise launched, walked through. Rachel told her what we were doing—talking about her career break—and as her daughter exited admonished her, "Don't do it, don't do it." Throughout our interview her demeanor was almost apologetic, and at one point she offered that "I don't feel particularly proud of my last twenty years." She elaborated, citing the "cocktail party dilemma" we heard about so frequently

during our first study, which was still a lingering—and very live—
issue to Rachel and others like her who'd not yet returned to work:

> In this community, there are a lot of very highly educated women who
> have opted out. The women who are staying at home, you know, they're
> not deemed unworthy or anything.... So if you're a stay-at-home mom, you
> still have the education behind you for your own self- worth.... But I feel
> like it's ... [she sighs], you know, you go to a cocktail party and people go,
> "What do you do?" and you know, I don't take pride in saying, "Well I'm a
> stay-at-home mom," and now that I don't have kids at home I really can't
> say I'm a stay-at-home mom. So I have to come up with something to say.
> You know?

Though inclined to want to return to work, Rachel was still uncertain
about what to do. She was now more open to finance, drawing on her
degree and old skill set, but as a personal financial or estate planner, not a
trader. Ageism concerned her: "There's a lot of things that I could offer,
but I don't think I'm as attractive to employers as younger people would
be." Trying to find her path, she'd taken some classes in the past year,
including language classes, to see if she "could get excited about anything." Although she'd "been thinking about this" since her middle child
had entered college almost five years previously, she still had "no idea":

> I wish I had more of like a path, or a clear vision of what I would do. I think,
> I mean I've been thinking about it, but still nothing has ... really evolved,
> and I still do feel very torn between parents and children and trying to fig-
> ure out what I'm going to be doing.... But it's really hard because I don't
> feel like I have skills. I kept thinking, "Oh I'll go back to school and I'll
> learn something," but that takes a lot of effort and energy. And if they're not
> going to hire me anyway, I'm not sure.

Her lingering uncertainty about what she wanted to do, coupled with
her ebbing confidence and ongoing family demands (a husband who
still traveled a lot and a youngest child just heading off to college) combined to paralyze her with respect to taking any significant steps to get
back to the workforce. Married to a successful investment banker,

Rachel also had no economic imperative to return to work. She mused that "I think I'm too soft" and "I'm just not going to push myself that hard because I don't have to."

In general, the group Rachel represents—women who'd never returned to work—evinced little regret about having made the fateful decision to quit their careers, but they were more likely to reveal inner conflict and wrestle out loud with ambivalence about their current lives, giving poignant voice to the paradox of privilege. Patricia Lambert, with an MBA from another top school, and a husband with a lucrative career in finance, had forged a highly involved and successful at-home "career" of professional-level volunteer work, serving on multiple boards. Referring to her current life and the decision to opt out and focus on volunteer and community work instead, she said: "I think the thing that I'm just amazed at is the fullness I feel, and yet also the emptiness that also exists." In the same breath, she effectively chastised herself for even feeling pangs of regret and wrestled with her privilege:

> In my most honest moments I don't know that I'm giving really as much weight as I should to how darn lucky I am that I can be in this situation where I don't need to work. I can be in this situation where my husband makes enough money that we can live well and support our kids way longer than anybody should. That I can have, you know, unbelievable freedom to pick and choose the volunteer positions that I want. That I can play tennis when I'm asked. I mean, really. Huh? Exactly how bad is that? And I don't know that I really provide enough value to that. I'm embarrassed to provide the value that that really has.

Despite this, she still mourned her lost career. She "could have been a contender" and recognized that she'd made a trade-off she had never envisioned as a high-flying MBA:

> I don't think I have pushed myself to see what I am really capable of. I think I made the decision (that I don't regret) that I would take myself out of the job market, the officially determined job market, and even the entrepreneurial space … to focus on the kids and the family. I probably said this in 1999 too [the date of our first interview twelve years before, and she did],

but if someone told me when I was, say, in business school, or even in college [that I would have made the decision I did], I would say [laughing], "You're smokin' too much dope." I'm shocked. I'm a little surprised at myself. But we made that decision and don't regret it at all. And yet I regret the secondary impact of it, which was to not make my own accomplishment, and what I could do, a higher priority.

A LINGERING CHILL

The outsized proportion of nesters who had previously worked in male-dominated occupations suggests that features of male jobs may not only influence the type of work women pursue (or eschew) on reentry, leading to the larger trend of resegregation over the family life cycle, but perhaps also create a crisis of confidence—an Ophelia moment—that discourages them from reentering at all. Older women in this group of nonreturners, like Rachel, for example, were more likely to have been pioneers in their male-dominated work worlds. Rachel's current thinking was clearly influenced—negatively—by her prior experience. For younger women like Elizabeth, we saw how the demands of male fields with respect to time and travel were also discouraging. With their former careers deemed untenable, women were understandably awash and adrift, faced with the challenge of redirection. Many women met that challenge, but the longer younger women like Elizabeth remain at home, will memories of their former fields have a continuing chilling effect when they reach the empty nest stage, ruling out reentry?

WHAT IF? THE OPTING-OUT GAP AND LEADERSHIP LOSS

It had been seven years since Elizabeth gave up her partnership—itself a major career accomplishment—in one of the most well-respected management consulting firms in the country. Her interview reflects understandable uncertainty about her future employment, but when asked the hypothetical question "Where do you think you'd be if you'd continued working?" she stated confidently: "Senior vice president at [name of former company]." Kate Hadley thought she'd be at the same senior management level had she stayed in marketing. Diane Childs, who had never wanted to pursue the partnership track at a big-time accounting firm, had reached her career high as COO of a nonprofit. Meg Romano, who preferred being on the trading floor rather than management, had also attained her career pinnacle as a successful trader. Nan Driscoll, working part-time as a teacher's aide, envisioned herself as senior VP and editor-in-chief, positions she'd actually held before quitting. Denise Hortas, VP at a biotech pharmaceutical firm at the time of our follow-up interview, thought she'd be "right where I am now."

Women across the board replied like Elizabeth and the others—without missing a beat. Many, like Diane and Nan, had actually attained personal bests in their former fields before quitting. Others, who had left before doing so, replied very much like Elizabeth. Maeve Turner, a lawyer who'd been home twenty-four years and was among those who never tried to reenter, answered that she'd be a state or federal judge—tops in her field as a former litigator. Brooke Coakley, doing hospital management work on a freelance basis, saw herself becoming chief operating officer of a major hospital or health care system. In many cases, the difference between what women were doing by the time of the follow-up interview and what they perceived they could have been doing was pronounced.

While theirs may be wistful imaginings, and it's impossible to know how their predictions would have panned out, they are credible given these women's track records and promotion histories before opting out. Some women might have been overly optimistic—ignoring or discounting, for example, the glass ceiling and other forms of gender discrimination, but countering that, many had already achieved high levels of leadership in their fields. Further giving their claims credence, many supported their predictions with reference to former work colleagues who *had* continued working. A case in point is Patricia Lambert, the fifty-six-year old MBA continuously at home, who replied she'd "be the head of whatever I was doing." She backed this up with reference to the facts that "the person who replaced me is now the president of the company and all my peers have leadership positions." The exception proving the rule, one woman in our study was able to rebound and more— Denise Hortas, who'd left a job as director of research at a pharmaceutical company and worked her way into the position of vice president at a different firm. The difference between women's current position (after quitting and reentering) and the one they predicted they'd be in if they'd continued working captures what might be dubbed the opting-out gap and makes real the penalty attached to this strategy, in terms of lost leadership potential, at least as measured against the yardstick of the linear, male model of career. The opting-out gap also reveals the leaky pipeline in action and how and when the female talent pool dries up or goes empty. Women leave at two crucial points: either midcareer and ascendant (leaders whose potential is unrealized), which is well documented, or, less well documented, but clear in our results, at the top of their fields (leaders lost).

HAPPY ENDINGS?

Women who've opted out typically opt back in, though the path back to work is littered with dead ends and start-overs. In going back, their class privilege affords them a great deal of discretion as to whether or not to work. While their desire to work part-time or part year may be their own "choice," the structure of a highly gender-segregated and increasingly contingent labor market results in a lack of solid, secure, family-flexible jobs in these women's fields. Accordingly, they are forced to leave behind the more lucrative male professions many worked in before and channel themselves instead into lower-paying female-dominated professions and into contingent jobs that offer little in the way of job security, benefits, prospects for promotion, or even important assignments.

For these talented women, opting out sets in motion resegregation, loss of earnings and advancement opportunities, and marginalization over the course of their work lives, which largely takes them off the leadership track in their former fields. They find themselves starting over as new "old" kids on the block or on their own as freelancers, no longer anchored in organizations. Fortunately, because of what might be seen as the benevolent paternalism of how we as a society perceive highly gendered "women's work," women don't experience a precipitous drop in their occupational status (although recall that this sociologically derived measure doesn't take into account the prestige of the employing organization or other commonly perceived indicators of job status). While this might be considered a relatively empty consolation, at least women are able to broadly preserve status in their reentry fields and are spared the experience of blatantly downward mobility.

Despite these (mostly) objective negatives, of which women are well aware, subjectively, their stories (mostly) have happy endings. Women are delighted to be back at work and happy in their new jobs—happier, in fact, than they were in their former careers—and particularly pleased to have found in the historically female professions and the nonprofit sector the deep satisfaction of meaning and making a difference, with several even achieving leadership positions in these fields (e.g., executive director of a nonprofit). They are also happier and less conflicted than the women who remained at home. Their individual success stories, and satisfaction, however, obscure the larger loss of their talents, productivity, and potential from permanent jobs and from historically male professions—which many were helping to integrate before their career exits—and of which we get a measure when they tell us what they might have been. How do we reconcile individual stories of happy endings with the larger scenario?

SEVEN

The Paradox of Privilege and Beyond

LOOKING BACK, LOOKING AHEAD

As our interviews wound down, women often reflected back even as they looked to the future, which many were still actively building. These discussions were wide-ranging, but certain themes and topics recurred. Women repeatedly talked about options and choices, reinvention, and the sheer complexity of finding their way. They perceived themselves as on their own and self-reliant, developing private solutions to the challenges of career and family, career breaks, and reentry. And they wanted to "repay the favor" to their husbands, so to speak, by shouldering some, or even all, of the breadwinner burden.

The Marketing Executive to Management Consultant to What's Next?

Having "overdosed on the volunteer work" and "doing so much taking care of other people" during her most recent (and second) career break, Kate Hadley was ready "to do something selfish": "I want to get that identity of working and contributing to a bigger purpose back."

Looming large among her motivations to return to work was the performance of her husband's hedge fund, which had suffered big losses amid the market volatility of previous years. Kate was happy to help him out but knew that she'd have to continue shouldering the bulk of work on the family front, which informed her next steps: "So I want to do something that's sustainable. That's my big idea."

A big idea and *the* recurring problem, with—yet again—no easy solution in sight. By "sustainable," Kate meant a job she could do for more than the five years she'd spent in her last job. She was tired of short-term stints: "I don't want to do that again [work at a new job five years or less]. I want to do something that I can build my expertise and keep doing it while my kids are in college." "Sustainable" also meant avoiding the "high intensity" of project-based consulting work with its tight time lines. Kate acknowledged the challenges facing her and the constant process of reinvention on which she and others like her embarked, and the ephemeral nature of the solutions they cobbled together: "I feel like as long as *I keep trying to figure out* what works for me and my family, that's *really the only thing I can do*. I feel like *what works at one stage of life is not going to necessarily work at another stage.* I'm excited that I still want to go back to work and I feel like I can contribute and there are going to be opportunities for me" (emphasis added).

With degrees from the top schools and a résumé boasting employment at two premier firms ("good branding," as she put it in her marketing lingo), Kate was justifiably confident: "I'm very conscious and grateful for that. I don't think I can be cocky, but I can be comfortable, and I don't need to apologize." After our interview, Kate was off to an exploratory job interview with an executive search firm. This was a new field, but attractive because of its focus on career paths, something that she had thought a lot about ("I love understanding paths that people took") and had forged anew herself. The job turned out to be "too junior," but it helped jump-start her search, which she was beginning in earnest in September—starting over at forty-eight.

The CPA

Diane Childs, who'd been freelancing for years, was thinking about ramping up her solo accounting practice now that one kid was in college and another was not far off. With an established client base and special expertise in real estate tax law, she anticipated little problem in doing so. She had taken the trouble to post her résumé on LinkedIn because, she told us, as you get older, "If you're not on that kind of social media stuff you just seem like you're this old fogey." Like Kate, she'd had enough with volunteer work, which she was looking "to lose." And also like Kate, she was attuned to helping her husband by relieving some of the pressure of the primary-breadwinner role. As she explained, "I mean, his job is stressful, that wears on you, and so I guess, eventually, I'd like to do what I can to take the stress off him."

In addition to helping pay for college, Diane also saw her earnings as savings for "you know, the 401k and retirement so my poor husband [like her, age fifty-four] isn't working 'til he's seventy, and so that retirement will be peaceful.... My husband's job is very stressful and it's wearying, and it would be really nice if we could, who knows, maybe— I mean, who knows, we have to see how much money we end up with— after my son graduates from college, if there's any way my husband could, you know, maybe start his own business or not have the stress that he has now." While she may or may not be able to realize this vision, the course Diane has set with regard to reinvigorating her own career seems likely to succeed, carrying her and her husband to a successful retirement. Diane reflected not only on her future but on the big picture, beyond her own immediate situation, which was relatively rare: "Me, personally, I'm satisfied with my life. I think, I guess on a macro-view, you know, it's been how many years of women working? And there's still not enough support for families.... This individualistic American way of life is just very hard, it's a very hard life, I guess. I think that's my takeaway. Every family kind of reinvents the wheel, you know?" She followed this with a story involving the office manager of one of her clients who had returned to Slovakia after having a baby because "there was no family support. Like, the American Dream isn't all it's cracked up to be."

The Management Consultant Now Stay-at-Home Mom

Resuming her career was not on Elizabeth Brand's immediate to-do list. With three youngsters at home and a husband who's a busy CEO, the prospect clearly overwhelmed her. Notably, she saw no way to return to her former career and had yet to discover another avenue back. Her interview was studded with anxiety—she used the word frequently, and it was typically coupled with descriptions of falling short of her own perfectionist standards. Talking about her son, she noted, "Helping him has been a great challenge for me too but also has created anxiety at times. And you're always anxious, you know, not terribly anxious, but I get anxiety about the kids. I can be a worrier at times, because I want everything to work right and everyone to be perfect, and of course life doesn't work that way all the time."

Like Kate, what Elizabeth desired in a job was flexibility and responsibilities commensurate with her credentials and experience. Unlike Kate, she had been out a long time, was lacking in confidence, and had no financial incentive to work. In an archetypical example of the paradox of privilege, her anxiety and continuing inability to identify a career direction echoed the stories we heard from women who never resumed their careers. If we had to bet, it seemed likely Elizabeth would follow in their path and instead deepen her engagement with volunteering, which she'd already been doing and found gratifying.

The Editor Now Teacher

Unable to land her own classroom, Nan—at fifty-nine—envisioned working as a teacher's aide for five or six more years. Getting older further dimmed the prospect that she'd get her own class: "And frankly, the more time passes, the less likely it is for someone hiring me for my own class. I mean, why would they put the time into grooming me?" Although she was thinking ahead to retirement at age seventy, she was resistant to thinking *too* far ahead, perhaps informed by her own experience with teaching: "One thing I've learned in fifty-nine years is that I don't make plans too far into the future. You know, I really just, I try to make the best of the situations that come along. And, which is not to say that I don't focus on [pause] you know, I make plans, but not ... not firm plans. You know, I think it's foolish."

Her thoughts about the future turned to her three daughters: "As they grapple with [pause] choices of their own, and they're just starving to do that—boyfriends, careers—I am certainly encouraging them to prepare themselves to have a successful, interesting career. Mostly interesting, but they have to be able to support themselves." Talking about her oldest, who had just graduated from college, she again picked up on the futility of planning: "She's still very young, yeah. And I really do think that [pause] there's a limit to the value in setting your absolute sights on something, so much of which you're not able to really control. Between the economy, your ovaries. You know, I mean, there's just a lot of factors, so many variables you really have no control over. I really don't encourage them [her oldest and other two daughters] to create a five-year plan." Nonetheless, she did have one piece of advice: "I guess if I ... were to give my kids advice—depending on what they were doing when their kids were born—and if they were on the fence about [about whether or not to work part-time], I would say, 'You should try and do that. If you can continue to work part-time, I think it's a very wise thing for a woman to do.'" To which she quickly added the caveat (born of her own experience): "It's not always possible."

Nan, whose youngest was still at home, in high school, seemed likely to continue teaching until retirement. Despite some dissatisfaction with the way her teaching career had turned out, she'd made peace with her disappointment.

The Trader Now Nonprofit Executive

Meg reveled in her new career, delighted that she had been able to parlay her volunteer work into a job she loved, and one in which she felt her "different skill set" (from the for-profit business sector) made her a "unique voice." The income trade-offs she'd made were "well worth it," though Meg was not unmindful of being able to add to family coffers and echoed a concern about her husband, similar to those voiced by others. Speaking about his reaction to her return to work:

> He knew that I would be happiest if I were fully engaged. And quite truthfully, also, he felt—and I think it's not unique to men—I think he felt a tremendous amount of pressure, no matter how much money you make, unless you make so much money that you get trust funds kind of stuff. I think he had a certain amount of worry and anxiety about "Well, how am I going to make this all happen?" and to know that you have a helpmate in that process reduces the stress. I mean it's not that I make so much money here, but I make enough that it takes a chunk out of those college tuitions. So that ... strengthens our partnership in that he feels like it's not all on him.

At fifty-one, she foresaw retiring "when I'm sixty-five or so. My husband will start to cut back his clients most likely, and I'll probably at that point stop working and go back to volunteering.... . Gardening, that's just not me, I would have to be volunteering somewhere in some capacity. I just couldn't be home all day, I'd go crazy."

Given her record to date, Meg seemed likely to pursue her charted course. Her parting reflection, which she prefaced with "I imagine you're hearing this from all the women you're interviewing," was "I think if you leave the workforce with a certain confidence in your abilities and an understanding of what your skill sets are, then you find a path that utilizes them." Unfortunately, we did *not* hear this from all women; in fact, Meg was the rare case of someone with a high degree of confidence and clarity of vision. That most women nonetheless eventually found a path is a testimony to their persistence—and to their privilege, which opened some doors to new paths and closed others.

The Scientist

The only woman who was able to pick up pretty much where she had left off, Denise was loving being back in her new old career, where she was now being given opportunities—and was able to take advantage of them—for leadership positions. She was keenly aware of the privilege she'd enjoyed by being able to take time out: "Taking care of your kids is—it's a privilege! We're not having to do what the mothers at the school where I taught do. They work three jobs! They were house-cleaners by day, they cleaned offices at night, for heaven's sake!"

Reflecting on the choices she'd made, and the advice she gives to other women, Denise voiced a common refrain, heavy on self-reliance, improvisation, and making it up as you go along:

> I give this advice a lot. I think it depends entirely on the situation. I think that if you have a flexible work situation and it works for you and you like it, it's fantastic, and try to do it. Because it's wonderful to be able to do both. But my feeling is you have to make choices. It is very hard to be the CEO of the company and the mother of small children and keep your marriage together and see your friends. You just can't do everything. So you have to really figure out what's working and use your best judgment which, whatever you decide, is going to be good enough. For people who stay in the workforce, it generally works well. And for people who stay home, that works well too. But I think you really have to do a lot of soul searching.

Denise's reentry was notable because she took on the primary-breadwinner role, relieving her husband, who, after twenty years of corporate litigation, "was really tired of it." As we heard from other women, Denise was motivated to support her husband by a mingled sense of concern, fairness, and gratitude. She described his newfound routine with obvious satisfaction: working out of their house, a "mix of things, but extremely part-time," enabling him to pursue his many hobbies. He was, she said, "happy"—and she was obviously happy too that she could help make this new phase of life possible for him, in an arrangement that seemed likely to continue until their retirement.

DÉJÀ VU

As we conducted interviews and pored over transcripts, we often had a sense of déjà vu—and an accompanying sense of *plus ça change, plus c'est la même chose* ("The more things change, the more they stay the same"). When we first talked with them, high-achieving women for whom being a stay-at-home mom had never been part of their life plan were settling uneasily into their new role as "accidental stay-at-home mother" (and its socially devalued status). In the ensuing years until we talked with them again, they'd more fully embraced the privileged form of domesticity distinctive to their class, particularly its status-keeping function, the importance of which emerged as they prepared their children for an adulthood equal in achievement to their own. Although a major economic recession occurred in 2008 between our first and second studies, these women and their families occupied a safe niche, most (but not all) unbuffeted by it. The few who were drew on their prior professional experience to step in as primary breadwinners, sparing the family from a precipitous drop in fortune.

Women skillfully guided children through the thicket of upper-middle-class-dom while at the same time quietly keeping alive their hopes of returning to work, even though few had a compelling financial incentive to do so. They worked their way back to work in two distinct phases: initially, while their children were younger, a family-first period, characterized by serendipity and reactivity—when jobs found them—followed by a relaunch period when their children were older, characterized by strategic agency and proactivity—when they found jobs.

The follow-up study crystallized and made clearer many of the themes and nascent trends we had initially identified. Even while living the lives of seemingly traditional stay-at-home moms, women maintained their professional identities and their desire to realize them. It was especially significant that already at the first interview we were seeing signs that women, while still out of the labor force, were turning away from former careers from which they had felt effectively shut out and whose time demands were omnivorous. We were also seeing a growing interest, grounded in their experiences at home, in the female-dominated caring occupations—a radical shift in direction for most of our women. Was it a romantic flirtation or the real deal? we wondered at the time. Would they even try to return? And could they? The answers are now clear—they could, they did, and it *was* the real deal, resulting in a pattern of resegregation and marginalization over the course of their lives.

Women's reentry to the world of work was déjà vu all over again, since the need for flexibility and part-time hours, which had been key reasons for interrupting their careers in the first place, continued to be paramount considerations even as children got older. Less frequently articulated, but also carrying over from what we originally observed, was the quietly assumed deference to their husbands, whose career primacy and disengagement from home responsibilities had only increased over time. Women implicitly pursued reentry paths, whether changing fields or working contingently, that tucked neatly around and didn't compete with their husbands' careers.

We saw how women deployed their privilege to prepare for and pursue paths that optimized meaning, self-actualization, and social contribution over remuneration, many working for far less than they had earned in their former fields before opting out and many starting over at entry level. These second acts, however much of a comparative objective loss they represented (in pay and position), were for the most part successful and gratifying. They represented the end of a hard-fought and often circuitous but necessary process of midlife reinvention that was occasioned by the unchanging, still family-hostile nature of jobs in their former corporate and professional places of employment—places to which they couldn't (and no longer wanted to) go home again.

NEW INSIGHTS

Thanks to its long-term perspective, our research extends previous research in important ways. It answers, in the overwhelming affirmative, that women who opt out want back in, though it often takes them much longer than initially intended to fully act on and realize their intentions. While previous research finds that women have a difficult time reentering and end up in jobs far beneath their qualifications, we find more positive outcomes, and—because we take a longitudinal approach—reveal the process of reentry to have two distinct phases. The first phase does indeed see women working at jobs below their qualifications, but this turns out to be a temporary, transitional phase from which they rebound—a rebound missed by the short-term cross-sectional nature of previous research. Even though they rebound, for the most part women never fully attain the level of their former careers. However, by exploring their decision-making in depth, our research further shows that this ostensible loss is the long-term end result of innumerable smaller choices—ones that have been made within the constraints and parameters of privileged domesticity. Women change fields or change to freelancing modes by choice, leaving former fields and employers in the dust—their privilege both requiring and allowing them to step down and step back. One thing is clear: women don't *resume* their careers, they restart and reconstruct them. And their success in returning to work—overcoming the gap in their résumés—is probably the result, in no small part, not only of the advantages they enjoy, but of their radical reinvention and their willingness to start over.

Our study not only allows us to closely dissect the complicated process of labor force reentry and career relaunch but, by virtue of its qualitative, in-depth design, reveals the full complexity of, and myriad pressures on, women's decision-making in a way not captured by surveys. Notably, we document how the family continues to be a major shaper of women's work far past children's entry to school and even beyond the empty nest. And our results make clear that for women like the ones we study, husbands are too often overlooked. Much as the long hours of husbands' extreme, high-paying jobs put pressure on women's initial decisions to quit, they continue to spill over and restrict women's options on reentry, contributing to women's decisions in favor of female-dominated and contingent jobs. The breadth of our study draws attention to the many contexts of women's decision-making—family/household and workplace, class, and gender—to show clearly the mutually reinforcing nature of the work-family system.

THE PARADOX OF PRIVILEGE

These women, urged to "lean in," are leaning out. They are in the crosshairs of the paradox of privilege, buffeted by its pressures and crosscurrents at numerous points across the life course, which we see more clearly from the long-term view afforded by our follow-up. The highly educated are most egalitarian with regard to gender ideology, yet most traditional in family structure.[1] Class works to privilege career for men of the upper-middle, professional class and to exempt them from family responsibilities that aren't tied to career; in fact, their primary family responsibility *is* their career, breadwinning. Men don't have to do it all, but in an era of ascendant or at least nascent gender egalitarianism, women do. This makes it hard for women of all backgrounds, but high-achieving professional women face pressures unique to their class. These pressures, as we've seen, are especially undermining of their sustained pursuit of elite professional careers—and especially harmful because these careers require sustained pursuit to succeed. The career penalties for taking time out and for motherhood and related accommodations are much higher for professional women than for those in other kinds of work. While we don't ask you to feel sorry for women who've led seemingly rich and satisfying lives—and they would certainly not want you to—it's important to understand the contradictory structural and cultural pressures high-achieving women face in trying to combine careers and motherhood, a nexus that makes up what we call the "paradox of privilege" and explains, in part, why so few women like these make it to the top.

We defined the paradox of privilege to mean the phenomenon whereby the gender-based interests of high-achieving women—for professional accomplishment, gender egalitarianism, and economic independence—are at odds with their class interests, which place a premium on their family roles as caregivers and status keepers. In other words, women who are best positioned to succeed and achieve leadership in elite careers, in part by virtue of their class advantage, are undermined by that same privilege once they become mothers. The paradox exhibits itself in many ways, at numerous critical junctures. It's perhaps not a single paradox but a series, interlinking and reinforcing across the life course and the work-family system. Here's a shorthand list of the ten paradoxes that we saw play out in the lives of the high-achieving women we studied:

Paradox 1: Marriage to professional equals created unequal professionals.

Paradox 2: Marriage to equals created unequal marriages.

Paradox 3: Highly career-committed women were judged to be less committed.

Paradox 4: Highly recruited women were easily let go.

Paradox 5: Barriers to career entry were high; barriers to career exits were low.

Paradox 6: Good jobs were not as good as they appeared.

Paradox 7: Elite employers, the "best places to work," were hostile workplaces.

Paradox 8: Professional women had flexibility they couldn't use without incurring a penalty.

Paradox 9: Women left male fields to which they'd flocked for female fields they'd eschewed.

Paradox 10: Women's economic privilege freed them to pursue care work (paid and unpaid) that economically marginalized them.

More broadly, we saw how class interests worked repeatedly against gender interests to make opting out a functional response to the untenable double bind of work and family, both sides of which have witnessed a speedup. On the work side, increasing overwork in elite jobs represents an intensification of ideal-worker norms that privileges male workers and disadvantages mothers. Intensified ideal-worker norms (especially longer hours) in top-paying jobs also intensify the maternal wall (motherhood discrimination), making opting out an economically rational choice for wives of men with top jobs. The ongoing gender pay gap and gendered ideals about intensive mothering mean that wives are almost always the ones to marginalize their careers "for the good" of the family. Opting out represents the most extreme form of marginalization, but we see it in a variety of other so-called "neotraditional" work-family configurations, for example, when wives downshift to less demanding jobs or work part-time.

On the family side, an increasingly precarious economic climate triggers increasing status anxiety among the upper-middle class, with attendant intensification of parenting ideals and practices. Competitive pressures in the affluent enclaves in which these women live exact ever more demanding standards of motherhood, putting pressure on them, in turn, to become or embody the "ideal mother" who is fully at home and fully available. Ironically, there is no evidence that the efforts of at-home mothers give their children an edge over the children of working moms, even among this privileged group. In fact, if anything, the evidence favors working mothers, whose daughters—especially those whose mothers were employed in highly skilled professional fields—

are more likely to be successful at work and whose sons are more likely to pitch in at home. And neither group has an edge on happiness in their adult lives: daughters and sons of working mothers are as happy as children of at-home mothers.[2] Nonetheless, for women displaced from their careers, for whom their own children's outcomes are still to be revealed, successful children are the goal. Motherhood becomes their new career, and they embody a throwback form of motherhood with continuing cultural currency. Their embodiment of this ideal extends beyond their class, perpetuating stereotypes about mothers among employers and creating expectations that are hard for all mothers to meet but impossible for most, who lack the resources—time and money—to emulate these women.

Initially a short-term strategy used by professional women to cope with inflexible workplaces and absent, overworked husbands, over the long term opting out has the paradoxical consequence of enhancing women's role in maintaining family class privilege while reinforcing their gender subordination in the family and workplace. Once women are out of paid employment, their family's dependence on them as keepers of class status grows, both to help leverage husbands' careers (and the intensified earning power associated with their extreme-hour jobs) and to increase the social capital of their children. The high-level volunteer work that women engage in (e.g., serving on the boards of local community organizations) also serves the status-keeping function of raising their social influence and family profile in the community as well as partially compensating them for their career marginalization. Women's role as status keepers comes to be seen as more valuable to the family than their ability to generate income given their husbands' earning capacity. As purveyors of family values and cultural and social capital, they are perceived as virtually irreplaceable.

After opting out, women's class position also enables a privileged form of domesticity—devoid of the drudgery of housework, filled with meaningful and pleasurable aspects of motherhood and community engagement. The seductive dynamics of privileged domesticity further prolong their time out and cause them to change their values and preferences around work. Marriage to highly successful men also undermines their rationale for working, their motivation to work, and the legitimacy of working in their former high-paying, corporate jobs while also giving them freedom to find meaningful, albeit lower-paid work in female-dominated fields and/or the nonprofit sector.

Privileged domesticity beckons women with its rewards and pleasures even as it subordinates them as dependents in a patriarchal bargain. Via this cycle, opting out reinforces both the inflexible, sexist structure of work and women's gender subordination in the family, while at the same time enhancing class and male privilege among the elite. Women become not only status keepers but keepers of patriarchy. One of perhaps the greatest ironies in our findings is that women groom their daughters (and equally, but less directly, their sons) to repeat the cycle of high achievement and career subordination they themselves experienced. While espousing equality and encouraging ambition and achievement in their daughters, they model very different behavior, thereby perpetuating opting out and the paradox of privilege in the next generation.

As a result of their affluence and privilege, these women face pressures unique to their class. These pressures are not more important and certainly not harder to surmount and deal with day to day than the work-family pressures facing women of other classes who have far fewer resources to draw on. The constraints and pressures on women who "have it all" are, however, invisible, not only to the outside world—who can easily dismiss them as poor little rich girls with rich people's problems—but even to high-achieving women themselves. By cloaking their decision-making in the language of choice and discretion, and framing it euphemistically as reinvention, women obscure the barriers placed in their way, the stifled opportunity for advancement and leadership in their former careers, and the considerable difficulty of finding their way back to work. Women who resented seeing their careers cut off when we first talked with them metamorphosed to acceptance and accommodation, in line with their class, not gender interest. On the one hand, and in light of the constraining realities of their former occupations and the seductive rewards of privileged domesticity, such an accommodation may have come to seem rational. On the other hand, and in yet another example of the paradox of privilege, they fail to recognize that they've re-created the very scenario they railed against—workplaces dominated by male bosses and colleagues with stay-at-home wives who sustain working conditions inimical to the working moms they were and mostly are (or hope to be again).

FORCED CHOICE VERSUS PRIVILEGED CHOICE?

Although the care-oriented jobs that women return to are less lucrative and elite by conventional standards, women derive meaning and satisfaction from them, and often to a greater degree than previous jobs. By reinventing themselves in this way, might we alternatively conclude that in doing so they are liberated, not just constrained, by their economic privilege? After all, less economically privileged women (and perhaps many of their male counterparts too) may envy our women's seemingly unfettered access to domesticity's ample family time. Opt-out women's affluence may also be viewed as freeing them to eschew corporate workplaces experienced as dehumanizing in their time-devouring demands, singular focus on the bottom line, and frequently misogynistic environments. Instead, family privilege permits women the time and resources to redirect to work that is socially meaningful and enjoyable and that provides a space for deeper connection to family and community—job qualities that most workers want, including men. In fact, by our follow-up interview we heard many women describing their husbands as "burnt out" and eager to get off the relentless corporate wheel in order to retire early or, like themselves, pursue a "second act" career in a "giving" profession. In other words, women's surprisingly positive attitude toward career change may have represented both acquiescence, as mothers, to the near-impossibility of conforming to a hegemonic male career model—a forced choice—and at the same time, their delighted or at least thankful rejection of it—a privileged choice.[3]

And yet, as may be obvious by now, this was not a win-win for women. In yet another paradox, women's privilege may have freed them to exchange the bottomless demands of mother-hostile workplaces for jobs with flexibility and social purpose; but this same choice also marginalized them economically, reduced their social and marital power, and blocked their pathways to leadership in elite professions. The question follows, is such a trade-off inevitable? Or are there public and/or private solutions that would permit women and men alike to better reconcile both realms of human identity—love and achievement, family and work?

RELAUNCH PROGRAMS

Back to our opening scene—a room full of women like the ones profiled here, taking first and tentative steps to restarting their careers. Scenes like this one are becoming increasingly common, and we saw them played out across the country. Career relaunch is now a growth industry, targeting the affluent zip codes where these women live and the elite schools from which they graduated. Initially driven by the "supply side," in recognition of the needs of returning women, these programs are increasingly driven by the "demand side," as employers in a tightening labor market seek to capitalize on this untapped talent pool and diversify their workforce. To learn more about these programs, we spoke with career reentry expert Carol Fishman Cohen, founder and CEO of iRelaunch, one of the first programs of its kind and still a leader in the field, and author of the go-to how-to book on career reentry.[4] Herself an "opt outer," with an MBA from Harvard, Cohen saw an opportunity to create a business that reached out to and supported women like her as they attempted to go back to work—women (and men) for whom, as she framed it, "the career path includes a career break." From her vantage point as a pioneer in this space, Cohen saw the issue as having reached a "tipping point" around 2010, when career reentry was "swirling around" and benefited from the increased attention being given larger issues of women and work by "a whole succession of high-profile articles and books."

iRelaunch's target audience is women like its founder, and like the women we study. They are highly educated, about two-thirds with graduate degrees; they have considerable work experience, "they're really mid-career or senior"; and they have been out of the workforce "from one to over twenty years." Through partnerships with professional associations and colleges and universities, which view her workshops as important offerings for their at-home alumnae, iRelaunch offers programs that address many of the needs we identified. In Cohen's experience, and reflected in our results, the biggest challenge facing relaunchers is "figuring out exactly what you want to do": "It kind of drives the whole thing, you know. You cannot put language and materials together about how you can add the most value to an employer unless you have that complete clarity on what your career goals are. And so, I think it's really hard to get people to go through a thorough proper career assessment process, but I think it is the most important part of the process." And one entailing a long and winding search, as we also saw, for which some women might not have time. She counsels them to take "the not-so-perfect job" which "may become a stepping-off point they can build on," and not to "shy away from temp work," which "gets you in the door" and "might morph into something permanent." Both pieces of advice have been followed by women in our study.

Cohen is an advocate of internships (also called "returnships" in this context) as a pathway back to work and promoted them in an influential article in the *Harvard Business Review* titled "The 40-Year-Old Intern."[5] Since its publication in 2012, there has been a pronounced increase in such programs, the earliest of which date to 2008. As she recounted,

"All of a sudden [in 2013–14], MetLife, Crédit Suisse, Morgan Stanley, and JP Morgan started programs." A check at the iRelaunch website shows dozens of companies now offering their own versions with names like Re-Ignite (Johnson & Johnson) and Take Two (General Motors). iRelaunch was initially focused on providing support to women (the vast majority of their clients) through one-day seminars and other forms of training, but since 2014, with corporate interest continuing to escalate, it has also "become a recruiting hub for [corporations and their reentry] programs." Cohen advises companies to "go after your regrettable losses, you know, your high performers."

While there is variation across these programs from company to company, their essential features are the same. A small number of paid internships are offered to what turns out to be a large and competitive pool. According to Cohen, "They have hundreds of people applying and they only pick a few. So ... it's a high-caliber group." Entry requirements relate to the length of time out; some programs set a fairly tight minimum of two years or less, while others are more expansive, putting virtually no limit on it. Required, too, is prior experience in the industry in question as well as a willingness to work full-time during the internship, which typically ranges from ten to twelve weeks. Some programs have other requirements, such as GPAs or a relevant up-to-date professional certificate, but generally there is a downplaying of formal requirements, which might be daunting to returnees.

According to Cohen, these programs are "a test run" for both employers and interns. Employers make clear in their description that there is no guarantee of a job on completion of the internship. Typically, as is also made clear up front, successful interns, those offered jobs, will be expected to work full-time, though some programs offer flexible hours. In selecting successful candidates, companies "are looking not only for credentials, but they're looking for readiness"—*readiness* meaning, in effect, being committed to returning to work on a full-time basis.

These programs, while promising, are new and proprietorial, and Cohen confirmed that there is, as yet, little evaluation of their effectiveness, whether judged by how many women turn internships into jobs or by less hard criteria such as the extent to which they've increased women's workplace readiness. She identified two "real burning issues in the career reentry conversation," which were similarly front and center in our interviews: "One is part-time and the other is ageism." She elaborated on the former. Part-time on the order of fifteen to twenty hours is not a viable option on reentry, but Cohen cautioned not to confuse part-time with face time and offered a workaround solution: "If it's really face time in an office that's an issue, and you could work equivalent to a full-time job—knowing that some jobs are more than forty hours a week—then it's more of an issue that you have to work at home part of the time or you have to work nontraditional hours." She did offer that she'd seen the tiniest beginnings of a shift with employers around flexibility (of all kinds, not only part-time), with a very few willing to broach it with prospective employees "right in initial interviews" rather than "once you've proven yourself and paid your dues." She was working on "reentry programs with a flexible element," but she admitted, "It's really hard." This view was echoed, by the way, by others in the reentry space with whom we spoke. A headhunter in Palo Alto, California, for instance, seeking to connect employers with reentering women, opined that "In Silicon Valley, flexibility is the F word." Part-time, reduced-hour work remains a stumbling block. Many women with whom Cohen worked initially wanted part-time but came to realize that "things were not going to happen for me unless I shifted and was open to full-time," which, "after some hiccups along the way, was okay."

Ageism was also complicated. Cohen finds that it is often exaggerated in returning women's minds, its effect so overwhelming that "it keeps people from even starting the process" of reentry (something we also observed). According to Cohen, the single most important thing to combat ageism is "to get really, really up to date in your field." This could mean formal credentials, but more important in her experience were more informal ways of keeping abreast—reading, being au courant with emerging issues in the field, things that gave the reentrant something to talk about in an "energetic and enthusiastic way" that countered ageist stereotypes.

The growing proliferation of programs and supports for career reentry is evidence of increased recognition of opting out or career breaks as a work-family strategy among high-achieving women, who are being courted and curried. These programs are potentially an important part of the privatized and privileged strategies to which women like the ones we study have access, and our findings underscore the need for them. Our observation of them, while not a systematic evaluation, shows them to provide both the "soft" emotional and vocational support and the "hard" skill-building support that reentering women seek. And they provide a critical brokering role, and a sheltered space, between returning women and employers.

While employers are showing interest in and receptivity to returning women—a plus—their internship programs highlight some problems and raise a red flag. First, the companies offering these programs, so-called "employers of choice," who perennially appear on "best places to work" lists and compete for top talent, are also characterized by extreme-hour jobs and ideal-worker cultures. They are the very type of companies from which women opted out. Second, the programs require a demonstration of commitment to the ideal worker model— that women show "readiness" and be willing to work full-time. These companies appear to be making little change to their cultures of overwork, effectively asking working mothers to drop out, thereby setting in motion the processes of displacement and reinvention we observed, and the women's return to the same old unchanged workplaces they had left behind. Our results suggest, however, that in restarting their careers women will be wary of a return to these kinds of firms unless and until they become receptive to more flexible ways of working and change their work environments.

OPTING OUT, OPTING BACK IN,
AND GENDER INEQUALITY

Opting out, or career interruption, sets in motion a domino-like process of cascading events. Women are penalized for their time out of the labor force per se, but when they opt back in we find that they pursue strategies that carry additional penalties. While the opting-out strategy maximizes the class privilege of upper-middle-class families in the context of the all-or-nothing nature of high-level professional jobs, it marginalizes women's careers by forcing them to first exit, then scale back significantly on their careers for many years. Moreover, this takes place at a critical midcareer juncture, when they, or at least their male counterparts, are at a takeoff point. The long-term consequences of opting out for women take three different forms, each of which reinforces gender inequality in upper-middle-class families and gender inequality overall: (1) never returning to the workforce; (2) redirecting to completely different fields that are more family flexible, but often female-dominated and lower paying than previous careers; and (3) returning to their former professions by taking jobs in the lower-paid, less secure, and contingent secondary sectors of their professions.

Many of those in the first group, who never fully returned to paid employment, experienced significant floundering and feelings of having failed to live up to their potential. Women in the other two groups felt their career sacrifices for family were worth it, and had traded jobs with pay and status for those perceived to have social meaning. Women's career redirection to lower-paid caring labor upon reentry can be seen as a process of occupational resegregation over the life course, where professional women started their careers breaking gender barriers and ended them by re-creating the sex-segregated status quo, widening rather than closing the gender divide. Women's marginalization in the secondary contingent labor market further perpetuated gender disadvantage—making them more economically vulnerable (through episodic employment and lack of pensions, for example) and sidelining them from the leadership track they'd been on. Thus, through interruption and ensuing redirection, both parts of the opt-out process—the initial decision and the eventual decision to opt back in—exacerbated gender inequality among this high-promise, high-potential group of women.

TRANSCENDING THE PARADOX OF PRIVILEGE

In opting out and in their reentry strategies, even privileged women operate within a range of relatively narrow options. They forge individual, private solutions and, though they are in a good position to do so, bear the attendant costs and risks. The apparent disconnect between the satisfaction and happiness they feel about their new careers and the objective losses they've incurred reveals the limitations of private solutions to public problems. Highly educated professional women find themselves having to make costly trade-offs for family that, while maximizing their class interests, work against their gender interests and the larger agenda of gender equality. In an example of the so-called "tragedy of the commons," whereby individual members of a group, each seeking their own personal gain, hurt the group as a whole, high-achieving women's solutions work for them but harm working mothers in general by perpetuating stereotypes about mothers being less committed and by leaving in place and reinforcing ideal worker norms and practices that are detrimental to their own interests in resuming careers. It should be acknowledged that husbands are hurt too by current work and family structures and the attendant phenomenon of opting out. As wives are effectively forced out of their careers, husbands are effectively forced out of the family and into the breadwinner burden of never-ending hours in the office (the penalty or underside of their male privilege).

A more privatized, individual understanding of opting out and reentry as reflecting women's relatively unfettered choices and preferences also overlooks the bigger picture, which is one of brain drain and talent loss from the elite professions. Our research suggests that in these fields there is a large reservoir of underutilized talent among women like those we study. We need to find ways to break the opting-out cycle of high achievement and career subordination and derailment to fully utilize this talent while also enabling women (and men) to realize their aspiration for a life that combines—simultaneously, not sequentially—career and family.

Moreover, going beyond privatized solutions is necessary to give professional women with families more freedom to truly determine their career direction. Some women will still make the decision to not opt back into their former elite careers in legitimate pursuit of a more philanthropic or care-oriented career, and that choice should not continue to be a marginalizing one. But given the right supports, we think many women in high-level professions would choose to maintain their existing careers; by contrast, only stressing private solutions won't create the incentives needed.

More broadly, a focus on individual explanations and solutions can obscure the larger role played by economic and social forces that impinge on and constrain individual decision-making, such as the ongoing pressures of work speedup and increasing economic insecurity. Stepping even further back, opting out is a phenomenon linked to historical changes in marriage patterns whereby we see increasingly high rates of marriage between equals (homogamy) at the top.[6] Such underlying conditions, especially those involving the economy, could and should be addressed, though this would require a large political and policy shift (discussed later in this chapter). Meanwhile, more proximate, intermediate-level policies are needed to at least mitigate the conditions that cause opting out and to ameliorate its most harmful effects.

How can we move from disrupted careers, false starts, and do-overs to support women like the ones we studied? How can we promote continuity and flow, retention and advancement throughout their work lives so as to take full advantage of their talents and skills? How can we put their careers on an equal footing with those of their husbands (while at the same time permitting husbands' access to greater family flexibility and involvement)? We recommend focusing policy efforts in three broad areas. First, creating a family- and parent-friendly workplace with respect to work time. Second, eliminating gender disparities with respect to pay and status within and across traditionally male- and female-dominated occupations. Third, changing the household division of labor to loosen the hold of the male breadwinner/female caregiver model. Addressing these areas requires a multilevel policy response. Experience with a variety of relevant policies on, for example, pay equity and pregnancy discrimination illustrates the importance of developing policy at all levels—local, state, and federal—to buffer against strong polarizing political forces at the federal level. Policy changes are also needed to encourage and promote efforts in the private sector, where leading firms, like the ones women left and did not return to, shape best practices in their respective industries. It is also in their best interest to create and implement—as well as model—policies and practices that will retain the best female talent, helping them meet their avowed diversity goals, including bringing more women into leadership roles.

CREATING A FAMILY-FRIENDLY WORKPLACE: REINING IN WORK TIME

As a category of workers, professionals have the most control over their work. Control is a key feature of flexibility and a key factor in successfully combining work and family lives.[7] Offsetting this advantage, however, are demands in the professions for long hours, face time, and 24-7 availability, which no amount of discretion and control can surmount. Furthermore, the stigma attached to flexibility undercuts its use and effectiveness. Our research and that of others point to the enduring detriment of extreme hours and related features of professional employment, which are especially pronounced among leading top-tier firms, for families coping to combine work and family. Research is piling up to show that extreme hours have a deleterious effect on a variety of other important outcomes such as productivity and health. Companies need to limit work hours, which are the immediate, proximate cause of opting out and a major consideration shaping reentry, because, as we so clearly saw, men's overwork is women's underwork (and vice versa). This unintended consequence is now long apparent, and elite companies can no longer ignore that the way they structure work is a generator of male career advantage (though one that comes with potential health and family costs for men) and female career disadvantage, promoting retention among men and turnover among women.

Companies are on the front lines, but their track record in creating sustained change to reduce or control work hours is mixed at best. A quick overview of a large body of research and anecdote on what companies call "flexibility" yields the following answers: How extensive is it? Relatively limited. Who uses it? Primarily professional employees and women (the exception being men in sales, whose jobs exhibit flexibility of both time and place). Under what circumstances? To address mothering/caregiving needs of children (and increasingly, elders). How effective is it in meeting the needs of employees who availed themselves of it as well as company needs? Employees working flexibly rate higher on job satisfaction, performance, and company loyalty. Companies tout flexibility but often fail to implement it widely or consistently, making it vulnerable to being cut because of manager discretion or larger economic vicissitudes, as appeared to have happened in the face of the 2008 recession and its aftermath. Even as the economy heats up, the usual suspects—finance, law, management consulting—appear to be reverting to their old ways. Newly emerging industries are no better, with the high-tech world's geek bro culture replicating the rest of corporate America's frat boy culture (face time in T-shirts instead of ties).

Private-sector efforts are to be encouraged, but as this track record illustrates, employers cannot be relied upon to initiate and consistently implement flexibility and reduced hours options. Why? In the short term, these efforts are costly for companies, and unless all employers are held to the same standards, they are likely to be perceived (erroneously) as bad for the bottom line. For this reason, public policy solutions are necessary. One especially direct solution would be to make long hours expensive to employers by requiring them to pay overtime to professionals and managers, extending the overtime provisions of the Fair Labor Standards Act to a class of workers who have long been exempt from them. As hours get longer and professional/managerial employment is threatened by technology and deskilling, the historical antipathy of professionals to working by the clock is being eroded, and calls for this type of solution are increasing. Other efforts to control and tame working time are already long-established policy in other countries, particularly European Union countries, who have mandated flexibility and caps on working time. They also have part-time parity laws to guard against well-documented penalties to working part-time per se, a dollars and cents manifestation of flexibility stigma. Workers in these countries have the *right* to request part-time jobs, with the onus placed on the employer to demonstrate a credible business case to refuse. Both with regard to long hours and what Europeans call nonstandard hours, which are a growing problem in the US (not so much among professionals as among workers in manufacturing and service industries), EU and other countries provide an array of tested policies that can serve as a template for efforts here at any level of government.

ENDING GENDER DISCRIMINATION WITHIN AND ACROSS OCCUPATIONS

Gender discrimination at work means that, other things being equal, women—even high-achieving women with credentials comparable to their husbands'—are likely to earn less than their husbands and to have poorer prospects for career growth. Market inequality between women and men translates into career inequality between wives and husbands, the implications of which we saw play out. To level the playing field requires addressing both good old-fashioned gender discrimination and variants such as motherhood discrimination. We have antidiscrimination laws on the books to address the most blatant cases where women are paid less for doing equal work or are not promoted though best qualified. These laws need to be aggressively enforced, as do pregnancy discrimination laws, which are as close as we come to addressing discrimination against motherhood per se.

But existing law, even if fully enforced, addresses only a fraction of the gender earnings gap, the bigger share of which is due to occupational segregation—the fact that men and women do far different types of work, and female-dominated occupations are lower paying, largely because women do them and are crowded into them, which further drives down wages.[8] Increasing the earnings of female jobs to reflect their requirements and responsibilities and purge them of the depressant effects of their gender composition requires a different approach: equal pay for female-dominated jobs that are comparable (not the same as or equal) to male-dominated jobs. This policy, known as pay equity or comparable worth, has seen limited implementation at the state and local levels but to be fully effective needs to be enacted at the federal level.

This policy is especially good at remedying the underpayment of the so-called female "semi"- or "quasi"-professions, such as teaching, which require considerable formal credentials yet are relatively low paid.[9] These occupations employ large numbers of highly educated women and, as we saw, are especially attractive to reentry women, most of whom did not even consider them as they transitioned from school to work and initially formulated their career goals. Here we see yet another manifestation of the systematic devaluation of "female" occupations: it makes them an unsuitable aspiration for ambitious, high-achieving upper-middle-class women, who are prepared (and preparing their own daughters in turn) for the "better things" offered by male professions. This artificial, systemic, and discriminatory devaluation obscures the fact that the care work involved in traditionally female-dominated occupations is intrinsically valuable (in fact, fundamental to the functioning of the economy) and meaningful (for many, more meaningful than their former careers). It forces women into having to make a false trade-off between remuneration and other desirable qualities of jobs (which economists call "compensating differentials"), something we saw them doing. If female jobs were fairly compensated, resegregation wouldn't necessarily be a problem, and the solution wouldn't be getting women to work and stay in traditionally male jobs. Properly valuing women's work would not only enhance and validate a wider range of options for women but also attract men to these fields. In conjunction with the more conventional strategy to move more women into men's fields, integrating men into traditionally female fields would go a long way toward enhancing gender equality.

ENCOURAGING MEN TO CO-PARENT

Parenthood marks a critical transition in work and family for both women and men, and a moment when we see real class and gender differences emerge. The identification of parenthood with motherhood crosses all classes, but the male breadwinner advantage is most pronounced among the affluent upper-middle class, making the decoupling of gender and caregiving especially challenging. Just as evidence suggests that, among women, the motherhood penalty is especially large, there is also evidence that the fatherhood penalty to caregiving is too. Professional men, virtually the only group of workers who have access to paid or unpaid parental leave, are penalized for taking it and, not surprisingly, are hesitant to take it or take only a small portion of the leave available to them. Beyond days of work missed, men's use of leave appears to violate deeply held masculinity norms associated with the ideal worker. Calling into question their masculinity calls their competence and commitment into question as well. Overcoming this flexibility stigma is another reason we need public policy, not private solutions.

As challenging as it is to devise policies to address market-based inequality, it is perhaps even more challenging to end—or begin to chip away at—gender inequality in the caregiving work of home and family. Just as we need to value paid care work more highly in the labor market, so too do we need to better value and support the unpaid work of care in the home. The larger goal is to design a new care infrastructure that both recognizes care work as a public good and calls on men to step up their share of care, or to truly co-parent. Here again, we can look to other countries for example and precedent. Their experience shows, for instance, that men are more likely to take leave when it is paid, to offset the temporary loss of their typically higher earnings; unpaid leave, such as we have in the US through the Family and Medical Leave Act, favors women's uptake and reinforces the traditional division of labor in the home and women's secondary position in the market. To avoid this, Sweden offers an example of how to induce men to take paid leave. Through a universal social insurance system, Swedes allocate separate and nontransferable amounts of paid leave to mothers and fathers in the same household, thereby introducing incentives for fathers to use it or lose it. Even a country as progressive as Sweden has been surprised at the policy's success. Not only are men taking leave in far larger numbers, but the experience of doing so has had a long-term effect on cultural attitudes about men's engagement with fathering— validating their caregiving as normative.[10] So transformed are larger attitudes that there is evidence to suggest that Swedish fathers who do *not* take the maximum paternal leave are the ones feeling the sting of stigma.

A similar "use or lose it" paternity leave program in Quebec, Canada, has seen huge success in both its uptake and its effects on fathers' share of caregiving. The number of recent fathers taking paid paternity leave shot up from just 28 percent in 2005 (just before the "daddy quota" system started) to 86 percent in 2015. Even more startling, research shows that by 2010 men who had taken the leave and had since returned to work were spending 23 percent more time doing housework and child care compared to men in other parts of Canada. The same study found that just as fathers increased their time at home, mothers spent less time at home and more time at work. Similarly, Iceland's daddy quota has resulted in remarkable progress. Ninety percent of Icelandic fathers choose to use rather than lose their dedicated paternity leave, and according to one study the proportion of married and cohabiting parents who report sharing child care equally has roughly doubled since the law's passage. Apparently, the strategic use of public policy can make significant and lasting impact on gender dynamics within households, including father involvement in child-rearing.[11]

SYSTEMS CHANGE

Clearly the changes proposed above would require making a significant shift in the orientation of American society—away from an economy that is increasingly unequal, as well as still male dominated. The specific policies suggested to give working parents more time, equalize the valuation and compensation of gendered work, and encourage men to fully co-parent are likely to come about only in a society that is redirected toward more humane and egalitarian priorities in general. Without a strong politics that challenges the larger status quo, it is unlikely that a wide range of progressive policies, including the ones we've proposed, will ever be enacted. In sum, we need a significant shift in the social system (and balance of power) in the United States. Our prevailing form of capitalism (also known as "neoliberalism") and patriarchy as we know it have to change.

Systemic change of this sort is not only needed to bring about the particular policies we advocate but imperative for creating a larger economic and cultural context conducive to helping high-achieving mothers flourish in their careers without interruption or derailment. Reducing the economic inequality and insecurity now squeezing most Americans would ease the economic and class anxiety experienced by upper-middle-class families. This would diminish the fierce pressures on mothers, like the ones we studied, to engage in extreme (one might call it "defensive") parenting, thereby helping them to stay in their careers. Creating a more gender-equitable society in which care work is treated as the public good that it is—the work that makes all other work possible—and is appropriately valued, rewarded, and equally shared by men and by society as a whole is also a critical goal for addressing the paradox of privilege.[12] Such a transformation would facilitate the structural changes in market work and family life (e.g., a reduced workweek, good part-time jobs, co-parenting) that would level the playing field between high-achieving women and their male counterparts in elite professions. At the same time, such a change would ease men's breadwinning burden and grant them the freedom to engage with and enjoy the satisfactions of family and community life more deeply.

The same systemic transformations described above would also help women who still would choose to redirect away from former careers. A more egalitarian economic system, through stronger labor laws and regulations, would address key problems that face all contingent workers, including women who return to their former professions as freelancers (problems such an absence of benefits and a lack of work continuity and security). At the same time, a more humane and gender-neutral society would reward rather than socially and economically marginalize women (and men) who choose to reorient their careers to the caring professions.

It's worth noting that the aforementioned systemic changes would benefit not just the women we studied but many less privileged women as well. Clearly a more equitable, care-oriented economy would provide a better work and family life for the vast majority of women and their families, who generally have suffered from growing economic stress and anxiety over the last few decades as well as a whittling away of their ability to control the growing incursion of work into family life. This coincidence of interests between privileged and nonprivileged women in this kind of change could help create a basis for the viable transformational politics needed.

Some readers may question whether such progressive change is possible or realistic. Importantly, we can note again that it has already occurred to a greater or lesser extent in other capitalist societies, which have developed stronger welfare states and a more egalitarian social structure than the United States. As illustrated earlier, the largest such change has happened in Scandinavian countries. While the US may appear to be inherently impervious to any shift in that direction, it actually has happened repeatedly in the past—during the Progressive Era, the New Deal, and the Great Society period of the 1960s, when a wide range of social democratic policies previously thought to be unobtainable were enacted. These changes came about through sustained social pressure, and there is no compelling reason to assume that this can't happen again.

ME TOO?

While opting out is clearly a problem specific to privileged women, as discussed in the Introduction, it can also be seen as a manifestation of a problem faced by all women. Whether the issue is long hours (professional women) or unpredictable schedules and a lack of access to paid parental and sick leave (low- and moderate-income women), the inflexible workplace marginalizes all women economically and forces almost all mothers to scale back their work, pay, and prospects for advancement. This confluence of interests may present important opportunities for women collectively to demand change.

But what of the high-achieving women highlighted here? Will they be change makers or guardians of the status quo? We were more optimistic before the follow-up, which found that women spent the ensuing decade largely securing their own class advantage, via volunteer work that benefited their own interests and others like them. They channeled any feelings of displacement and resentment not into building a movement to create more family- and mother-friendly workplaces but into realizing their dreams and aspirations for their children and, secondarily, into reimagining and reinventing themselves. These women find creative solutions to the double bind of career and family among the upper-middle, professional class—but they are solutions that involve changing themselves, rather than changing the institutions and systems that created their predicament. Can women like these break out of their gilded cages to be a part of creating more fundamental change of the sort we call for? Doing so will require them to put aside the seductive comforts of racial and economic advantage—strong incentives to maintain their complicity with patriarchy, for sure—and to instead unite with other women across color and class divides in order to challenge unjust work and family structures that hold all women back.

This may be the historical moment to imagine this happening. Not only is gender discrimination rising in public consciousness, and feminism seeing a resurgence among younger women, but the emergence of the #MeToo movement offers a new vehicle for change.[13] Originally created by a black woman, Tarana Burke, as a grassroots movement for victims of sexual assault in low-income communities, it is now being extended to sexual harassment in the workplace and to equal rights.[14] It wouldn't necessarily be a huge leap to extend it further to issues of workplace flexibility and gender equity at home and at work.

What makes #MeToo so compelling and promising is that, in a classic feminist formula, it combines the personal—shared, intimate testimonials—with the political—connecting and mobilizing women of diverse backgrounds through social media. #MeToo calls out behavior that was formerly taken as given, and taken for granted, behavior that was hiding in plain sight, made normal by its matter-of-factness and the tacit silence that surrounded it. In much the same way, extreme hours and overwork are being challenged as inherent features of elite jobs. Instead they are increasingly being recognized as key drivers of gender inequality and as inhumane and unhealthy for all workers. Gender roles, and gender itself, are being reimagined as more fluid and less determinative.

In identifying and dissecting the paradox of privilege, we hope to inspire another #MeToo moment. Paradoxes juxtapose two seemingly incompatible, contradictory, yet coexisting states. The juxtaposition makes us see things in new ways, inconsistency highlighting the taken-for-granted status quo and its dysfunction: like recruiting highly accomplished women to jobs that face them with all-or-nothing choices about work and family, or forcing them to constantly reinvent new ways of working that underutilize their skills and talent. In 1989, Mary Catherine Bateson wrote a seminal book, *Composing a Life*, about "the personal and career obstacles women face in achieving success," showing the extent to which the women profiled, most of whom came of age and started careers in the 1960s and '70s, had to live "life as an improvisational art form."[15] Little has changed—these women's daughters and granddaughters are still improvising. And our policy recommendations are depressingly familiar—echoing ones that scholars and activists have been making for the last twenty years but that are still unrealized.

But there are currently reasons for greater hope. As we write, we are in a larger moment of political change for women, witnessing a veritable revival of feminist anger and activism activated by Trump's election and the subsequent surge of women and particularly women of color running for and winning political office in 2018. Where could the women we studied fit into this political transformation? Social change happens when larger trends outpace institutions or when emerging trends collide. The paradox of privilege tells us we're at just such a moment. It's time for women of privilege to heed the call. A recent *New York Times* article is cause for hope and despair.[16] Despair because it's about an alleged case of pregnancy discrimination—a job offer as museum curator rescinded when the employer learned the woman he'd offered the job to was pregnant. Hope because the woman bringing the suit was inspired by the #MeToo movement to use her privilege to help herself and other women too: "I'm very lucky. I'm privileged, I'm a middle-class white woman. I have a partner with a good job who's able to support me if the worst happened. I thought, if I'm afraid to speak up, who will speak up?" Our hope is that our research affords women like the ones we study, including those who have not yet opted out, a similar eureka moment: the realization that they, too, in concert with other diverse and less privileged women, can use their voices to leverage change. Together, and as part of a larger movement for progressive change, they can help build a more humane, egalitarian society—one that permits all women (and men) to enjoy the work and family lives they deserve. It's about time—and time's up (#TimesUp).

STUDY METHODOLOGY

STUDY DESIGN

The research for this book is based on a set of two linked studies. The first study, the subject of *Opting Out?*, explored the lives of women at home who had made the decision to leave their careers,[1] and the second one followed these same women over ten years later to find out what had happened in their work and family lives as a result of their earlier career exit. The two studies together constitute a longitudinal or panel design. The strength of this design rests on its ability to follow the same set of participants over an extended period of time to describe and explicate how earlier life events may affect later changes and dynamics in the life course. Accordingly, many aspects of the follow-up study's methodology, such as its sample, were largely predetermined by the original study (for details of which, see the appendix to *Opting Out?*). We give an overview here of our research methodology, focusing on differences between the first (original) and second (follow-up) waves.

STUDY PARTICIPANTS

The original sample consisted of fifty-four women, all of whom had previously worked in professional or managerial occupations, were married with children at home, and were out of the labor force taking care of children at the time of interview. They were identified through snowball or referral sampling, relying primarily on alumnae networks of four highly selective colleges and universities. Interviews were conducted throughout the United States in seven metropolitan areas located in four broad regions of the country—the Northeast (which accounted for the largest share of the interviews), the Southeast, the Midwest, and the Far West. Women were recruited whose former careers reflected a mix of classic male-dominated professions as well as gender-integrated or mixed fields and female-dominated ones. Age quotas ensured roughly equal numbers of younger women aged thirty to forty ($n = 24$) and older ($n = 30$).

The immediate goal—and major challenge—of any follow-up study is to secure a high response rate, that is, to locate and reinterview as many of the original participants as possible. A high response rate is in pursuit of the larger goal of obtaining a follow-up sample whose features closely match the original's or at least show no discernible bias, which can result if respondents in the second wave are somehow different from first-wave respondents (so-called nonresponse bias). To increase the follow-up response rate, it is necessary to locate the first-wave respondents and then secure their participation.

With approximately twelve years having elapsed since the first interview (initial interviews having been carried out over a period of several years), we anticipated that locating respondents would not be easy. It wasn't, but it was made easier by the fact that, as it turned out, these women had lived remarkably stable lives, the majority still living in the same house. Those who had moved were harder to locate, but we did so by using various internet services like White Pages and Spokeo. Once women were located, we reached out to them repeatedly, if necessary, to obtain their consent to participate. Initially, we sent a series of letters and reminder postcards. If these overtures resulted in silence, we phoned women directly or, in a few cases where we had valid addresses, emailed them.

We were able to locate all but one woman from the original sample. For those for whom we had a valid address and phone number ($N = 53$), six declined to be reinterviewed and four never replied. The final follow-up sample consisted of forty-three of the original fifty-four women, for a response rate of 80 percent, which is considered very high for follow-ups generally, but especially given the extended time that had elapsed between the two studies. Table 1 presents a thumbnail sketch of each of the women in the follow-up.

A comparison of the follow-up sample ($N = 43$) with the original ($N = 54$) shows remarkable similarity on key demographic characteristics, suggesting that nonresponse did not introduce any significant bias. The original sample of women represented a broad spectrum of professions, including doctors, lawyers, scientists, bankers, management consultants, marketing and nonprofit

TABLE I

Follow-up study participants at a glance (listed alphabetically by first name)

Name	Age	Education	Former Occupation	Current Occupation	Total Years Out of Labor Force	Youngest Child's Age	Husband's Occupation
Amanda Taylor	51	PhD*	Banking executive	Research scientist	10	24	Retired***
Bettina Mason	53	JD	Lawyer	Not working	19	22	Lawyer
Blair Riley	69	JD	Lawyer	Lawyer	9	25	Designer
Brenda Dodd	62	BS	Medical technician	Dental assistant	15	25	Doctor
Brooke Coakley	60	MBA	Health care executive	Health care consultant	5	20	Sales executive***
Christine Thomas	53	BA	Marketing executive	Marketing consultant	1	18	Sales executive
Claire Lott	61	MBA	Telecom executive	Freelance language teacher	9	16	Executive coach***
Denise Hortas	57	PhD	Pharmaceutical executive	Pharmaceutical executive	1	23	Lawyer in private practice***
Diane Childs	54	CPA	Nonprofit executive	Freelance accountant	1	16	Real estate developer
Donna Haley	57	JD	Lawyer	Lawyer	4	23	Retired***
Elizabeth Brand	47	MBA	Management consultant	Not working	9	4**	Corporate executive
Emily Mitchell	48	BA	Customer service supervisor	Small business owner	18	21	Accountant
Felice Stewart	60	BA	Teacher	Teacher	10	19	Engineer
Frances Ingalls	53	BA	Teacher	Office manager	21	23	Commodities trader
Helena Norton	51	MPA	Educational administrator	Educational administrator	12	15	Hedge fund manager***
Jessica Beckman	47	MBA	Marketing executive	Marketing consultant	9	14	Marketing executive

Joan Gilbert	45	BA	Nonprofit administrator	Not working	9	11	Defense contractor***
Karen Gordon	40	MS	Engineer	Engineering consultant	2	4**	Engineer
Kate Hadley	48	MBA	Marketing executive	Management consultant	7	10	Hedge fund manager***
Kristin Quinn	47	MEd*	Teacher	Teacher	4	16	Comptroller
Lauren Quattrone	55	JD	Lawyer	Nonprofit fund-raiser	20	19	Lawyer
Leah Evans	57	MA*	Health care executive	Adjunct professor	4	24	Retired***
Lily Townsend	51	JD	Lawyer	Office administrator	12	16	Divorced***
Lisa Bernard	63	MPH	Health care executive	Not working	13	25	Professor and academic administrator***
Maeve Turner	65	JD	Lawyer	Not working	24	19	Lawyer
Marina Isherwood	58	MBA	Health care executive	Health care consultant	11	22	Doctor
Martha Haas	42	BA	Education fund-raiser	Education fund-raiser	12	7**	Professor
Meg Romano	51	BA	Trader	Education fund-raiser	9	15	Financial planner
Melanie Irwin	59	HS	Marketing executive	Small business owner	18	24	Divorced***
Melissa Wyatt	41	BA	Nonprofit administrator	Not working	12	10	Venture capitalist
Mirra Lopez	44	BS	Engineer	Not working	12	10	Engineer
Nan Driscoll	59	MEd*	Editor	Teacher's aide	18	16	Lawyer
Naomi Osborn	66	MBA	Investment banker	Not working	17	29	Investment banker
Nathalie Everett	51	MEd*	Marketing executive	Publisher sales representative	6	11**	Contractor and remodeler***
Olivia Pastore	54	JD	Lawyer	Career services director	1	22	Lawyer
Patricia Lambert	56	MBA	Marketing executive	Not working	18	22	Investment banker
Rachel Berman	56	MBA	Trader	Not working	21	18	Investment banker
Sarah Bernheim	39	BA	Marketing executive	Not working	11	3**	Software engineer
Tess Waverly	53	AA	Medical products manager	Patient care associate	13	17	Business owner***

TABLE I

Follow-up study participants at a glance (listed alphabetically by first name)

Name	Age	Education	Former Occupation	Current Occupation	Total Years Out of LF	Youngest Child's Age	Husband's Occupation
Theresa Land	69	BA	Computer programmer	Not working	23	26	Retired***
Trudy West	58	BS	Computer programmer	Library aide	12	21	Deceased***
Vita Cornwall	57	MBA	Nonprofit executive	Not working	22	21	Entrepreneur***
Wendy Friedman	53	BA	Editor	Freelance editor	1	18	Architect

NOTE: These names are pseudonyms. The information reported pertains to the time of the follow-up interview except for former occupation, which is the last occupation held before exiting the workforce as reported at the initial interview.

*For education, the current degree represents a change from the initial interview (i.e., the participant has subsequently obtained the degree indicated).

**For youngest child's age, child was born since initial interview.

***For husband's occupation, there has been a change since initial interview.

executives, editors, and teachers. In the original sample, just over half (54 percent) had worked, before opting out, in male-dominated, high-prestige professions such as law, business, medicine, or science and engineering, compared to just under half (44 percent) of the follow-up sample. Approximately one-third (37 percent) of the original sample had worked in mixed or transitional fields, such as publishing, public relations, marketing, and nonprofit administration, compared to 35 percent of the follow-up. The remainder of the original sample (9 percent) had worked in traditionally female-dominated professions such as teaching versus 21 percent in the follow-up. Thus, with regard to their former careers, the two samples are similar, with most women having worked in male-dominated professions, followed in popularity by mixed-gender and female ones. In both samples, women typically had two children when they were initially interviewed. They were identical with regard to education. Approximately half of each wave had an advanced degree (52 and 54 percent, respectively) when originally interviewed, with MBAs and JDs being the most common. By design, roughly half the women in the original sample were in their thirties, half in their forties, with a median age of forty-one; for women included in the follow-up sample, median age at first interview was forty-two. Their median age at the time of follow-up was fifty-four, with an age range from thirty-nine to sixty-nine.

INTERVIEWING

Details of Administration

As in the original study, information in the follow-up phase was collected via in-depth interviews, typically lasting two hours, utilizing a life history approach. Aspects of data collection differed between the original and follow-up, with changes being based largely on cost and logistic considerations. Notably, in the original study, interviews were conducted face to face by Stone and Lovejoy. For the follow-up, because of cost constraints, interviews were conducted mostly by phone (with a few in-person exceptions) by Stone, Lovejoy, and under our supervision and training, a small team of advanced graduate student assistants. For both phases, interviews typically lasted about two hours and were audiotaped and fully transcribed. Women were guaranteed confidentiality: that is, their true identities would be known only to us or our assistants. This ensured that women could speak freely about their work experiences and family lives without fear of reprisal or concern about their comments coming back to haunt them or otherwise embarrass them. While we have no way of assessing whether the changes we made in the interview procedure affected the results, it is our judgment that neither who conducted the interview nor the method of administration affected the interview process or the quality of the information collected. Respondents in both phases appeared to be relaxed, engaged, and fully forthcoming, with no discernible differences between the interviews we conducted and those of our students.

About the Interviews

Interviews in the first wave of the study were semistructured and elicited women's work and family histories. It was important for the purposes of this study to use a method that would foreground women's experiences and not impose a preexisting framework; life history narratives provided a particularly natural device for doing so. The interview typically began with a general prompt, asking the respondent to describe work and family trajectories from college graduation until the decision to quit her job. The narratives these women told were typically highly articulate, complex, and fluid, with little need for interviewer prompting, although all participants received probes to elaborate on certain key topics if they did not emerge spontaneously. These topics included the participant's job satisfaction, as well as characteristics of the workplace environment, and the role of husband, children, and other family members in the decision to return to work or not. Women were also asked to describe their lives at home since their career exit.

The follow-up interview also employed the life history narrative approach, using the time of original interview as a starting reference point. In an innovation from the prior study, we supplemented interviews with information from a work and family history form providing yearly highlights. We asked women to complete this prior to the interview, both to jog their memories and to provide us with a time line of critical occurrences (e.g., birth of child, return to work). These interviews focused particularly on women's decision to return to work (or not) and the process of reentry, probing to understand the factors influencing this decision and, for those who were working, aspects of their work experience.

DATA ANALYSIS

Interviews in both phases were audiotaped, transcribed, and coded. Here we discuss analysis for the follow-up, which entailed several steps, similar to those we used in the original study as well (for details of which, see *Opting Out?*). In the first step, a narrative summary was written for each participant, typically by the person who conducted the interview. In the second step, narrative summaries and interview transcripts were reviewed multiple times in order to develop an initial set of themes informed by the longitudinal and holistic context of women's work and family trajectories. In a third step, the initial coding scheme was further developed and refined through systematic application of the codes to the interview transcripts using ATLAS.ti, a software program for qualitative data analysis. In a final step, a set of broader and cohesive conceptual themes and constructs were identified from analysis of the finer-grained codes, and these were developed into an explanation of the dynamics of opting back in.

PRESENTATION OF RESULTS

As is common practice in qualitative research, we sometimes present findings in terms of percentages and fractions of the sample. These numbers are not meant to be statistically representative of tendencies in the larger population. Rather, we use them to develop an *explanation* of the dynamics of opting back in that may have much broader applicability beyond our sample (what qualitative researchers call "analytic generalization").[2]

The names and identifying details presented here, with the exception of women's ages, the number and ages of their children, their years of work experience, and other objective characteristics, are changed to protect women's identity. We "anonymize" participants in a number of ways. Typically, we omit or change details and/or describe women's characteristics in very broad terms so as to preclude their identification. For example, all names, whether of companies, place of residence, or children and husbands, are changed or described only in general or broad categories (e.g., financial industry). At the same time, to provide verisimilitude and punch, we did not want to obscure the details of women's lives to such an extent that they came across as cardboard figures. Thus, primarily with respect to where they had gone to school and where they lived, we used real names but changed them to places that were roughly comparable. For example, a woman who graduated from Harvard Business School might be identified as having graduated from Wharton and vice versa. With respect to undergraduate schools, which are not as explicitly a professional credential, we typically used a general descriptor: for example, Harvard would be described as an Ivy League school, and the University of Michigan or University of North Carolina as a public Ivy (i.e., a highly selective public school).

NOTES

INTRODUCTION

1. Belkin (2003).

2. Stone and Lovejoy (2004); Stone (2007a, 2007b); Boushey (2005, 2008).

3. Cohen and Rabin (2007); Shellenbarger (2004).

4. We put "opting out" in quotation marks here to indicate our skepticism about the story line this term conveys with regard to women's career and labor force exits. See Stone (2007a) for the development of this argument. For ease of reading, in the rest of the book we dispense with quotation marks around this or related phrases, but they are implied.

5. Ely, Stone, and Ammerman (2014).

6. Stone (2007a, 2007b).

7. Steiner (2007); Cohen and Rabin (2007).

8. Hirshman (2006); Bennetts (2007).

9. Weisshaar (2018).

10. Hewlett and Luce (2005); McGrath et al. (2005); Shaw, Taylor, and Harris (1999).

11. Hewlett and Luce (2005); Cabrera (2009); Herman (2015); Evertsson, Grunow, and Aisenbrey (2016).

12. Chao and Rones (2007).

13. Malkiel (2016).

14. Sandberg (2013); Slaughter (2015).

15. Statistics compiled from AAMC (2016); ABA (2017); Catalyst (2018); Warner (2014).

16. Hess et al. (2015).

17. Goldin (2014, 1095). The wage gap is much larger when we use a more nuanced (and, many would argue, more realistic) measure of the earnings gap, which looks not at earnings for one year only but at total earnings across fifteen years for all workers who worked at least one year. According to a report by the Institute for Women's Policy Research (Rose and Hartmann 2018), women's earnings in 2015 were only 49 percent—less than half—of men's earnings, for a wage gap of 51 percent. The same study also found that the penalty to spells out of the labor force has increased over time. Prior to 2001, women who took off one year earned 12 percent less than those who worked continuously, a penalty that expanded to 39 percent after 2001.

18. Goldin (2014).

19. Goldin (2014).

20. Goldin and Katz (2008).

21. Goldin (2014, 1106).

22. Buchmann and McDaniel (2016).

23. England et al. (2016).

24. Cha and Weeden (2014).

25. Belkin (2003).

26. Martin (2015); Wolitzer (2008).

27. Miller (2015).

28. Ely, Stone, and Ammerman (2014). Another study of elite business school graduates showed women finessing the career-versus-kids dilemma altogether by forgoing children: only 42 percent planned on becoming mothers in 2012 compared to 78 percent in 1992 (Friedman 2013).

29. Rivera and Tilcsik (2016).

30. Rivera and Tilcsik (2016, 1097).

31. Hersch (2013).

32. Kuperberg and Stone (2008); Hersch (2013); Williams and Boushey (2010).

33. Landivar (2017).

34. Williams and Boushey (2010).

35. Hersch (2013).

36. Amott and Matthaei (1996); Landivar (2017).

37. Kossek, Su, and Wu (2017).

38. Stone (2007b, 19).

39. Cooper (2014); Pugh (2015).

I. GREAT EXPECTATIONS

1. Portions of some of these background sketches originally appeared in *Opting Out?* (Stone 2007a).

2. A huge literature on social mobility in the US reveals that the status of a person's family of origin (especially parents' education and income) plays a major role in one's own social standing. The effect of family transmission of status operates directly and indirectly (the more sizable influence) through its influence on educational attainment. See, for example, the classic *The American Occupational Structure* (Blau and Duncan 1967). A separate literature documents the long-lasting advantages of family wealth on children's own wealth, mobility, and educational outcomes as adults. See *Toxic Inequality* (Shapiro 2017, 26–27) for a summary of this research.

3. This overview is based on the previous study. For detailed results, see Stone (2007a).

4. Damaske (2011).

5. On the historical run-up in work hours, see Schor (1991) and Cha and Weeden (2014).

6. Clawson and Gerstel's (2014) study of jobs in the health care industry underscores the tyranny of time norms in the professions, where doctors were seen to work much longer hours than those in support positions, with the associated effect on the home front that doctors had more traditional families than, for example, EMT workers: more stay-at-home wives and a more highly gendered, less egalitarian division of household labor. Blair-Loy's (2003) study of finance executives is illuminating in showing how these time-based material manifestations of work take on strong cultural meanings that exercise their own particularly compelling hold.

7. Stone and Hernandez (2013).

8. Since the term *opting out* was first coined by Lisa Belkin in 2003, a recent review by Zimmerman and Clark (2016, 603–4) notes that research on the topic "has markedly increased across various disciplines."

9. Bertrand, Goldin, and Katz (2010).

10. Hewlett and Luce (2005).

11. Metz (2011).

12. Herr and Wolfram (2012).

13. Fox and Quinn (2015).

14. Cha (2013, 177).

15. Shafer (2011).

16. Cha (2010).

2. THE SIREN CALL OF PRIVILEGED DOMESTICITY

1. This length of time at home does not include two very part-time and short-lived jobs she started and stopped along the way in an effort to test her interest in making a fuller reentry. As we will see in the next chapter, this often brief and temporary dip into the labor force prior to a fuller career relaunch was a common pattern among these women.

2. Stone (2007a).

3. Walzer (2010).

4. Pyke (1996).

5. See Jacobs and Gerson (1998); Williams (1999).

6. According to Cha and Weeden (2014), other macrostructural factors contributing to the increased prevalence of overwork and its rising wage premium are deindustrialization, globalization, and the emergence of a bifurcated labor market in which higher-paid core employees are overworked while contingent workers who work part-time or in temporary positions work for lower pay. They also find that the increasing prevalence of overwork (defined as working fifty or more hours a week) and the rising hourly wage returns for this behavior have contributed to stalled progress in narrowing the gender gap in hourly pay. As compared to women, men with family responsibilities are better able to engage in overwork and therefore are better positioned to take advantage of the rising return on overwork.

7. Hays (1996).

8. Lareau (2003).

9. Lareau (2003).

10. J. Wallace (2014).

11. Lareau (2003).

12. Parker and Wang (2013).

13. Cooper (2014); Lareau (2003); Vincent and Ball (2007).

14. Cooper (2014, 107).

15. This insight is inspired in part by Aida Hurtado's (1989) seminal intersectional analysis of the racial dynamics of gender subordination in her article "Relating to Privilege: Seduction and Rejection in the Subordination of White Women and Women of Color." Hurtado develops the idea that gender subordination for women privileged by race often operates through a process of seduction: that is, their connection by marriage or blood ties to white men grants them access to racial/class privileges as long as they remain subordinate as women. Thus white women, as a group, are subordinated through seduction; women of color, as a group, through rejection.

3. PUTTING FAMILY FIRST

1. See Belkin (2003) for a classic example of how the media have framed the phenomenon of opting out, and Kuperberg and Stone (2008) for a scholarly analysis of its media depiction.

2. See Chaker and Stout (2004); Hannon (2013); Light (2013); O'Kelly (2013); Schulte (2011); Schulte (2014); and K. Wallace (2013).

3. Sylvia Ann Hewlett and her associates (Hewlett and Luce 2005; Hewlett et al. 2010) conducted two national surveys of highly educated women (aged twenty-eight to fifty-five) and their patterns of career exit and reentry. Both studies found that the overwhelming majority of women with children who had taken a career break had eventually sought to return to the workforce (93 percent in 2004 and 89 percent in 2009), and three-quarters of them had been successful in doing so.

4. Hewlett and associates (Hewlett and Luce 2005; Hewlett et al. 2010); McGrath et al. (2005).

5. The slang term *gig economy* has been variously defined, but here we use a broad definition that equates it with nonstandard work arrangements that tend to lack long-term employment contracts, such as contingent labor (Bracha and Burke 2016). According to the Bureau of Labor Statistics (DiNatale and Boraas 2002), *contingent labor* refers to work that is implicitly or explicitly temporary in nature. The four types of contingent arrangements identified by the BLS are independent contractors, on-call workers, temporary help agency workers, and contract company workers.

6. Kalleberg (2011).

7. Bertrand, Goldin, and Katz (2010); Grant-Vallone and Ensher (2011); Fehring and Herring (2012); Hewlett and Luce (2005); Hewlett et al. (2010); McKie, Biese, and Jyrkinen (2013).

8. Grant-Vallone and Ensher (2011).

9. Seligson (2008); K. Wallace (2013); Chaker and Stout (2004) .

10. Schulte (2014); Hannon (2013); Light (2013); O'Kelly (2013); K. Wallace (2013); Schulte (2011); Chaker and Stout (2004).

11. Zolfagharifard (2016).

12. "The reserve army of labor" is a concept that Karl Marx (2000) used to describe the unemployed or underemployed in a capitalist society who can be easily hired and then disposed of again as the needs of capital dictate.

13. Cabrera (2007); Herman (2015); Hewlett et al. (2010, 11); McGrath et al. (2005).

14. The results of a well-regarded longitudinal panel study (Katz and Krueger 2016) found that in a ten-year span alone, from 2005 to 2015, the

percentage of workers engaged in contingent work (as defined by the Bureau of Labor Statistics) rose from 10 percent to 16 percent.

15. Carré and Tilly (1998); Kalleberg (2011).

16. Bateson (1989); Cabrera (2013, 2009); Hewlett and Luce (2005); Hewlett et al. (2010); Mainiero and Sullivan (2005); McKie, Biese, and Jyrkinen (2013).

17. Hewlett et al. (2010, 11).

4. CAREER RELAUNCH

1. The eighteen women who never relaunched their careers include nine women who were still in the "family-first" phase by the follow-up interview, and nine women who never returned to the labor force at all.

2. The socialist feminist notion of women as a "reserve army of labor" in the capitalist economy (Bruegel 1979; Simeral 1978) is here applied to wives' role in the new traditional household, where their labor may be seen as a convenient but only temporarily needed backup in times of financial strain.

3. See Thompson (2009) for reference to "mancession."

4. Concierge parenting—a variant on intensive parenting—is a phenomenon originally described by Julie Lythcott-Haims (2015) in her book *How to Raise an Adult: Break Free of the Overparenting Trap and Prepare Your Kid for Success.* It has been elaborated by sociologists Hamilton, Roksa, and Nielsen (2018) as a dynamic prevalent among affluent parents who provide their college children with enriched "academic, social and career supports and access to exclusive college infrastructure"—a pattern that they claim reproduces class inequality among college students.

5. QUESTING AND REINVENTION

1. Lovejoy and Stone (2012); McGrath et al. (2005); Tomlinson (2005).

2. Schneer and Reitman (1990, 1997).

3. Hewlett and Luce (2005).

4. Cabrera (2007, 2009); Fehring and Herring (2012); Herman (2015); Hewlett and Luce (2005); Hewlett et al. (2010); McGrath et al. (2005); McKie, Biese, and Jyrkinen (2013); Shaw, Taylor, and Harris (2000).

5. Tronto (1993); Ruddick (1990).

6. Jung (1971); McAdams (2001); Erikson (1964).

7. Freedman (2006); Schaefers (2012).

8. See Mainiero and Sullivan (2005, 2006). Research by O'Neil and Bilimoria (2005) also finds three similar age-related phases in women's career trajectories.

9. A similar theme is noted in Catherine Bateson's book *Composing a Life* (1989), in which she observes that women's lives are more contingent, nonlinear, and improvisational because of their responsibilities for care.

10. "Low bar for leaving" is an expression used by Professor Emeritus Bruce Roberts (of Stanford University's Department of Computer Science) and emerged in a personal communication with him.

11. This term is adapted from the concept of "life course innovation," which refers to the adoption of new life course patterns or roles that come to prefigure the institutionalization of that way of life (Giele 1998; Kohli 1986).

6. THE BIG PICTURE

1. To access occupation-specific national data on gender composition, earnings, and prestige for each job, we match women's job titles (informed by industry as necessary) to the over four hundred detailed occupational titles available from the SOC (Standard Occupational Classification).

2. Kalleberg (2011).

3. In this chapter, we cite various numbers and proportions to describe patterns internal to our sample. These are not to be generalized to larger populations but are for broad descriptive purposes only.

4. Wikipedia, "Occupational Prestige," last modified January 2017, accessed 2018, https://en.wikipedia.org/wiki/Occupational_prestige.

5. England (1979); Bose and Rossi (1983); J. Fox and Suschnigg (1989).

6. England (1979).

7. Because contingency is a feature of particular jobs, not of broad occupations, a few women who changed course, i.e., changed occupations, also worked contingently in a job in their new field. Claire Lott, for example, left a full-time job in telecommunications marketing to teach Spanish part-time on a short-term contract basis.

8. While not shown, at their initial reentry virtually all women worked contingently, which, as we've seen in prior chapters, was a key transition back-to-work strategy in the family-first phase of the process of relaunching careers.

9. Pipher (1994).

7. THE PARADOX OF PRIVILEGE AND BEYOND

1. Clawson and Gerstel (2014).

2. See McGinn, Castro, and Lingo (2018), who also provide a comprehensive summary of this body of research.

3. See, for example, the conclusion reached by Stromberg (2017).

4. Cohen and Rabin (2007).

5. Cohen (2012).

6. Schwartz and Mare (2005).

7. Lyness et al. (2012).

8. Bergmann (1974).

9. Stone and Kuperberg (2006).

10. Haas and Hwang (2008).

11. Patnaik (2017); Arnalds, Eydal, and Gíslason (2013).

12. Slaughter (2015).

13. Vagianos (2017).

14. Gaudiano (2017).

15. Bateson (1989).

16. Ryzik (2018).

APPENDIX

1. Stone (2007a).

2. Yin (2003).

REFERENCES

AAMC (American Association of Medical Colleges). 2016. "The State of Women in Academic Medicine: The Pipeline and Pathways to Leadership, 2015–2016." https://www.aamc.org/members/gwims/statistics/.

ABA (American Bar Association). 2017. "A Current Glance at Women in the Law." January. https://www.americanbar.org/content/dam/aba/marketing/women/current_glance_statistics_january2017.authcheckdam.pdf.

Amott, Teresa L., and Julie A. Matthaei. 1996. *Race, Gender, and Work: A Multicultural Economic History of Women in the United States.* Boston: South End Press.

Arnalds, Ásdís A., Guðný Björk Eydal, and Ingólfur V. Gíslason. 2013. "Equal Rights to Paid Parental Leave and Caring Fathers: The Case of Iceland." *Icelandic Review of Politics and Administration* 9 (2): 323–44.

Bateson, Mary Catherine. 1989. *Composing a Life.* Harvard East Asian Monograph No. 142. New York: Atlantic Monthly Press.

Belkin, Lisa. 2003. "The Opt-Out Revolution." *New York Times*, October 26. https://www.nytimes.com/2003/10/26/magazine/the-opt-out-revolution.html.

Bennetts, Leslie. 2007. *The Feminine Mistake: Are We Giving Up Too Much?* New York: Voice/Hyperion.

Bergmann, Barbara R. 1974. "Occupational Segregation, Wages and Profits When Employers Discriminate by Race or Sex." *Eastern Economic Journal* 1 (2): 103–10.

Bertrand, Marianne, Claudia Goldin, and Lawrence F. Katz. 2010. "Dynamics of the Gender Gap for Young Professionals in the Financial and Corporate

Sectors." *American Economic Journal: Applied Economics* 2 (3): 228–55. https://doi.org/10.1257/app.2.3.228.

Blair-Loy, Mary. 2003. *Competing Devotions: Career and Family among Women Executives.* Cambridge, MA: Harvard University Press.

Blau, Peter M., and Otis Dudley Duncan. 1967. *The American Occupational Structure.* New York: John Wiley.

Bose, Christine E., and Peter H. Rossi. 1983. "Gender and Jobs: Prestige Standings of Occupations as Affected by Gender." *American Sociological Review* 48 (3): 316–30.

Boushey, Heather. 2005. "Are Women Opting Out? Debunking the Myth." Center for Economic and Policy Research Briefing Paper, November. http://cepr.net/documents/publications/opt_out_2005_11_2.pdf.

Boushey, Heather. 2008. "'Opting Out?' The Effect of Children on Women's Employment in the United States." *Feminist Economics* 14 (1): 1–36. https://doi.org/10.1080/13545700701716672.

Bracha, Anat, and Mary A. Burke. 2016. "Who Counts as Employed? Informal Work, Employment Status, and Labor Market Slack." SSRN Scholarly Paper ID 2935535, Social Science Research Network, Rochester, NY. https://papers.ssrn.com/abstract=2935535.

Bruegel, Irene. 1979. "Women as a Reserve Army of Labour: A Note on Recent British Experience." *Feminist Review,* no. 3: 12–23. https://doi.org/10.2307/1394707.

Buchmann, Claudia, and Anne McDaniel. 2016. "Motherhood and the Wages of Women in Professional Occupations." *Russell Sage Foundation Journal* 2 (4): 128–50. https://doi.org/10.7758/RSF.2016.2.4.05.

Cabrera, Elizabeth F. 2007. "Opting Out and Opting In: Understanding the Complexities of Women's Career Transitions." *Career Development International* 12 (3): 218–37.

Cabrera, Elizabeth F. 2009. "Protean Organizations: Reshaping Work and Careers to Retain Female Talent." *Career Development International* 14 (2): 186–201. https://doi.org/10.1108/13620430910950773.

Cabrera, Elizabeth F. 2013. "Opting Out and Opting In: Understanding the Complexities of Women's Career Transitions." *Career Development International* 12 (3): 218–37. https://doi.org/10.1108/13620430710745872.

Carré, Françoise, and Chris Tilly. 1998. "Part-Time and Temporary Work." *Dollars and Sense,* January 1998. www.dollarsandsense.org/archives/1998/0198carre.html.

Catalyst. 2018. "Quick Take: Women in the Workforce: United States." March 28. www.catalyst.org/knowledge/women-workforce-united-states.

Cha, Youngjoo. 2010. "Reinforcing Separate Spheres: The Effect of Spousal Overwork on Men's and Women's Employment in Dual-Earner Households." *American Sociological Review* 75 (2): 303–29.

Cha, Youngjoo. 2013. "Overwork and the Persistence of Gender Segregation in Occupations." *Gender and Society* 27 (2): 158–84.

Cha, Youngjoo, and Kim A. Weeden. 2014. "Overwork and the Slow Convergence in the Gender Gap in Wages." *American Sociological Review* 79 (3): 457–84. https://doi.org/10.1177/0003122414528936.

Chaker, Anne Marie, and Hilary Stout. 2004. "After Years Off, Women Struggle to Revive Careers." *Wall Street Journal,* May 6. www.wsj.com/articles/SB108379813440903335.

Chao, Elaine, and Philip Rones. 2007. "Women in the Labor Force: A Databook." Bureau of Labor Statistics. www.bls.gov/opub/reports/womens-databook/archive/women-in-the-labor-force-a-databook-2014.pdf.

Clawson, Dan, and Naomi Gerstel. 2014. *Unequal Time: Gender, Class, and Family in Employment Schedules.* New York: Russell Sage Foundation.

Cohen, Carol Fishman. 2012. "The 40-Year-Old Intern." *Harvard Business Review,* November. https://hbr.org/2012/11/the-40-year-old-intern.

Cohen, Carol Fishman, and Vivian Steir Rabin. 2007. *Back on the Career Track: A Guide for Stay-at-Home Moms Who Want to Return to Work.* New York: Warner Business Books.

Cooper, Marianne. 2014. *Cut Adrift: Families in Insecure Times.* Berkeley: University of California Press.

Damaske, Sarah. 2011. *For the Family? How Class and Gender Shape Women's Work.* New York: Oxford University Press.

DiNatale, Marisa, and Stephanie Boraas. 2002. "The Labor Force Experience of Women from 'Generation X.'" Bureau of Labor Statistics, March. www.bls.gov/opub/mlr/2002/03/artifull.pdf.

Ely, Robin J., Pamela Stone, and Colleen Ammerman. 2014. "Rethink What You 'Know' about High-Achieving Women." *Harvard Business Review,* December 1. https://hbr.org/2014/12/rethink-what-you-know-about-high-achieving-women.

England, Paula. 1979. "Women and Occupational Prestige: A Case of Vacuous Sex Equality." *Signs: Journal of Women in Culture and Society* 5 (2): 252–65.

England, Paula, Jonathan Bearak, Michelle J. Budig, and Melissa J. Hodges. 2016. "Do Highly Paid, Highly Skilled Women Experience the Largest Motherhood Penalty?" *American Sociological Review* 81 (6): 1161–89. https://doi.org/10.1177/0003122416673598.

Erikson, Erik H. 1964. *Childhood and Society*. New York: Norton.

Evertsson, Marie, Daniela Grunow, and Silke Aisenbrey. 2016. "Work Interruptions and Young Women's Career Prospects in Germany, Sweden and the US." *Work, Employment and Society* 30 (2): 291–308.

Fehring, Heather, and Katherine Herring. 2012. "Voices from the Working Lives Project: The Push-Pull of Work and Care." *International Education Studies* 5 (6): 204–18. https://doi.org/10.5539/ies.v5n6p204.

Fox, Annie B. and Diane M. Quinn. 2015. "Pregnant Women at Work: The Role of Stigma in Predicting Women's Intended Exit from the Workforce." *Psychology of Women Quarterly* 39 (2): 226–42.

Fox, John, and Carole Suschnigg. 1989. "A Note on Gender and the Prestige of Occupations." *Canadian Journal of Sociology/Cahiers Canadiens de Sociologie* 14 (3): 353–60.

Freedman, Marc. 2006. "The Social-Purpose Encore Career: Baby Boomers, Civic Engagement, and the Next Stage of Work." *Generations* (San Francisco) 30 (4): 43–46.

Friedman, Stewart. 2013. *Baby Bust: New Choices for Men and Women in Work and Family*. New York: Wharton Digital Press.

Gaudiano, Nicole. 2017. "'Me Too' Movement Fuels Equal Rights Amendment Push." *USA Today*, November 18. https://www.usatoday.com/story/news/politics/2017/11/18/me-too-movement-renews-equal-rights-amendment-push/875903001/.

Giele, Janet Z. 1998. "Innovation in the Typical Life Course." In *Methods of Life Course Research: Qualitative and Quantitative Approaches*, 231–63. Thousand Oaks, CA: Sage Publications.

Goldin, Claudia. 2014. "A Grand Gender Convergence: Its Last Chapter." *American Economic Review* 104 (4): 1091–119. https://doi.org/10.1257/aer.104.4.1091.

Goldin, Claudia, and Lawrence F. Katz. 2008. "Transitions: Career and Family Life Cycles of the Educational Elite." *American Economic Review* 98 (2): 363–69. https://doi.org/10.1257/aer.98.2.363.

Grant-Vallone, Elisa J., and Ellen A. Ensher. 2011. "Opting in Between: Strategies Used by Professional Women with Children to Balance Work and Family." *Journal of Career Development* 38 (4): 331–48. https://doi.org/10.1177/0894845310372219.

Haas, Linda, and C. Philip Hwang. 2008. "The Impact of Taking Parental Leave on Fathers' Participation in Childcare and Relationships with Children: Lessons from Sweden." *Community, Work and Family* 11 (1): 85–104.

Hamilton, Laura, Josipa Roksa, and Kelly Nielsen. 2018. "Providing a 'Leg Up': Parental Involvement and Opportunity Hoarding in College." *Sociology of Education* 91 (2): 111–31. https://doi.org/10.1177/0038040718759557.

Hannon, Kerry. 2013. "7 Ways Women Can Opt Back into the Workforce." *Forbes,* August 14. www.forbes.com/sites/nextavenue/2013/08/14/how-opt-out-women-can-opt-back-into-jobs/.

Hays, Sharon. 1996. *The Cultural Contradictions of Motherhood.* New Haven, CT: Yale University Press.

Herman, Clem. 2015. "Rebooting and Rerouting: Women's Articulations of Frayed Careers in Science, Engineering and Technology Professions." *Gender, Work and Organization* 22 (4): 324–38. https://doi.org/10.1111/gwao.12088.

Herr, Jane Leber, and Catherine D. Wolfram. 2012. "Work Environment and Opt-Out Rates at Motherhood across High-Education Career Paths." *ILR Review* 65 (4): 928–50.

Hersch, Joni. 2013. "Opting Out among Women with Elite Education." *Review of Economics of the Household* 11 (4): 469–506. https://doi.org/10.1007/s11150-013-9199-4.

Hess, Cynthia, Jessica Milli, Ariane Hegewisch, Stephanie Román, Julie Anderson, and Justine Augeri. 2015. "The Status of Women in the States: 2015." Institute for Women's Policy Research. https://iwpr.org/publications/the-status-of-women-in-the-states-2015-full-report/.

Hewlett, Sylvia Ann, Diana Forster, Laura Sherbin, Peggy Shiller, and Karen Sumberg. 2010. *Off-Ramps and On-Ramps Revisited.* New York: Center for Work-Life Policy.

Hewlett, Sylvia Ann, and Carolyn Buck Luce. 2005. "Off-Ramps and On-Ramps: Keeping Talented Women on the Road to Success." *Harvard Business Review,* March 1. https://hbr.org/2005/03/off-ramps-and-on-ramps-keeping-talented-women-on-the-road-to-success.

Hirshman, Linda R. 2006. *Get to Work: A Manifesto for Women of the World.* New York: Viking.

Hurtado, Aída. 1989. "Relating to Privilege: Seduction and Rejection in the Subordination of White Women and Women of Color." *Signs* 14 (4): 833–55.

Jacobs, Jerry A., and Kathleen Gerson. 1998. "Who Are the Overworked Americans?" *Review of Social Economy* 56 (4): 442–59.

Jung, Carl. 1971. *The Portable Jung.* New York: Viking Press.

Kalleberg, Arne L. 2011. *Good Jobs and Bad Jobs: The Rise of Precarious and Polarized Employment Systems in the United States, 1970s to 2000s.* New York: Russell Sage Foundation.

Katz, Lawrence, and Alan Krueger. 2016. "The Rise and Nature of Alternative Work Arrangements in the United States, 1995–2015." National Bureau of Economic Research, Working Paper 22667, September. https://doi.org /10.3386/w22667.

Kohli, Martin. 1986. "The World We Forgot: A Historical Review of the Life Course." In *Later Life: The Social Psychology of Aging,* edited by V. W. Marshall, 271–303. Beverly Hills, CA: Sage Publications.

Kossek, Ellen Ernst, Rong Su, and Lusi Wu. 2017. "'Opting Out' or 'Pushed Out'? Integrating Perspectives on Women's Career Equality for Gender Inclusion and Interventions." *Journal of Management* 43 (1): 228–54. https:// doi.org/10.1177/0149206316671582.

Kuperberg, Arielle, and Pamela Stone. 2008. "The Media Depiction of Women Who Opt Out." *Gender and Society* 22 (4): 497–517. https://doi.org/10.1177 /0891243208319767.

Landivar, Liana Christin. 2017. *Mothers at Work: Who Opts Out?* Boulder, CO: Lynne Rienner.

Lareau, Annette. 2003. *Unequal Childhoods: Class, Race, and Family Life.* Berkeley: University of California Press.

Light, Paulette. 2013. "Why 43% of Women with Children Leave Their Jobs, and How to Get Them Back." *Atlantic,* April 19. www.theatlantic.com /sexes/archive/2013/04/why-43-of-women-with-children-leave-their-jobs-and-how-to-get-them-back/275134/.

Lovejoy, Meg, and Pamela Stone. 2012. "Opting Back In: The Influence of Time at Home on Professional Women's Career Redirection after Opting Out." *Gender, Work and Organization* 19 (6): 631–53.

Lyness, Karen S., Janet C. Gornick, Pamela Stone, and Angela R. Grotto. 2012. "It's All about Control: Worker Control over Schedule and Hours in Cross-national Context." *American Sociological Review* 77 (6): 1023–49.

Lythcott-Haims, Julie. 2015. *How to Raise an Adult: Break Free of the Overparenting Trap and Prepare Your Kid for Success.* San Francisco: iDream Books.

Mainiero, Lisa A., and Sherry E. Sullivan. 2005. "Kaleidoscope Careers: An Alternate Explanation for the 'Opt-Out' Revolution." *Academy of Management Executive* 19 (1): 106–23. https://doi.org/10.5465/AME.2005.15841962.

Mainiero, Lisa A., and Sherry E. Sullivan. 2006. *The Opt-Out Revolt: Why People Are Leaving Companies to Create Kaleidoscope Careers.* Mountain View, CA: Davies-Black.

Malkiel, Nancy Weiss. 2016. *"Keep the Damned Women Out": The Struggle for Coeducation.* Princeton, NJ: Princeton University Press.

Martin, Wednesday. 2015. *Primates of Park Avenue: A Memoir.* New York: Simon and Schuster.

Marx, Karl. 2000. *Capital.* Vol. 1. London: Electric Book Company. http://ebookcentral.proquest.com/lib/brandeis-ebooks/detail.action?docID=3008518.

McAdams, Douglas. 2001. "Generativity in Midlife." In *Handbook of Midlife Development*, edited by Margie E. Lachman, 395–443. New York: John Wiley and Sons.

McGinn, Kathleen L., Mayra Ruiz Castro, and Elizabeth Long Lingo. 2018. "Learning from Mum: Cross-national Evidence Linking Maternal Employment and Adult Children's Outcomes." *Work, Employment and Society,* published online April 30. https://doi.org/10.1177/0950017018760167.

McGrath, Monica, Marla Driscoll, Mary Gross, Penny Bamber, and Kerriann Axt. 2005. "Back in the Game: Returning to Business after a Hiatus." Philadelphia: Wharton Center for Leadership and Change. http://citeseerx.ist.psu.edu/viewdoc/summary?doi=10.1.1.214.53.

McKie, Linda, Ingrid Biese, and Marjut Jyrkinen. 2013. "'The Best Time Is Now!': The Temporal and Spatial Dynamics of Women Opting In to Self-Employment." *Gender, Work and Organization* 20 (2): 184–96. https://doi.org/10.1111/gwao.12019.

McKinsey and Company. 2017. "Women in Law Firms." Featured Insights, October. https://www.mckinsey.com/~/media/mckinsey/featured%20insights/gender%20equality/women%20in%20law%20firms/women-in-law-firms-final-103017.ashx.

Metz, Isabel. 2011. "Women Leave Work Because of Family Responsibilities: Fact or Fiction?" *Asia Pacific Journal of Human Resources* 49 (3): 285–307.

Miller, Claire. 2015. "More Than Their Mothers, Young Women Plan Career Pauses." *New York Times,* July 22. https://www.nytimes.com/2015/07/23/upshot/more-than-their-mothers-young-women-plan-career-pauses.html.

O'Kelly, Allison. 2013. "Off-Ramping? Not So Fast." *Huffington Post,* May 30. www.huffingtonpost.com/allison-okelly/offramping-not-so-fast_b_3353820.html.

O'Neil, Deborah, and Diana Bilimoria. 2005. "Women's Career Development Phases: Idealism, Endurance, and Reinvention." *Career Development International* 10 (3): 162–88.

Parker, Kim, and Wendy Wang. 2013. "Modern Parenthood." *Pew Research Center's Social and Demographic Trends Project* (blog), March 14. www.pewsocialtrends

.org/2013/03/14/modern-parenthood-roles-of-moms-and-dads-converge-as-they-balance-work-and-family/.

Patnaik, Ankita. 2017. "Reserving Time for Daddy: The Consequences of Fathers' Quotas." SSRN Scholarly Paper ID 2475970. Rochester, NY: Social Science Research Network. https://papers.ssrn.com/abstract=2475970.

Pipher, Mary Bray. 1994. *Reviving Ophelia: Saving the Selves of Adolescent Girls.* New York: Putnam.

Pugh, Allison J. 2015. *The Tumbleweed Society: Working and Caring in an Age of Insecurity.* New York: Oxford University Press.

Pyke, Karen D. 1996. "Class-Based Masculinities: The Interdependence of Gender, Class, and Interpersonal Power." *Gender and Society* 10 (5): 527–49.

Rivera, Lauren A., and András Tilcsik. 2016. "Class Advantage, Commitment Penalty: The Gendered Effect of Social Class Signals in an Elite Labor Market." *American Sociological Review* 81 (6): 1097–131.

Rose, Stephen J., and Heidi Hartmann. 2018. *Still a Man's Labor Market: The Slowly Narrowing Gender Wage Gap.* Washington, DC: Institute for Women's Policy Research.

Ruddick, Sara. 1990. *Maternal Thinking: Toward a Politics of Peace.* New York: Ballantine.

Ryzik, Melena. 2018. "Curator Says MoMA PS1 Wanted Her, Until She Had a Baby." *New York Times,* July 9. https://www.nytimes.com/2018/07/06/arts/design/moma-ps1-discrimination-suit-baby.html.

Sandberg, Sheryl. 2013. *Lean In: Women, Work, and the Will to Lead.* New York: Alfred A. Knopf.

Schaefers, Kathleen Galvin. 2012. "Working for Good: The Encore Career Movement." *Career Planning and Adult Development Journal* (San Jose) 28 (2): 84–95.

Schneer, Joy, and Frieda Reitman. 1990. "Effects of Employment Gaps on the Careers of M.B.A.'s: More Damaging for Men Than for Women?" *Academy of Management Journal* 33 (2): 391–406. https://doi.org/10.2307/256330.

Schneer, Joy, and Frieda Reitman. 1997. "The Interrupted Managerial Career Path: A Longitudinal Study of MBAs." *Journal of Vocational Behavior* 51: 411–34.

Schor, Juliet. 1991. *The Overworked American: The Unexpected Decline of Leisure.* New York: Basic Books.

Schulte, Brigid. 2011. "Movement to Keep Moms Working Is Remaking the Workplace." *Washington Post,* May 5. https://www.washingtonpost.com/local/movement-to-keep-moms-working-is-remaking-the-workplace/2011/05/05/AFMTqOLG_story.html.

Schulte, Brigid. 2014. "Programs to Help Women Relaunch Careers Plummeted during Recession." *Washington Post,* October 17. www.washingtonpost .com/news/local/wp/2014/10/17/back-to-work-women-whove-opted-out-face-stigma-struggle-to-get-back-in/.

Schwartz, Christine R., and Robert D. Mare. 2005. "Trends in Educational Assortative Marriage from 1940 to 2003." *Demography* 42 (4): 621–46. https:// doi.org/10.1353/dem.2005.0036.

Seligson, Hannah. 2008. "Off Ramp to On Ramp: It Can Be a Hard Journey." *New York Times,* December 7.

Shafer, Emily Fitzgibbons. 2011. "Wives' Relative Wages, Husbands' Paid Work Hours, and Wives' Labor-Force Exit." *Journal of Marriage and Family* 73 (1): 250–63.

Shapiro, Thomas M. 2017. *Toxic Inequality: How America's Wealth Gap Destroys Mobility, Deepens the Racial Divide, and Threatens Our Future.* New York: Basic Books.

Shaw, Sue, Mary Taylor, and Irene Harris. 1999. "Jobs for the Girls: A Study of the Careers of Professional Women Returners Following Participation in a European Funded Updating Programme." *International Journal of Manpower* 20 (3/4): 179–89.

Shellenbarger, Sue. 2004. "A Bellwether Working Mom Returns to the Office." *Wall Street Journal,* May 4. www.wsj.com/articles/SB108362148104000689.

Simeral, Margaret H. 1978. "Women and the Reserve Army of Labor." *Insurgent Sociologist* 8 (2–3): 164–79. https://doi.org/10.1177/089692057800800217.

Slaughter, Anne-Marie. 2015. *Unfinished Business: Women, Men, Work, Family.* New York: Random House.

Steiner, Leslie. 2007. "Back in Business." *More Magazine,* June 2007.

Stone, Pamela. 2007a. *Opting Out? Why Women Really Quit Careers and Head Home.* Berkeley: University of California Press.

Stone, Pamela. 2007b. "The Rhetoric and Reality of 'Opting Out.'" *Contexts* 6 (4): 14–19.

Stone, Pamela, and Lisa Ackerly Hernandez. 2013. "The All-or-Nothing Workplace: Flexibility Stigma and 'Opting Out' among Professional-Managerial Women." *Journal of Social Issues* 69 (2): 235–56.

Stone, Pamela, and Arielle Kuperberg. 2006. "Anti-discrimination vs. Anti-poverty? A Comparison of Pay Equity and Living Wage Reforms." *Journal of Women, Politics and Policy* 27 (3–4): 23–39. https://doi.org/10.1300/J501v27n03_03.

Stone, Pamela, and Meg Lovejoy. 2004. "Fast-Track Women and the 'Choice' to Stay Home." *Annals of the American Academy of Political and Social Science* 596 (1): 62–83.

Stromberg, Lisen. 2017. *Work Pause Thrive*. Dallas, TX: BenBella Books.

Thompson, Derek. 2009. "It's Not Just a Recession. It's a Mancession!" *Atlantic,* July 9. https://www.theatlantic.com/business/archive/2009/07/its-not-just-a-recession-its-a-mancession/20991/.

Tomlinson, J. 2005. "Examining the Potential for Women Returners to Work in Areas of High Occupational Gender Segregation." Final Report to the Department for Trade and Industry, London, October. https://www.escholar.manchester.ac.uk/uk-ac-man-scw:75229.

Tronto, Joan C. 1993. *Moral Boundaries: A Political Argument for an Ethic of Care.* New York: Psychology Press.

Vagianos, Alanna. 2017. "The 'Me Too' Campaign Was Created by a Black Woman 10 Years Ago." *Huffington Post,* October 17. https://www.huffingtonpost.com/entry/the-me-too-campaign-was-created-by-a-black-woman-10-years-ago_us_59e61a7fe4b02a215b336fee.

Vincent, Carol, and Stephen J. Ball. 2007. "'Making Up' the Middle-Class Child: Families, Activities and Class Dispositions." *Sociology* 41 (6): 1061–77. https://doi.org/10.1177/0038038507082315.

Wallace, Jennifer Breheny. 2014. "Should Children Be Held Back for Kindergarten?" *Wall Street Journal,* September 12, sec. Life and Style. www.wsj.com/articles/should-children-be-held-back-for-kindergarten-1410536168.

Wallace, Kelly. 2013. "Moms 'Opting In' to Work Find Doors Shut." CNN, August 13. www.cnn.com/2013/08/13/living/parents-mothers-opt-to-work/index.html.

Walzer, Susan. 2010. *Thinking about the Baby: Gender and Transitions into Parenthood.* Philadelphia: Temple University Press.

Warner, Judith. 2014. "The Women's Leadership Gap: Women's Leadership by the Numbers." Center for American Progress fact sheet, 1–7. https://www.americanprogress.org/issues/women/reports/2014/03/07/85457/fact-sheet-the-womens-leadership-gap.

Weisshaar, Katherine. 2018. "From Opt Out to Blocked Out: The Challenges for Labor Market Re-entry after Family-Related Employment Lapses." *American Sociological Review* 83 (1): 34–60.

Wikipedia. 2017. "Occupational Prestige." Last modified January 2017. Accessed 2018. https://en.wikipedia.org/w/index.php?title=Occupational_prestige&oldid=759663304.

Williams, Joan C. 1999. *Unbending Gender: Why Family and Work Conflict and What to Do about It.* New York: Oxford University Press, USA.

Williams, Joan C., and Heather Boushey. 2010. "The Three Faces of Work-Family Conflict." Center for American Progress, January 25. https://www.americanprogress.org/issues/economy/reports/2010/01/25/7194/the-three-faces-of-work-family-conflict/.

Wolitzer, Meg. 2008. *The Ten-Year Nap.* New York: Riverhead Books.

Yin, Robert. 2003. *Case Study Research.* 3rd ed. Thousand Oaks, CA: Sage.

Zimmerman, Lauren M., and Malissa A. Clark. 2016. "Opting-Out and Opting-In: A Review and Agenda for Future Research." *Career Development International* 21 (6): 603–33.

Zolfagharifard, Ellie. 2016. "Should Women Explain Gaps in Their Resume after Raising a Family?" *Daily Mail,* May 20. www.dailymail.co.uk/sciencetech/article-3601630/Should-women-explain-gaps-resume-raising-family-Controversial-study-says-honest-help-land-job.html.

INDEX

Founded in 1893,
UNIVERSITY OF CALIFORNIA PRESS
publishes bold, progressive books and journals
on topics in the arts, humanities, social sciences,
and natural sciences—with a focus on social
justice issues—that inspire thought and action
among readers worldwide.

The UC PRESS FOUNDATION
raises funds to uphold the press's vital role
as an independent, nonprofit publisher, and
receives philanthropic support from a wide
range of individuals and institutions—and from
committed readers like you. To learn more, visit
ucpress.edu/supportus.